Fran
Haute Provence

Adrian Berry

A rock climbing guidebook to the
Haute Provence area of France

All uncredited photos by Adrian Berry
Other photography as credited
Edited by Alan James
Printed by John Browns, Nottingham
Distributed by Cordee (www.cordee.co.uk)

Published by ROCKFAX Ltd. December 2009
© ROCKFAX Ltd. 2009
www.rockfax.com

ISBN 978 1 873341 27 8

This page: *No Man's Land* (7b) - page 285 - at Buoux.
Photo: Richard Kirby.
Cover: *Cent Patates* (7b+) - page 39 - at Céüse.
Photo: Adrian Berry

Céüse
Sisteron
Volx
Orpierre
Bellecombe
Baume Rousse
Ubrieux
Saint Julien
Saint Léger
Malaucène
Combe Obscure
Les Dentelles
Venasque
Buoux

Awesome Walls
Climbing Centre
www.awesomewalls.co.uk

e Ryall on *L'Haut de Là* (7a+) - *page 95* - Bellecombe.

Céüse · Sisteron · Volx · Orpierre · Bellecombe · Baume Rousse · Ubrieux · Saint Julien · Saint Léger · Malaucène · Combe Obscure · Les Dentelles · Venasque · Buoux

Guidebook Footnote

inclusion of a climbing area in this guidebook does not mean that you have a right of access or the right to climb upon it. The descriptions outes within this guide are recorded for historical reasons only and no reliance should be placed on the accuracy of the description. grades set in this guide are a fair assessment of the difficulty of the climbs. Climbers who attempt a route of a particular standard uld use their own judgment as to whether they are proficient enough to tackle that route. This book is not a substitute for experience proper judgment. The authors, publisher and distributors of this book do not recognise any liability for injury or damage caused to, or climbers, third parties, or property arising from such persons seeking reliance on this guidebook as an assurance for their own safety.

Céüse
Sisteron
Volx
Orpierre
Bellecombe
Baume Rousse
Ubrieux
Saint Julien
Saint Léger
Malaucène
Combe Obscure
Les Dentelles
Venasque
Buoux

The South of France contains the best sport climbing in the world, there's no 'some of' about it. While new sport climbing areas regularly take the limelight as the latest 'must visit' destinations, seldom is the quality of routes found on the limestone crags of southern France matched. In the same way that newly publicised bouldering areas are inevitably compared to Fontainebleau, so areas in the South of France such as Céüse and Buoux are the quality benchmarks of sport climbing. It's not uncommon to hear of newly developed crags being described lavishly - *"it's as good as Céüse"*, or more modestly assessed - *"brilliant, but no Buoux"*. And yet while climbers fly halfway around the world to queue for routes at the latest trendy area, the spiritual home of sport climbing is surprisingly quiet. Indeed, while producing this book, one of the challenges I had was finding people to photograph.

While raising the profile of French sport climbing was one of the objectives of this book, another was to raise the profile of less well known areas that offer a similar high quality climbing. Often it is the 'hard' crags that have the highest profiles as these are the ones where the latest super-routes are established, which generates lots of interest in the magazines and online. Yet there are many brilliant crags in France where the routes are largely in the 4s, 5s and lower-end of the 6s. Such venues are often deserted while better-known hard crags frustrate lower-grade climbers who will struggle to find good routes that aren't polished warm-ups. This book will help to redress this misapprehension by highlighting several superb venues across the Haute Provence area, places like Baume Rousse, Ubrieux, Saint Julien, Les Dentelles and Orpierre.

It is a terrible irony that we climbers have such a negative impact on the very environment that gives us such joy. A major driving force behind this book was the desire to publicise an area that can be reached by climbers in northern Europe without necessarily flying. Over the two years it took to produce this book, not one flight was taken to France. Also, in order to mitigate the fuel needed to drive from the UK to Provence, longer, less frequent trips were made. A typical research trip in early 2008 lasted four months and the average daily distance driven, including the drive down and back from northern England was less than 30 miles per day (48km). Additionally, this guidebook has the train symbol on the maps - showing where the nearest railway station is located. There is no doubt that taking the train is far less damaging to the environment than flying, and we hope that this book will help start a change in our behaviour for the better.

Adrian Berry, November 2009

Les Dentelles de Montmir

Céüse

Sisteron

Volx

Orpierre

Bellecombe

Baume Rousse

Ubrieux

Saint Julien

Saint Léger

Malaucène

Combe Obscure

Les Dentelles

Venasque

Buoux

Hamer on the classic *Piedra Salvage* (6b+) - *page 155* - at Saint Léger.

Katie Whittaker redpointing *Carte Blanche* (8a) - *page 43* - at Céüse.

Céüse
Sisteron
Volx
Orpierre
Bellecombe
Baume Rousse
Ubrieux
Saint Julien
Saint Léger
Malaucène
Combe Obscure
Les Dentelles
Venasque
Buoux

Access

All the areas covered by this book are well-publicised and popular, and unless indicated otherwise, you can assume there is a right of access. These rights have often been hard won and they should be respected since they can be lost in an instant by the thoughtless behaviour of one individual.

Park considerately - don't block access and be prepared to climb elsewhere if there's nowhere to park considerately.

Stick to the approach paths - avoid short cuts through someone's private land.

Keep the noise down at the crag - crags are often in areas popular with walkers who are keen to get away from all that.

Take your rubbish home with you - better still, make space for some of other people's rubbish, and remember that everything you bring to the crag is rubbish if you leave it there - even orange peel takes around two years to decompose - is it really that much of a chore to carry it home?

Local Guidebooks

Nearly all the areas covered by this guidebook are detailed in locally available publications. Local guidebooks include mor routes and may well be more up-to-date, an if you particularly like an area in this book, would be well worth tracking down the loca information.

In the introduction to each section, the curr 2009 local guidebook is featured so you kn what it looks like. You can usually get hold these from the tourist information office or, if there is a climbing shop in the area, then that is an obvious place to look. The web site **www.topostation.com** has an extensi stock and does online ordering.

It is not the policy of Rockfax to replace loc guidebooks, but rather to introduce climber to the areas covered by this book, typically climbers who may be unaware of the wealt of climbing and who are unable to acquire information via local sources. Rather than competing with local guidebooks, we expec that the increased number of visitors will le to more sales of quality local guidebooks a a general boost to the local economy.

The walk-in to Céüse

Feedback - Online Route Database

The database at **www.rockfax.com** contains a listing of every route in the book with the opportunity for you to lodge comments and vote on grades and star ratings This information is essential to help us ensure complete and up-to-date coverage for all the climbs. We can then produce updates and make sure we get it right in subse quent editions. To make this system work we need the help of everyone who climbs in the areas covered by th book, so if you think you have found a badly graded rou or discovered a hidden gem that we have only given a single star to, let us know about it. Your general commen on all other aspects of this book are also welcome.

Adrian Berry off *Sault Qui Peut* (8a) - *page 152* - at Saint Léger. Photo: Phil Vickers

Céüse

Sisteron

Volx

Orpierre

Bellecombe

Baume Rousse

Ubrieux

Saint Julien

Saint Léger

Malaucene

Combe Obscure

Les Dentelles

Venasque

Buoux

Céüse

Sisteron

Volx

Orpierre

Bellecombe

Baume Rousse

Ubrieux

Saint Julien

Saint Léger

Malaucène

Combe Obscure

Les Dentelles

Venasque

Buoux

Die Klettermöglichkeiten in Südfrankreich gehören zu den besten der Welt. Oft stehen neue Sportklettergebiete im Rampenlicht, die man unbedingt besuchen muss; doch nur wenige erreichen die Qualität der Routen im südfranzösischen Kalk. Dieses Buch versammelt eine Reihe von spitzenmäßigen Gebieten in der Haute Provence, von den majestätischen Wänden Ceüses bis zu den wundervoll gelöcherten Felsen von Buoux, und noch einige dazwischen. Insgesamt gibt es 2345 Routen in 14 Gebieten – genug, um viele Kletterer für viele Jahre glücklich zu machen.

Zugang

Für die meisten Routen in diesem Buch gibt es keine Zugangsbeschränkungen und sie können jederzeit beklettert werden. Häufig wurde dies mit einigen Verhandlungen zwischen den Kletterern und Landbesitzern bzw. Anliegern erreicht. Bitte folgt daher genau den beschriebenen Zustiegen in den Gebietsbeschreibungen. Beachtet bitte außerdem jegliche Schilder in Gebietsnähe, die neue Informationen beinhalten könnten.

Der Kletterführer

Dieses Buch enthält sämtliche Informationen, die Du benötigst, um die besten Felsen des Gebietes zu finden und einzuschätzen - auch wenn Englisch nicht Deine Muttersprache ist. Topos und Symbole veranschaulichen die Art der Routen in diesem Buch.

Ausrüstung

Die meisten Routen in diesem Kletterführer sind voll eingerichtete Sportkletterrouten, für die lediglich ein Satz Expreßschlingen und ein langes Seil benötigt wird. Ein 70 Meter Seil ist angebracht, um sicher abseilen zu können. Wenn Du beabsichtigst, Mehrseillängenrouten zu klettern, sind 9mm Doppelseile mit 50 Metern Länge zum Abseilen nötig.

Internet

Alle beschriebenen Aufstiege dieses Kletterführers sind in der Routendatenbank von Rockfax auf der Internetseite - www.rockfax.com - enthalten. Hier findest Du auch mehr Informationen über die einzelnen Routen, sowie Votings zu Schwierigkeitseinstufungen und Kommentare anderer Kletterer. Wenn Du Routen kletterst und nicht mit diesem Kletterführer übereinstimmst, dann besuche unsere Datenbank, um uns Deine Meinung mitzuteilen.

Rockfax

Rockfax veröffentlicht seit 1990 Kletterführer, darunter 30 Bücher zu Gebieten in Europa und vier Bücher zu Gebieten in den USA. Darüber hinaus sind auf der Rockfax-Website mehr als 50 Miniguides im PDF-Format verfügbar. In letzter Zeit haben wir eine Serie von Büchern zum Thema Training veröffentlicht. Weitere Informationen findest Du auf unserer Internetseite - **www.rockfax.com**

Symbole

☼1 Lohnende Kletterei.

☼2 Sehr lohnende Kletterei, eine der besten Routen an diesem Felsen.

☼3 Brilliante Kletterei, eine der besten Routen im Gebiet.

Technisch anspruchsvolle Kletterei, die eine gute Balance und Technik erfordert oder komplexe und trickreiche Züge beinhaltet.

Anstrengende, kraftvolle Kletterei; Dächer, überhängender Fels oder maximalkräftige Züge.

Durchweg anstrengende Kletterei; entweder mit vielen harten Zügen oder überhängender Fels, der zu dicken Armen führt.

Kleingriffige Kletterei

Potentiell weite Stürze bzw. weite Hakenabstände

Weite Züge, morpho

Eine Route, die nicht vollständig mit Bohrhaken ausgerüstet ist - Absicherung durch Klemmkeile und Friends notwendig.

Möglicherweise lockerer Fels im Routenverlauf.

Felsymbole

Steilheit des Zugangsweges mit ungefährer Zeitangabe.

Ungefähre Zeit, zu der der Felsen in der Sonne liegt (wenn sie scheint!).

Überhängende Wände, die trockenen Fels bei Regen bieten.

Klettern an geneigtem Fels, plattig.

Klettern an senkrechtem Fels.

Klettern an stark überhängendem Fels.

Menschenleer - Zur Zeit wenig besucht und meistens ruhig. Langer Anmarsch und / oder weniger lohnende Routen.

Ruhig - Weniger beliebte Sektoren an Hauptfelsen, oder gute Felsen mit langem Zugangsweg.

Belebt - Plätze, an denen Du selten allein sein wirst, besonders an Wochenenden. Lohnende Routen und leichter Zugang.

Zum Brechen voll - Die populärsten Felspartien, an denen ständig Hochbetrieb herrscht.

Farbig markierte Routennummern

Die Seillängen sind farblich nach Schwierigkeit geordnet:

1 Grad V+ und darunter

2 Grad VI- bis VII-

3 Grad VII bis VIII

4 Grad VIII+ und darüber

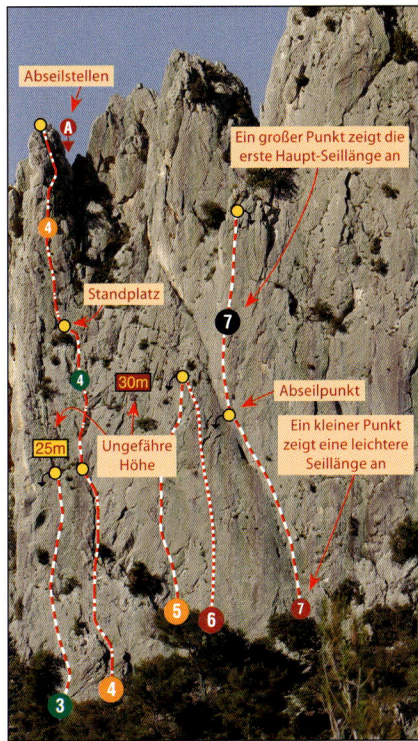

Abseilstellen

A

Ein großer Punkt zeigt die erste Haupt-Seillänge an

Standplatz

30m

Abseilpunkt

Ein kleiner Punkt zeigt eine leichtere Seillänge an

25m

Ungefähre Höhe

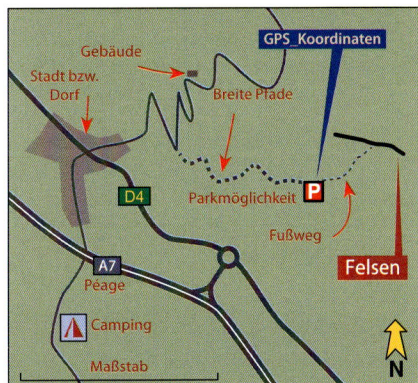

GPS_Koordinaten

Gebäude

Stadt bzw. Dorf

Breite Pfade

Parkmöglichkeit

Fußweg

Felsen

Péage

Camping

Maßstab

N

Céüse · Sisteron · Volx · Orpierre · Bellecombe · Baume Rousse · Ubrieux · Saint Julien · Saint Léger · Malaucène · Combe Obscure · Les Dentelles · Venasque · Buoux

Before crediting those whose efforts have been directed at making this book, credit must go to those who created the routes we describe. Creating a sport route is a lot of work, some of which is skilled, some of which is just sheer effort, and placing bolts on overhanging rock is particularly difficult. It is interesting how the experience of having developed new routes makes one far more understanding of the difficulties of the job - and more forgiving of minor mis-judgements that lead to bolts not being exactly where one may wish they were. And so to all those who have toiled, sweated, bled, cursed, wondered why they were doing it, vowed never to do it again, and created such wonderful climbs: thank you.

Though there is only one name on the cover, this book is the result of the efforts of a great many more people. There are many whose names I have forgotten to add to this list, and to each of them go both my thanks and my apologies.

An extra big thanks to the following for going well beyond the remit of helpfulness:

Chris Singer for spending several winter months with only myself for company deserves credit for that alone, much of the research of the climbs in and around Buis-les-Baronnies is his work, his efforts in inadvertent bolt-testing should also be appreciated by all. Steve McClure was the source of the detailed descriptions of many of the hard routes that make up his astounding tick-list. Audrey Seguy helped as a photographic subject, French language proofer, and patient partner. Simon Richardson was of great help in sourcing addition photos and in getting information on Saint Léger long before the local guidebook came out. Toby Dunn offered his detailed knowledge of Saint Léger as well as posing for some great photos. Ian Fenton contributed significantly to checking the accuracy of the information at Orpierre where he offers guiding and instruction.

A big thanks to all the following for, amongst other things: putting up with me dressing them up in bright clothes to take photos, contributing photos of their own and giving feedback on the routes they've climbed:

Darren Stevenson, Richie Betts, Wayne Smith, Al Downie, Jonathan Read, Craig Entwistle, Adam Gill, Phil Vickers, Stephen Blacket, Chris Keag, Sam Hamer, Ed Hamer, Hugh Sibring, Dave Bond, Stuart Littlefair, Erin Macri, Carrie Cojocari, Dave Simmonite and Andy Gudgeon.

Lastly, for help in checking the text and sharing their wisdom, thanks to Chris Craggs, Jack Geldard, Cedric Larcher, Sherri Davy, Karsten Kurz and Sarah Burmester.

Adrian Berry, November 2009

Rockfax is grateful to the following companies who have supported this guidebook.

Guiding / Instruction

Climb France - Page 17
Buis les Baronnies, France.
Tel: +33 475 265 320
www.climbfrance.com

Services

BMC Insurance - Inside back cover
West Didsbury, Manchester.
Tel: 0161 445 6111
www.thebmc.co.uk

Gear Shops

V12 - Page 23
The Old Baptist Chapel, Llanberis.
Tel: 01286 871534
www.v12outdoor.com

Climbing Walls

Awesome Walls - Page 2
St. Alban's Church, Liverpool.
Tel/Fax: 0151 298 2422
The Engine House, Stockport.
Tel: 0161 494 9949
www.awesomewalls.co.uk

Outdoor Gear

Berghaus - Inside front cover
Extreme Centre, Sunderland.
Tel: 0191 516 5700
www.berghaus.com

Black Diamond - Outside back cover
Tel: 0162 958 0484
www.blackdiamondequipment.com

Climbers' Web Resource

Climb Europe - Opposite
www.climb-europe.com

ClimbinFrance - Cover flap
www.climbinfrance.com

Céüse
Sisteron
Volx
Orpierre
Bellecombe
Baume Rousse
Ubrieux
Saint Julien
Saint Léger
Malaucène
Combe Obscure
Les Dentelles
Venasque
Buoux

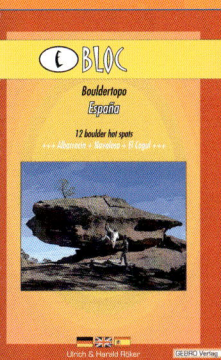

Haute Provence Logistics

Céüse | Sisteron | Voix | Orpierre | Bellecombe | Baume Rousse | Ubrieux | Saint Julien | Saint Léger | Malaucène | Combe Obscure | Les Dentelles | Venasque | Buoux

Photo: Simon Richardson/DarkPeakImages

Céüse

Sisteron

Volx

Orpierre

Bellecombe

Baume Rousse

Ubrieux

Saint Julien

Saint Léger

Malaucène

Combe Obscure

Les Dentelles

Venasque

Buoux

Céüse

Sisteron

Volx

Orpierre

Bellecombe

Baume Rousse

Ubrieux

Saint Julien

Saint Léger

Malaucène

Combe Obscure

Les Dentelles

Vénasque

Buoux

Train

Eurostar operates a direct service from London to Avignon during the summer months. At other times of year, an indirect service is possible on the TGV. Luggage restrictions are far less than those imposed by budget airlines, and the journey only takes around 8 hours station to station.

Flying

There are a number of airports in the South of France served by budget airlines. Marseille and Avignon are the closest but Grenoble, Montpellier, Nîmes, Lyon and Nice are also options. Expect to pay more at popular times like weekends, the summer months and school holidays.

Driving

The French autoroutes are fast and usually uncrowded. If you've got a long drive, it makes sense to break the journey, sleeping in rest areas is acceptable, but if you're looking for a bed without spending too much, find a Formula 1 (**www.hotelformule1.com**) or, a bit nicer, an Ibis (**www.ibishotel.com**) or Etap (**www.etaphotel.com**).

Getting around without a car

A number of areas covered in this guide can be accessed quite easily by public transport, and if you are visiting at the right time of year, you will doubtless find other climbers with cars who you can share rides with. The municipal campsite in Apt is an easy place to get to on public transport (about one hour from Avignon) and there are always plenty of climbers driving in to Buoux each day. Some crags can be done without cars altogether - Céüse and Buis for example have campsites near to the climbing areas.

Guiding Services

There are also a number of guides operating in the areas covered, and some will pick you up at the train station or airport, put you up, take you to the crags, climb with you each day and then drop you off.
ClimbFrance - www.climbfrance.com

Satellite Navigation

The key parking spots for the crags in this book have a GPS co-ordinate box. These are in the standard DMS system which is accepted by most makes of SatNav.
Bear in mind that SatNavs often get it horrib wrong and will delight in taking you through an endless chain of tiny villages when you could have been cruising along on the Autoroute. Also note that there are many places in France with the same name - key- 'Saint Léger', and you could find yourself taking the scenic route to completely the wrong place. The best policy is to use your SatNav in conjunction with a map. The map the facing page gives rough locations. Each chapter has a closer map which should hom you in to your chosen crag but a detailed local area map will also be found useful.

Staying

A comprehensive listing of all the places to stay in the South of France would require every page of this book to cover. Camping in the South of France is very well provided for. Driving around, you will notice that there are signs for campsites everywhere. The be campsites are listed in the introductions to the areas covered in this book. Apartments and gîtes are best found using the Internet: search the web for 'gites france' and you wi access a number of listings sites that allow you to book online. Tourist information office are found in most towns, and are happy to find you somewhere to stay, and something keep you busy on a rest day.

Travel Insurance

UK citizens have reciprocal health care righ in France under the EHIC. Despite this it is strongly recommended that personal travel insurance is taken out to cover rescue, medical and repatriation following an accident.
BMC Travel Insurance - www.thebmc.co.

Grenoble

TGV

Valence

Die

Crest

A7

TGV

Montélimar

Gap

Ceuse

Serres

A51

Laragne-
Montéglin

Bellecombe

Nyons

Ubrieux

Baume Rousse

Buis-les-
Baronnies

Orpierre

Bollène

Malaucène

Saint Julien

Saint Léger

Sisteron

**Dentelles de
Montmirail**

Malaucène

Sisteron

Orange

Mont
Ventoux

Combe Obscure

Sault

Carpentras

A9

TGV

Avignon

Venasque

Apt

Avignon
Airport

Volx

A51

Cavaillon

Manosque

Buoux

Salon-de-
Provence

Pertuis

A54

A7

A8

TGV

Aix-en-Provence

Nice

TGV

About 20km

N

Marseille
Airport

Ceüse · Sisteron · Volx · Orpierre · Bellecombe · Baume Rousse · Ubrieux · Saint Julien · Saint Léger · Malaucène · Combe Obscure · Les Dentelles · Venasque · Buoux

While researching this book, the author spent February, March and April in Buis-les-Baronnies. In a three month period, there were less than five days of bad weather. Climbing in the sun on a winter's day in France is always delightful. If you want to climb on the south-facing crags, winter is definitely a good time for it. Spring and autumn are the best times for the lower crags when you can choose between optimum cool climbing conditions in the shade or relish the warmth of the sun. Summer may not be the best time for climbing on low level sunny crags, but there are plenty of north-facing venues, alternatively, get up to some of the high crags. The sheer number and variety of crags in France means there's always somewhere to climb, no matter what time of year you choose to visit.

Average Temp °C	Jan	Feb	Mar	Apr	May	Jun	Jul	Aug	Sep	Oct	Nov	De
Gap (maximum)	7	8	12	15	19	23	27	27	21	17	10	8
Gap (minimum)	-3	-2	1	3	7	10	12	12	10	6	1	-1
Buis (maximum)	10	12	16	18	22	27	29	29	25	19	13	10
Buis (minimum)	2	3	6	8	11	14	18	18	13	10	7	3
Apt (maximum)	11	12	16	18	22	27	30	30	25	20	15	12
Apt (minimum)	3	4	6	9	12	15	18	18	16	12	8	5

The average rainfall for the areas covered by in book is relatively low. The high figures in September to November tend to result from storms rather than full days of rain. This may mean that there is a bit of seepage on some routes but you are very unlikely to lose too mu climbing time.

Rainfall cm / month	Jan	Feb	Mar	Apr	May	Jun	Jul	Aug	Sep	Oct	Nov	De
Gap (average)	3.3	2.9	2.9	4.3	3.9	4.0	3.3	3.7	4.6	6.4	4.9	3.
Buis (average)	3.7	2.3	2.5	4.7	4.6	2.5	2.1	2.9	6.6	6.0	5.3	3.
Apt (average)	3.5	2.1	2.2	4.0	2.7	1.5	0.8	1.8	5.7	5.2	3.9	2.

Looking east on the road between Buis and Orpierre in February. It was possible to climb at both locations at the time if a little chilly.

Céüse

Sisteron

Voix

Orpierre

Bellecombe

Baume Rousse

Ubrieux

Saint Julien

Saint Léger

Malaucène

Combe Obscure

Les Dentelles

Venasque

Buoux

Steep rock on the magnificent Berlin Sector at Céüse

Haute Provence Climbing

Ceüse

Sisteron

Volx

Orpierre

Bellecombe

Baume Rousse

Ubrieux

Saint Julien

Saint Léger

Malaucène

Combe Obscure

Les Dentelles

Venasque

Buoux

Céüse
Sisteron
Volx
Orpierre
Bellecombe
Baume Rousse
Ubrieux
Saint Julien
Saint Léger
Malaucène
Combe Obscure
Les Dentelles
Venasque
Buoux

Grades

The routes in this book are graded using the usual sport grade system, or 'French Grade' as it is often known. Many of these venues were developed in the early days of sport climbing and, as is often the case, this means that they later acquire a reputation for stiff grading, certainly in the lower and mid grades. This is definitely true of Céüse and Buoux which will be regarded as 'hard' by many climbers.

Route Grades

Sport Grade	British Trad Grade (for well protected routes only)	UIAA	USA
1	Mod (Moderate)	I	5.1
2	Diff (Difficult)	II, III	5.2
2+	VDiff (Very Difficult)	III+	5.3
3	HVD (Hard Very Difficult)	IV	5.4, 5.5
3+	Sev (Severe)	IV+	5.6
4	HS (Hard Severe); VS (Very Severe) 4a–4c	V-, V	5.7
4+		V+	5.8
5	HVS (Hard Very Severe) 4c–5b	VI-	5.9
5+		VI	5.10a
6a	E1 5a–5c	VI+	5.10b
6a+	E2 5b–6a	VII-	5.10c
6b		VII	5.10d
6b+	E3 5c–6a		5.11a
6c		VII+	5.11b
6c+	E4 6a–6b	VIII-	5.11c
7a		VIII	5.11d
7a+	E5 6a–6c	VIII+	5.12a
7b			5.12b
7b+		IX-	5.12c
7c	E6 6b–6c	IX	5.12d
7c+		IX+	5.13a
8a	E7 6c–7a	X-	5.13b
8a+			5.13c
8b	E8 6c–7a	X	5.13d
8b+		X+	5.14a
8c	E9 7a–7b	XI-	5.14b
8c+		XI	5.14c
9a	E10 7a–7b		5.14d
9a+		XI+	5.15a

Colour-coding

The routes and pitches are colour-coded corresponding to a grade band. The idea is to give a rough comparison between trad routes and sport routes. For example, if you are happy on orange grades on trad, then you should consider routes given orange spot sport grades.

Green Spots - Everything at grade 4+ and under. Mostly these should be good for beginners and those wanting an easy life.

Orange Spots - 5 to 6a+ inclusive. General ticking routes for those with more experience.

Red Spots - 6b to 7a inclusive. Routes for the very experienced and keen climber.

Black Spots - 7a+ and above. The hard stuff!

Multi-pitch Colour-codes

There are plenty of multi-pitch routes covered in this guide in particular at crags like Saint Julien, in the Dentelles and at Buoux. Often you may not want to tackle all the pitches of a route, particularly if there is a single hard pitch high up with some great easier pitches leading to it. In this guide for the first time we have given each pitch a colour-code to aid location of these different pitches. Each route has a single large number which is given to the first significant pitch. The other pitches are all given smaller dots corresponding to their colour-code grade band.

Belays and Extensions

routes are bolted so that an ascent ends when you have clipped the belay, grabbing belays is not the custom. Multi-pitch routes are graded assuming you are taking each belay. Single pitches often have additional sections added to them to offer a longer and more difficult route, these are known as extensions - Céüse in particular is a crag with a lot of extensions. Most extensions are given extra grades in the route description, and often have different names. Extensions are not second pitches, and the grade of an extension assumes you have not rested on the belay - which would make it easier than graded. Extensions are given small spots in our colour-code system even if they are harder than the main pitch.

Sport Climbing+

The Rockfax publication Sport Climbing+, by Adrian Berry and Steve McClure, makes great companion to this book and it should enable you to get even more out of your trip to the Haute Provence crags.

The book takes a practical approach, focusing on the improvements that climbers can make immediately, without embarking on a lengthy training program. It is available from **www.rockfax.com**

Le Dame de Flair (6b) - *page 231* - St. Christophe, Les Dentelles.

Céüse
Sisteron
Volx
Orpierre
Bellecombe
Baume Rousse
Ubrieux
Saint Julien
Saint Léger
Malaucène
Combe Obscure
Les Dentelles
Venasque
Buoux

Céüse | Sisteron | Volx | Orpierre | Bellecombe | Baume Rousse | Ubrieux | Saint Julien | Saint Léger | Malaucène | Combe Obscure | Les Dentelles | Venasque | Buoux

Ropes, Route Lengths and Lowering Off

The most crucial item of gear is your rope. At the very least, you need a 60m rope, but if you're buying a new rope for a trip to France, we strongly recommend getting a 70m rope or longer. Single ropes are now available in thicknesses previously associated with half-ropes. The thinner your rope, the lighter it is to hike up to the crag, the easier it is to pull up to clip, and the softer it is to fall onto. Thicker ropes last longer and are better for working projects. For multi-pitch routes requiring an abseil descent, you may find that using a pair of half-rope is preferable, alternatively, if you have a 100m single rope, you can make all the abseils and have the convenience of leading on a single rope.

The photo-topos have approximate heights, rounded up to the nearest 5m, indicated next to some lower-offs. These are guideline heights only and it is important to remember that crag bases are not always level and people stand in different places when belaying. Also, many climbers don't even know exactly how long their rope is having chopped worn sections off the ends in the past. **The golden rule is always tie a knot in the end of the rope to prevent dropping a climber when lowering off.**

Other Gear

Only a few routes in this guidebook require more than a single rope and a set of quickdraws - 14 quickdraws is plenty for all but the longest of pitches. For the belays on multi-pitch route a couple of screwgate carabiners and a sling each is a good idea. The few routes which nee gear (11 of them) are denoted with the ⬚ symbol.

Make sure your belay device is suitable for your rope: too grabbing and you'll be cursing it each time you pay out rope, too slick and you may struggle to hold your partner. A belay device that you are happy to abseil on is also a good idea.

Beyond these essentials you may find tape useful for bandaging your fingers if the prickly rock starts to take its toll. For multi-pitch routes a small sack with a water bladder, a long-sleeve shirt and a sun hat are good ideas. A good pair of approach shoes are also worth packing as a number of the walk-ins are long.

Chris SInger belaying at Saint Léger.

Crag Table

	Routes	up to 4+	5 to 6a+	6b to 7a	7a+ and up
Céüse	*198*		20 ✓✓	61 ✓✓✓	117 ✓✓✓✓
Sisteron	*75*	5 ✓	32 ✓✓✓	27 ✓✓✓	11 ✓
Volx	*49*		4	5 ✓	40 ✓✓✓
Orpierre	*212*	12 ✓✓	98 ✓✓✓	61 ✓✓✓	41 ✓✓
Bellecombe	*40*		13 ✓✓	14 ✓✓✓	13 ✓✓
Baume Rousse	*87*	10 ✓✓✓	31 ✓✓✓	21 ✓✓	25 ✓✓
Ubrieux	*109*	17 ✓✓	36 ✓✓✓	36 ✓✓✓	20 ✓✓
Saint Julien	*89*	3 ✓	39 ✓✓✓	39 ✓✓✓	8 ✓
Saint Léger	*291*		8	74 ✓✓	209 ✓✓✓✓
Malaucène	*64*	2 ✓	11 ✓	18 ✓✓	33 ✓✓
Combe Obscure	*52*	1	26 ✓✓	18 ✓✓	7 ✓
Les Dentelles	*360*	21 ✓✓✓	171 ✓✓✓	168 ✓✓✓	86 ✓✓✓
Venasque	*130*		28 ✓✓	64 ✓✓✓	38 ✓✓✓
Buoux	*404*	4	76 ✓✓✓	173 ✓✓✓✓	151 ✓✓✓✓

Eastern Crags: Céüse, Sisteron, Volx, Orpierre

Buis-les-Baronnies: Bellecombe, Baume Rousse, Ubrieux, Saint Julien, Saint Léger, Malaucène, Combe Obscure

Buoux Area: Venasque, Buoux

Side tabs: Céüse, Sisteron, Volx, Orpierre, Bellecombe, Baume Rousse, Ubrieux, Saint Julien, Saint Léger, Malaucène, Combe Obscure, Les Dentelles, Venasque, Buoux

Quality and range of routes in different grade bands: ✓✓✓ - Excellent   ✓✓ - Good   ✓ - Okay   NO TICK - Not worth a visit

Approach	Sun	Multi-pitch	When wet	When hot	When cold	Summary	Page	
60 to 75 min	Morning		✓	✔	✘	A crag whose situation reflects its stature - high on a mountain top, Céüse Is a popular summer destination. Though famed for its world-famous super routes, there is plenty of interest in the mid-grades, just be prepared for a bit of a walk-in. Although very steep, the walls run with water during heavy rain.	28	Céüse
2 to 4 min	Lots of sun	Multi-pitch	✘	✘	✔	A road-side urban crag with an immaculate slabby south face that gets plenty of sun and offers great rock and a series of inviting routes winding their way to the top. It can get hot here though and there is the only shelter from the sun and rain is on a small north-facing wall with a few hard routes.	48	Sisteron
10 min	Lots of sun		✔	✘	✔	In some ways the epitome of hard sport climbing, though hardly beautiful. The climbing is good, steep and possible in all states of weather making Volx a popular destination for those avoiding rain. It is getting a bit polished now so probably worth keeping in reserve for a rainy day, and it only offers hard routes.	58	Volx
10 to 30 min	Sun and shade	Multi-pitch	✓	✓	✔	An extensive area with something for everyone, from beautiful slabs covered with friendly single pitches, to long multi-pitch offerings on some very impressive walls. It can get hot in the summer, but it is possible to chase the shade, and there is also a single shady and ever-dry hard wall covered here.	66	Orpierre
4 min	From mid morning	Multi-pitch	✘	✘	✔	A novel fin of rock that has enough to keep anyone entertained for a while. Although not an extensive crag, it does offer a wide variety of routes on excellent rock, often following compelling natural features and the location is superb. It will get hot in summer but is too exposed to be much of a winter sun-trap.	90	Bellecombe
5 to 12 min	Lots of sun		✓	✓	✔	An impressive concentration of high quality routes spanning the full grade range. All but the very best climbers could easily spend a week here and still have routes to go at. Facing a variety of directions, Baume Rousse is a winter sun-trap, but there is often something in the shade in summer.	98	Baume Rousse
0 to 20 min	From mid morning		✘	✓	✔	A treat for those looking for technical routes up sunny grey limestone, covering a range of routes from friendly first-leads through to some desperately thin wall climbs. Steep, sustained routes of all grades are also on offer at nearby Lou Passo which gets plenty of shade during summer.	110	Ubrieux
2 to 35 min	Lots of sun	Multi-pitch	✘	✘	✓	A beautiful crag with a sunny aspect, offering a wealth of multi-pitch routes on magnificent rock. Though fully bolted, Saint Julian has an adventurous feel to its climbing, and is an ideal destination for those looking for more than single pitch gymnastics. Sunny and exposed to the weather.	126	Saint Julien
10 to 30 min	Lots of sun		✔	✓	✔	An extensive crag which caters for those seeking the epitome of modern hard sport climbing. Facing every direction, Saint Leger offers both summer shade, a glorious winter sun-trap, and everything in between. Though there's not much to go at below 7a, there's a lifetime's worth of climbing above it.	142	Saint Leger
10 min	Not much sun		✓	✓	✘	A small area, but with excellent rock and a good variety of routes to go at, though you really need to be climbing at 6b or above to get the most of it. Malaucène can be a good summer venue until the sun arrives in mid-afternoon. It is less of a winter-sun option but late afternoons can be warm.	170	Malaucène
15 min	To mid afternoon		✘	✘	✔	A fine pair of walls consisting of some of the nicest limestone you will ever find. The rock offers superb routes in the lower grades, though there are certainly some technical test-pieces to be found. Depending on the time of day, you can find plenty of winter sun, or a little late summer shade.	180	Combe Obscure
2 to 25 min	Sun and shade	Multi-pitch	✔	✔	✔	An extensive area which has much for everyone. The majority of the rock faces south making it great for winter sun, although most areas are quite exposed to the wind. The north-facing Chaine de.Gogondas has routes across the grade spectrum for those after summer shade. There is one steep ever-dry wall.	188	Les Dentelles
0 to 5 min	Morning		✓	✓	✘	Offering a very different style from that offered by a typical French sport crag, Venasque is well worth checking out. A mixture of sloper-pulling technical climbs and steep jug-pulling extravaganzas, there's morning winter sun and afternoon summer shade on offer, plus the steep sections are sheltered in the rain.	234	Venasque
15 to 20 min	Lots of sun	Multi-pitch	✓	✘	✔	Probably the most recognisable crag in this book, Buoux is a jewel in the sport climbing crown. Though there is enough climbing below 6a to maintain interest for weeks, Buoux is at it best when you're climbing in the 7s. A bit hot in summer, and a bit cold in winter - though perfect in spring and autumn.	246	Buoux

✓ - Definitely worth a look   ✓ - Could be lucky   x - Probably not worth the effort   X - Forget it!

Céuse

Sisteron

Volx

Orpierre

Bellecombe

Baume Rousse

Ubrieux

Saint Julien

Saint Léger

Malaucene

Combe Obscure

Les Dentelles

Venasque

Buoux

The magnificent crag of Céüse is the main attraction in this area; a truly world class destination. Sisteron has a good sunny wall that will likely be in condition when it's too cold for Céüse, and conversely when it's too hot at Sisteron you can be sure of better conditions up at Céüse. Volx is included because it's such a useful place to know about when it rains.

Getting there and getting around

To arrive in style, the TGV will get you to Aix-en-Provence in the south, or Grenoble in the north. Gap has a SNCF station and it is possible to pick up a hire car from the station if you want the minimal drive. It is possible to climb at Céüse without your own car: get to Gap, then get a taxi to the campsite, in the summer there should be plenty of opportunities to get lifts to grocery shops. For those flying, the nearest major airports are in Marseille, Toulon, and Nice in the south, and Grenoble to the north.

Where to stay

The obvious place to stay at Céüse is the **Les Guérins** campsite situated some way beneath the crag. If you're looking for something more comfortable, the tourist information office in Gap will be happy to help (+33 4 92 52 56 56).
Sisteron also has a convenient campsite, **Camping Les Prés Hauts** (March - October) which is signposted from the roundabout at the base of the crag.
There is a municipal campsite in Volx, **Camping de la Vandelle** (June - October). **Camping des Princes d'Orange** (April - October) is well-situated in Orpierre.

Local guidebooks

The **Céüse** guidebook (€20), covering Céüse and four other nearby venues, is available from the Camping Les Guérins shop.
Topo Escalade Bleone Durance (€18) covers Sisteron, Volx and other areas. It is available from the TI office in Sisteron.
The **Orpierre** guidebook is available in the climbing shop in the village.

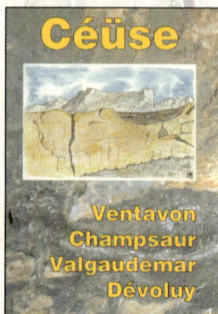

About 20km

N

D994
Gap
Céüse
N85
Sigoyer

N75
A51
D951
Orpierre
Sisteron
Sisteron

Digne-les-Bains

D951
N85

Forcalquier
D4
Volx
N100
Volx

Céüse

Ventavon
Champsaur
Valgaudemar
Dévoluy

ffme
TOPO D'ESCALADE BLEONE DURANCE
Volx
Sisteron "La Baume"
Sisteron "le Collet"
Chabrières
Château-Arnoux "St Jean"
Digne "Courbons"
Blegiers

Orpierre

Web links

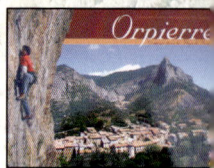

Céüse

Sisteron

Volx

Orpierre

Bellecombe

Baume Rousse

Ubrieux

Saint Julien

Saint Leger

Malaucene

Combe Obscure

Les Dentelles

Venasque

Buoux

Eastern Crags
Céüse - Sisteron - Volx - Orpierre

Audrey Seguy on *Hyper Mickey* (7c) - *page 33* - Cascade, Céüse.

Céüse

Sisteron

Volx

Orpierre

Bellecombe

Baume Rousse

Ubrieux

Saint Julien

Saint Léger

Malaucène

Combe Obscure

Les Dentelles

Venasque

Buoux

Céüse

La Cascade
Page 32

Tho...
Pag...

Face de Rat
Page 37

Berlin
Page 38

Biographie
Page 40

Demi Lune
Page 42

Un Pont
sur l'Infini
Page 44

La Maîtres
du Monde
Page 46

Junction to go to the
different sectors

Steep short cut for
Cascade sector

P

P

P

Cèüse · Sisteron · Volx · Orpierre · Bellecombe · Baume Rousse · Ubrieux · Saint Julien · Saint Léger · Malaucène · Combe Obscure · Les Dentelles · Venasque · Buoux

	No star	☼	☼☼	☼☼☼
Up to 4+	-	-	-	
5 to 6a+	1	2	12	5
6b to 7a	1	8	25	2
7a+ and up	3	8	46	6

Widely considered to be 'the best crag in the world', Céuse certainly has the strongest claim to being the best sport crag in France - and there's some pretty stiff competition! Although famed for long, steep, hard routes there is something brilliant here for everyone: from steep and juggy, to vertical and technical, plus a number of multi-pitch outings. The location is majestic - what could be more perfect? Well....

Approach

... there's always a catch, and this is it - the walk-in is a real pain! It takes between 45 minutes and an hour depending on how fit you are, and how much kit you've stashed on your previous visit.

From the campsite, follow a marked path past the concrete horse shed next to the camping until you reach a well-worn path leading upwards. Follow this past a staggered junction on a forest track until you get to a track that contours several hundred metres below the crag.
For Cascade: follow the path to the left, passing through a gate, a small path leads off to the right when you are under the sector.
All other sectors: follow the path to the right, the areas are clearly visible at this point, and paths lead up the hill. The path for Berlin is indicated by a painted-on sign on a rock, for Thorgal approach as for Berlin and walk left along the base. For sectors to the right of Berlin you can stay on the contouring path and pick one of several paths that lead up steeply to the base of the crag.

Conditions

Céuse is a summer crag. Even in the middle of August, the evenings can get cold, so bring your down jacket. Facing from southwest to east, you can follow the sun or the shade as you choose. Cascade gets sun until late morning; if you want Cascade in the shade you will need quite an early start. Leaving the campsite at around 1.30pm in the summer will get you to Berlin and sectors to its right just as they come into the shade. If it is particularly cold, or a strong breeze is blowing, it may be wise to aim to climb in the sun.

Céuse in the winter, probably best to climb somewhere else!

Céüse

Sisteron

Volx

Orpierre

Bellecombe

Baume Rousse

Ubrieux

Saint Julien

Saint Léger

Malaucène

Combe Obscure

Les Dentelles

Venasque

Buoux

on *Rosanna* (8a) - *page 33* - Cascade area at Céüse.

Céüse

Sisteron

Volx

Orpierre

Bellecombe

Baume Rousse

Ubrieux

Saint Julien

Saint Leger

Malaucène

Combe Obscure

Les Dentelles

Venasque

Buoux

La Cascade

Perhaps the most famous sector at Céüse. The routes here are steep and sustained, but with good holds on which to get pumped. Expect a fair bit of polish on the classic routes, as they get plenty of traffic. If you want the shade, get an early start, though there is some shade for belaying at the base even in the mid-day sun. If the waterfall is running, you can avoid carrying water to the crag by filling your bottles at its base.

① **Wake** 8b
1) 6b. Climb up the 'tree' and follow the groove.
2) 8b, 3) 7b+.

② **L'Espace Blue** 8a

③ **Gare au Goret** . . . . 7c+

④ **Unknown** . . . . ?

⑤ **Violente Illusion** 8b
A sharp (**V9**) boulder problem leads to 7b+ ground.

⑥ **Humble Heros** . . . . ?

⑦ **Ténéré** . . . . 7c+
The mantel over the top roof is a heart-breaker.
The extension is **8a**, or thereabouts.

⑧ **Mirage** . . . . 7c+
A classic.

⑨ **Unknown** . . . . ?

⑩ **Vagabond d'Occident** . . 7c
Soft for the grade.

⑪ **Blue Blanc Gioraphare** . 7c+
Hard and sharp.

⑫ **Blanches Fesses** 7c
Sustained and excellent.

⑬ **Correspondence Imaginaire** 7c+

⑭ **Corps Éntrager** . . . . 7b+
Formerly 7c+, so tough at this grade.

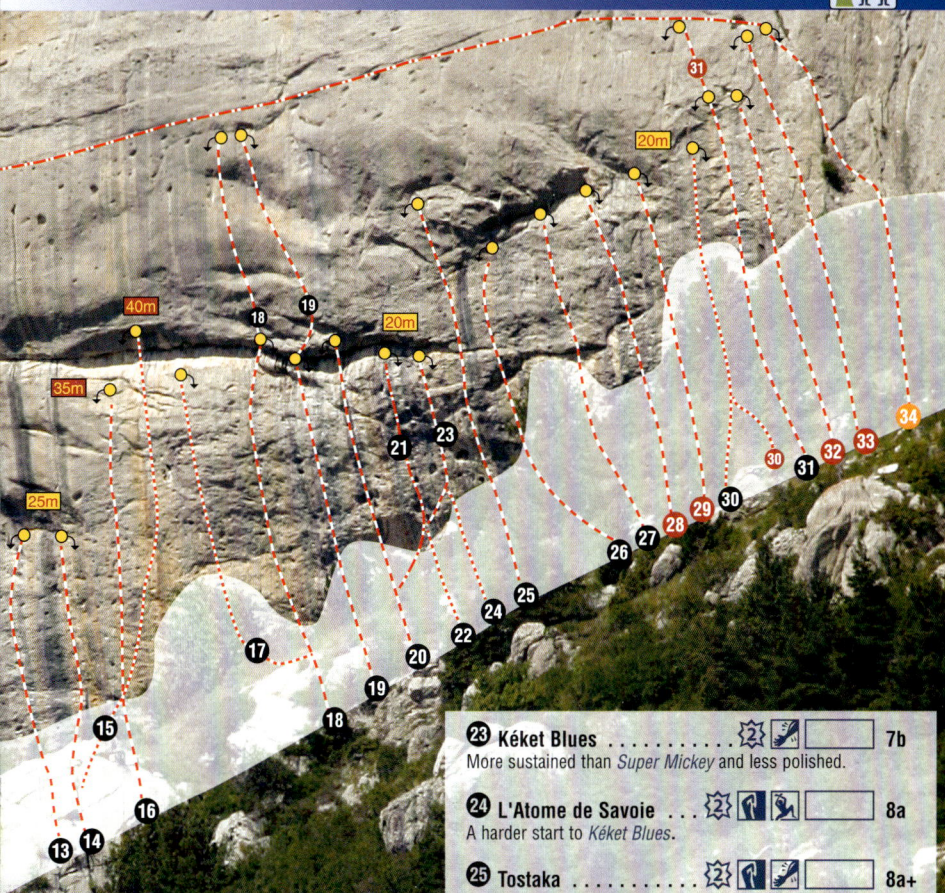

Céüse

Sisteron

Voix

Orpierre

Bellecombe

Baume Rousse

Ubrieux

Saint Julien

Saint Léger

Malaucène

Combe Obscure

Les Dentelles

Venasque

Buoux

23 Kéket Blues 7b
More sustained than _Super Mickey_ and less polished.

24 L'Atome de Savoie . . . 8a
A harder start to _Kéket Blues_.

25 Tostaka . . . . 8a+

26 La Tombe de Savoie . . 8a

27 Alabama . . . . 7b+

28 Ananda 7a
A classic of its grade. Is it possible to fall off holds this big?

29 Médecine Douce . . . . 6c+
Not quite 'first-route-of-the-day' material, but okay if you know
it. Has 'women' scratched at the start.

30 Women . . . . 7a+
An intense lower section. The first bolt is shared with _Medicine
Douce_ then trend right. There is an easier start out right.

31 Fletcher line . . . . 7b+
A bit painful. There is an extension at **7a**.

32 Les Sales Blagues à Nanard . . . 6c

33 Des Trous Direct 6b

34 Des Trous 6a
1) 5, 2) 5, 3) 5, 4) 6a

Association de Malfaiteurs 7c+
ong rising traverse.

Rosanna 8a
very bouldery crux. _See photo on page 31._

Questions d'Équilibre . . 8b

Pieds nus sous les Rodhodendrons
. . . . 7c+
ard start, then much easier. The extension is **Félicité, 8b**.

Le privilège du Serpent . . . 7c+
guably the best route here. The extension is **Magnificat, 8b**.

Fleur de Lotus 7c
rd at the grade - 8a has been suggested.

Super Mickey 7b
me very big pockets - still pumpy though, and a tricky finale.

Hyper Mickey 7c
V5) bouldery start to _Super Mickey_. _Photo on page 27._

65 min | From mid morning | Slabby | Vertical

Thorgal

In contrast to its steep neighbour down to the left, Thor has plenty of technical, slabby routes in the mid sixes.

1 Baie des Anges .... 7a+

2 Clochette Étalée 6c

3 Pony Boy .... 6c+
1) 6c. A hard slab at the top. 2) 6c+, 40m.

4 Colombine Panachée ..... 6b+
The last bolt and belay are left of the actual line. A technical slabby finish awaits!

5 Rumble Gish .... 6b+
1) 6b+, 2) 7a, 40m. The top pitch can be split - 6c, 7a.

6 La Femme Piége 6b

7 La Ballade de la Mer Salée 6b

8 Alinoé 6b

9 La Maître des Montagnes . 6b

10 Pulp Friction 6b

11 Les Daltons Courent Toujours 6b

12 La Touffe de ma Dalton 6a

Céüse · Sisteron · Volx · Orpierre · Bellecombe · Baume Rousse · Ubrieux · Saint Julien · Saint Léger · Malaucène · Combe Obscure · Les Dentelles · Venasque · Buoux

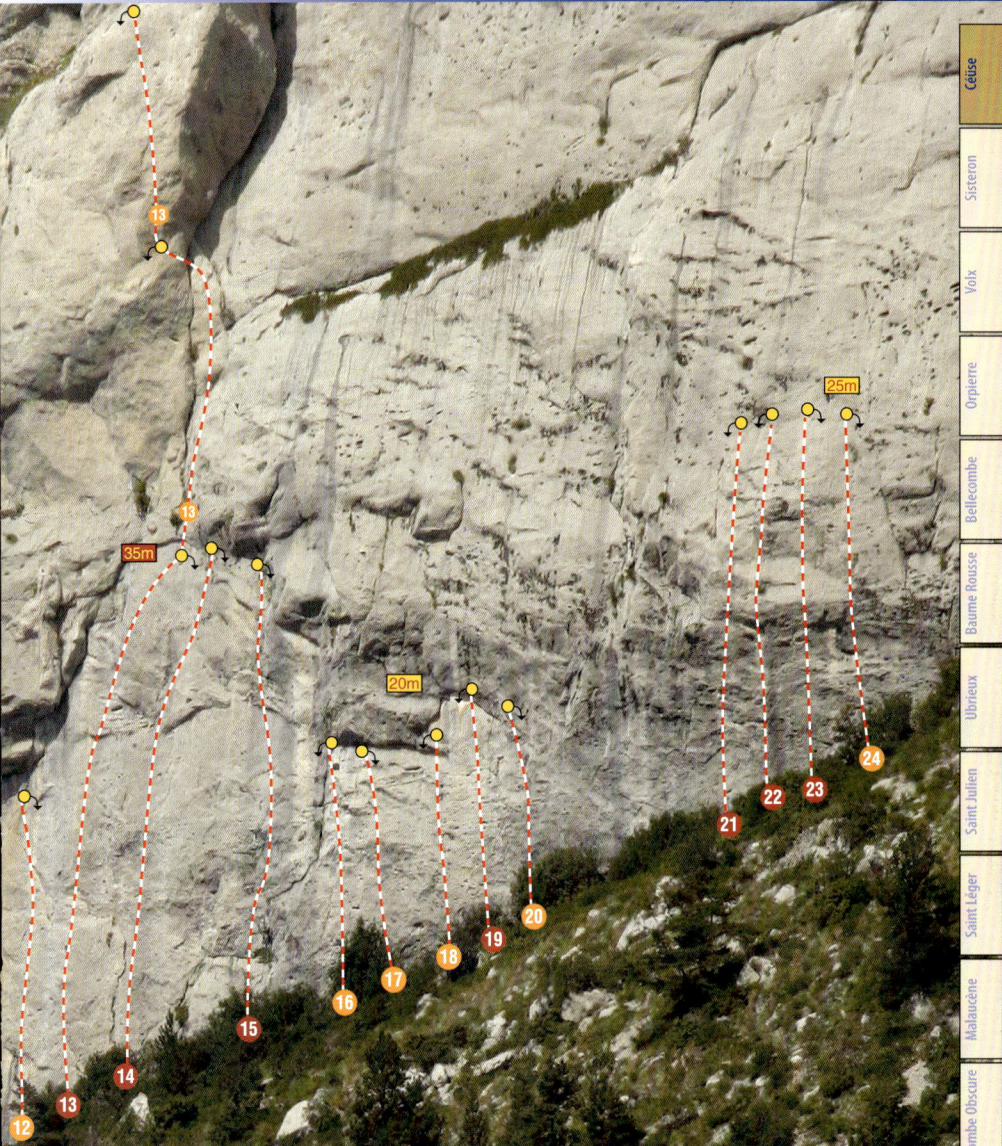

Céüse

Sisteron

Voix

Orpierre

Bellecombe

Baume Rousse

Ubrieux

Saint Julien

Saint Léger

Malaucène

Combe Obscure

Les Dentelles

Venasque

Buoux

L'évasion des Daltons				6b
6b, 2) 5+, 3) 5+				
Le Vol des Daltons				6b+
Les Daltons se Rachètent . .				6b
Les Yeux de Tanatloc				6a+
L'Épée Soleil				6a
La Forteresse Invisible				6a

19 Gondalf le Fou				6b
20 Au-delá des Ombres				5+
21 La Chute de Brek Zarinth . .				6c+
22 Entre Terre et Lumière				6b+
23 La Cité du Dieu Perdu . . .				6b
Photo on page 36.				
24 La Magicienne Trahie				6a+

Céüse

Sisteron

Volx

Orpierre

Bellecombe

Baume Rousse

Ubrieux

Saint Julien

Saint Léger

Malaucène

Combe Obscure

Les Dentelles

Venasque

Buoux

Reinhard Klier on *La Cité du Dieu Perdu* (6b) - *page 35*.

La Cascade
Page 32

Thorgal
Page 34

Face de Rat

Berlin
Page 38

Face de Rat

very impressive sector that is mostly undeveloped. The
ost noteworthy route is the one that gives the sector its
me, Face de Rat.

Un Temps Pour les Pierres . . . . 6c+

Héros Positif . . . . 7a+

Tempête sous un Crâne . . . 7b

Unnamed 7a

❺ Mon Ami le Coyotte . . . . ?

❻ L'Armée des Ombres . . 8b+

❼ Race de Fate 8b

❽ Face de Rat . . . . 8a+
A classic of the crag. Very long and sustained. Despite some
breathers the difficulties just keep coming. Put your technical
head on too, just pulling won't get you up this one.

❾ Rab de Farces 8b

40m

25m

35m

7

3   4   5   6   8   9

Céüse · Sisteron · Volx · Orpierre · Bellecombe · Baume Rousse · Ubrieux · Saint Julien · Saint Leger · Malaucene · Combe Obscure · Les Dentelles · Venasque · Buoux

Céüse
Sisteron
Voix
Orpierre
Bellecombe
Baume Rousse
Ubrieux
Saint Julien
Saint Léger
Malaucène
Combe Obscure
Les Dentelles
Venasque
Buoux

Berlin

Some would say that this is the best sector at Céüse, which would arguably make it the best sector in the World - now all you have to do is climb the best route here and you can retire! If anything the quality can be a bit overwhelming, and it's hard to appreciate individual routes when they are all so good. The bolts can be quite spaced here, but that just allows you to enjoy the climbing with less interruption, at least it does when you well within your grade - not the easiest thing. Just one warning: the slabby lower grade routes at the right-hand end aren't giveaways.

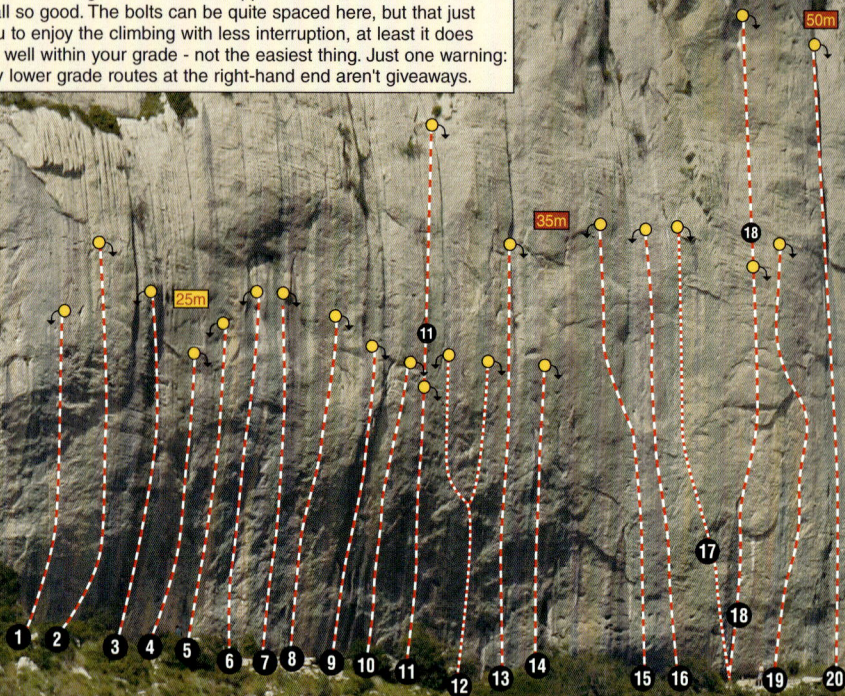

50m
35m
25m

❶ L'Errance d'une Passion 7c

❷ Monnaie de Singe 8a

❸ Blocage Violent . . . . . 7b+
A famous and popular 7b+. Considered tough for the grade.

❹ Dolce Vità . . . . 8a+
Tough for the grade, but a Céüse classic.

❺ Petit Tom 8a
Low in the grade.

❻ La Couleur du Vent . . . 8a
The grade is for a diversion left at the top - **8a+** direct.

❼ Berlin 7c
Follows the impressive blue streak. Hard for the grade,

❽ La Chose 7c

❾ Galaxy 7c
Given 7b+ locally.

❿ Makach Walou 7c

⓫ Queue de rat 7b
Clipping the belay is tricky. The amazing extension is **8a+**.

⓬ Unknown . . . . ?
A line of expansion bolts that splits into two.

⓭ Rat Man 8a

⓮ Bouse de Douze 8a

⓯ La Concombre Masqué . . 7c

⓰ Archetype 8b

⓱ Unknown . . . . ?

⓲ La Petite Illusion 7a
Tremendous climbing throughout. The runout bits aren't too hard, so keep on pulling! The extension is also **7a+**.

Céüse

Sisteron

Volx

Orpierre

Bellecombe

Baume Rousse

Ubrieux

Saint Julien

Saint Léger

Malaucène

Combe Obscure

Les Dentelles

Venasque

Buoux

Cucubau Setete . . . . 7b+

Le Bleu des Cousses . . 7b
ood line but can get dirty.

Casse-Noisette . . . . 7a+

Le Bleusard Pressé . . . . . 7a+

Ricoco 7b
e extension is **7b+**.

Zagreb 6c
ccellent climbing from start to finish.

Le Moustik Enragé 7a

Comme des Phoques 6b

Coup de Blues pour Dom . . . . . 6a+
ell-featured route, and always worthwhile.

28 **Super Mario** . . . . 6b+

29 **Le Petit Martien** . . . . 6b+
The extension is **6c+** but adds very little to the route.

30 **Bleu comme l'Enfer** . . . . . 6c+

31 **Monzob sur Mer** 7b
A bouldery finish.

32 **San John's Pécos** . . . . 7b+
Classic - a bouldery finish.

33 **Cent Patates** . . . . 7b+
A beautifully-situated route. *See photo on front cover.*

34 **Jungle Boogie** . . . . ?
Has had a lot of attention from a very talented climber, but it
remains unclimbed at time of writing.

Céüse
Sisteron
Voix
Orpierre
Bellecombe
Baume Rousse
Ubrieux
Saint Julien
Saint Léger
Malaucène
Combe Obscure
Les Dentelles
Venasque
Buoux

Biographie

A well-known sector, but out of reach for all but a few. There is a lot of work to be done here before this sector is fully developed.

70m

30m

20m

2

3 4 5 6 7 8 9 10

❶ Biographie . . . . . . 🔲🔲🔲🔲🔲 8c+

❷ Realization . . . . . . 🔲🔲🔲🔲🔲 9a+
A very significant extension.

❸ L'Étrange Ivresse des Lenteurs . . . . 🔲
An impressive project.

❹ Le Cadre . . . . 🔲🔲🔲🔲🔲 8c

❺ Three Degrees of Separation
. . . . 🔲🔲🔲🔲🔲 9a
Three big dynos provide much of the difficulty.

❻ La Part du Diable . . . . 🔲

❼ Les Colonnettes . . . 🔲🔲🔲🔲🔲 8a
With aid at the start it's only 7c+, but that's just cheating really. The cunning may find an upside-down no hands bat hang rest. The enormous extension is **The Black Beau, 8b+**.

❽ Chronique de la Haine Ordinaire
. . . . 🔲🔲🔲🔲🔲 8c

❾ No Futur . . . . 🔲🔲🔲🔲🔲 8c+
A long route! Falling from the top is liable to result in some swearing.

65 min | Morning | Steep

Céüse
Sisteron
Volx
Orpierre
Bellecombe
Baume Rousse
Ubrieux
Saint Julien
Saint Léger
Malaucène
Combe Obscure
Les Dentelles
Venasque
Buoux

30m

30m

20m

11 12 13 14 15 16 17 18 19 20

Work But No More Love

. . . . 2 8c+

med *Baa Baa Black Sheep* by the first ascensionist.

Ceredo Climbing Team . . . . 3 8a+

Tout n'est pas si Facile . . . . 1 7c+

me chipped holds to finish.

Nitassian 7a

ery hard start but a great tufa-pulling finish.

Wounded Knee 7b

Sitting Bull . . . . 7b+

16 Saint George's Picos 7a
A classic - hard for the first four clips, then easing.

17 J'Aime Lolo T 7a

18 La Femme Blanche . . . 8a+
A pumpy lower wall leads to a precarious slab at the top. Run-out but brilliant.

19 La Femme Noire 7c
High in the grade - run-out, but still good.

20 Le Chirurgien du Crépuscule 8b
High in the grade.

Céüse
Sisteron
Volx
Orpierre
Bellecombe
Baume Rousse
Ubrieux
Saint Julien
Saint Léger
Malaucène
Combe Obscure
Les Dentelles
Venasque
Buoux

65 min | Morning | Vertical | Steep

Demi Lune

A popular sector with a wide variety of grades on offer, although the harder routes are of better quality than the easier ones here.

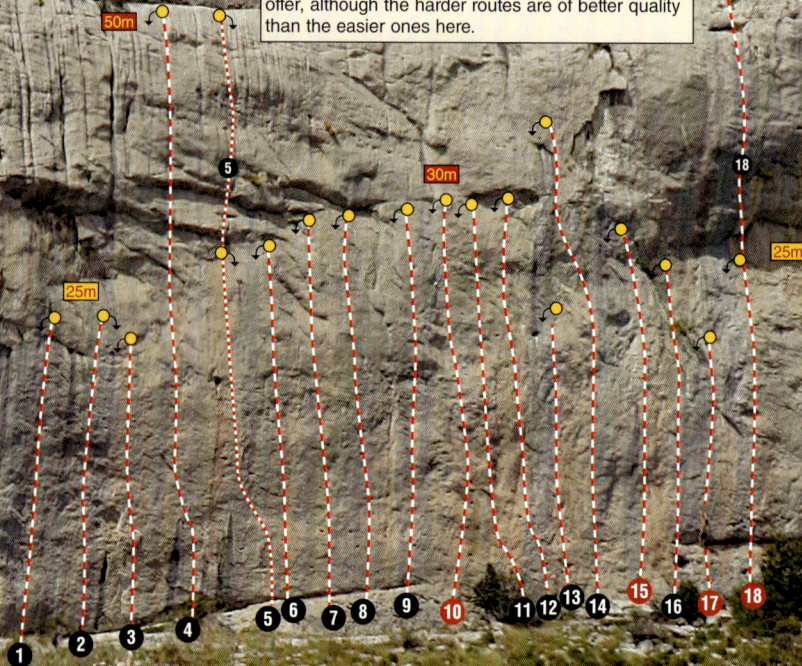

50m 25m 30m 18 25m 5

1 Le Poinçonneur des Lilas
. . . . 8a+

2 L'ami Caouette . . . 8a
A hard route epitomising the climbing in this area - fingery, technical and very sustained.

3 Changement de Look. . 7b+
The definitive line on this wall therefore a popular challange.

4 Joyeux Boucher . . . . . . 7c+

5 Marron Derrière. . . . . . 7b+
The extension is also **7b+**.

6 Jaune Devant . . . . 7b+

7 Vieille Canaille 7b

8 Angel Dust . . . . 7a+
Sustained, technical climbing.

9 Mélody Nelson . . . . . . 7a+
Easier than *Angel Dust*, yet difficult to onsight.

10 La Javanaise 7a
Great climbing with no tricks.

11 Great Blanc. 7b

12 Koumac Patom . . . . . 7b+

13 Esperanza . . . . 7a+
One particularly tough move. It used to have just four bolts, but is now more generously bolted.

14 Les Dingues et les Paumés
. . . . 7b+

15 El Daü . . . . 6c+
Will feel more like 7a+ for the vertically challenged.

16 Les Dessous Chics. . . . 7a+

17 Harley Davidson . . . . 6b+
An all-time classic.

18 Marylou 6b
The hard extension is **Minette á la Plage, 7c.**

Céüse
Sisteron
Voix
Orpierre
Bellecombe
Baume Rousse
Ubrieux
Saint Julien
Saint Léger
Malaucène
Combe Obscure
Les Dentelles
Venasque
Buoux

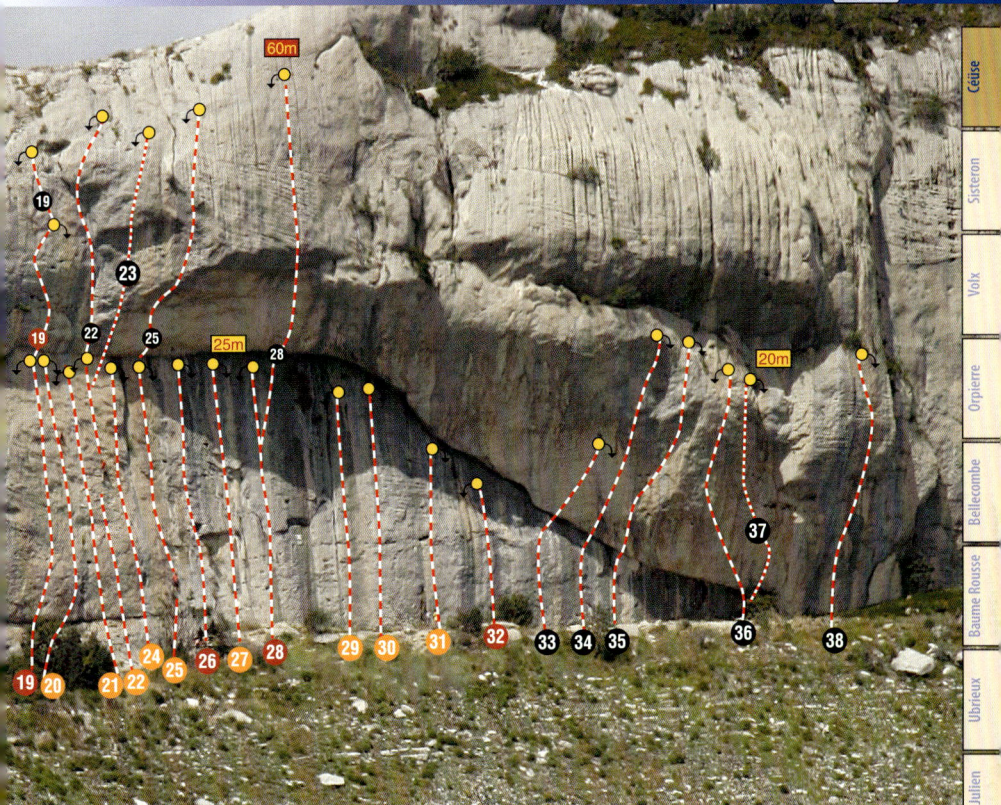

Chant de Cristal . . . . 🔻🔻 6b+
e first (recommended) extension, **Beauf Story, 6c** - a reach
ps at the start. The second extension is **7b**.

Papyrus . . . . 🔻🔻 6a+
ssic Céüse climbing, also giving a good pointer to Céüse
ding!

Katina . . . . 🔻🔻 6a

Carte Noire . . . . 🔻🔻 6a
e groovy extension is **Uniquemonde.com, 7c**.

Encore 🔻🔻 8a+
rt up *Carte Noire* then move right to follow this extension.

Sea Sex and Sun . . . . . . 🔻 6a
od climbing leads to a sharp finish

Les Sucettes à l'Anis . . . . 🔻🔻 6a
e three star extension is **Radote Joli Pépère, 8b**.

Canabis ou Nutella . . . . . 🔻🔻 6b

Face d'Iguane . . . . 🔻🔻 6a+

Tête d'Ampoule 6b
e vast extension is **Le Bazard Fait Bien les Choses, 8b+**.

29 **Petit Monstre** . . . . 🔻 6a
The crack, but don't expect to climb the crack.

30 **Couilles de Loup** . . . . . . 🔻 6a+

31 **À Patrick** . . . . 🔻 6a

32 **Bonny and Clyde** . . . . . . 🔻 6c
A bouldery start leads to easier climbing

33 **Lapinerie** . . . . 🔻 7b
A big move to get to the chain!

34 **Dures Limites** . . . . . . 🔻 8c
A popular 8c, with a technical finish.

35 **Suers Froides** . . . . . . 🔻 8a+

36 **Carte Blanche** . . . . . . 🔻 8a
A popular outing for the grade, feet are optional at the start.
Expect to queue at popular times. *Photo on page 5*.

37 **Sans Peur et Sanglier** . . . . 7c+
Start up *Carte Blanche* before moving right. A two-move wonder.

38 **Unnamed** . . . . ?
A project.

Céüse
Sisteron
Volx
Orpierre
Bellecombe
Baume Rousse
Ubrieux
Saint Julien
Saint Léger
Malaucène
Combe Obscure
Les Dentelles
Venasque
Buoux

Un Pont sur l'Infini

A good collection of wall climbs, the slightly longer walk-in means this area tends to be quieter than others. There have been a number of extensions added fairly recently, needless to say, you'll need a whopper of a rope to lower off from some of them in one go.

70 min | Morning | Vertical | Steep

60m
40m
30m

1 Machoire d'Âne ...... 7b+
Quite bouldery for the grade.

2 Au Sud de Nulle Part ..... 7b+
Low in the grade.

3 Pourquoi Pas .... 7a+
A steady classic, but with a sting in the tail.

4 Beaux Mouvements sur Fond Bleu
.... 7a+
Follow the beautiful blue streak. The extension is **7a+**.

5 Fissure Sans Nom 7a
The prominent crack.

6 Le Coeur des Hommes .... 7a+
Some brilliant steady climbing, after a broken start.

7 Désert Minéral 7b
Follow the undercut flake to start.

8 Déferlante de Prises ..... 7b+

9 Grand Mur Malade 7c

10 Petence Delly 7c

11 Oizeaudrome 8c
An insanely long pitch. A 120m rope may get you down.

12 Bourinator 8a
Two boulder problems on a route.

13 Unknown .... ?

14 Gelati Dolomiti 7a
A tough start - especially if you miss the key hold, but some great features lead the way.

15 Ça Cartoon .... 7a+

16 L'Anus en Décomposition .. 7a
A desperate slabby section awaits. The extension is **7b+**.

17 Douceur Candide .... 6b+
The first (good) extension is **6c+**, the second is **7a+**.

18 Oeil de Faucon .... 6b+
A bit powerful for a warm-up. The big extension is **7c+**.

Céüse
Sisteron
Volx
Orpierre
Bellecombe
Baume Rousse
Ubrieux
Saint Julien
Saint Léger
Malaucene
Combe Obscure
Les Dentelles
Venasque
Buoux

Equinoxe. **6c**
werful through the roof, then straight-up.

11 September 2001 ou la Bétise Humaine
. . . . **6c+**
e belay on *Théorème de Philippus* may help get down.

Théorème de Philippus. **6c**

Le Vol du Pilatus . . . . **6b+**

Requiem pour un Con **6c**
e extension is **6c**. The right-hand finish follows a crack.

Dietic Line **7b**
eat climbing, and low in the grade.

Opéra Vertical **7b**
me may find this a little too slabby.

2001 - L'Odyssée du Grimpeur. . . **7b**
eady climbing - just keep on going!

Mawoi . . . . **6b+**
ere are two extensions, the first is **6c+**, the second is **7b+**.

28 Un Pont sur l'Infini. **7a**
The extension is **6c**.

29 La Galère **7a**

30 La Reine des Pommes **7a**
A popular candidate for your first 7a onsight.

31 Noir sur Noir . . . . **7a+**

32 La Fin d'un Primitif . . . **7b**

33 Vas-y Tonton **7a**
The extension is **6b**.

34 Unknown. . . . . **?**

35 Retour en Afrique. . . . . **7a+**
Low in the grade - a good fun route. The extension is **7a**.

36 Silmarils. **6c**
Another one that is low in the grade, but good.

37 Bunny and Climb . . . . **6b+**

38 Le Coquelicot sur le Bouche. . . **6b+**

Céüse

Sisteron

Volx

Orpierre

Bellecombe

Baume Rousse

Ubrieux

Saint Julien

Saint Léger

Malaucène

Combe Obscure

Les Dentelles

Venasque

Buoux

75 min | Morning | Vertical | Steep

35m

40m

25m

20m

1

2 3

4 5 6 7 8 9

Les Maîtres du Monde

This area gives the last of the single-pitch routes before things get a lot bigger. It is possible to gain the top of the crag using a Via Ferrata at the left-hand side.

1 Via Ferrata . . . . N/A

2 Les Malvoyants 6b
A beautiful brass name plate leads the way.

3 La Renfougne 6b
Climb the wide crack/chimey.

4 Fécondation in Vito . . . . . . 6b+

5 Un Esprit Saint dans un Porcin . 7a+

6 Scène de Panique Tranquille . . . 7b

7 Unknown . . . . ?

8 Unknown . . . . ?

L'ami de tout le Monde
. . . . 8b
classic route and therefore quite polished. Quite bouldery.

Le Magicien de RIGA . . 7c+
rd for the grade.

Teuchipa 7c
se the first quickdraw as a hold. The tall can jump to a jug and
oid the aid at **7c+**, shorties may find the grade closer to **8a+**.

Bibendum . . . . 7b+
se the first quickdraw as a hold. After the break, the smallest
ld is a jug, which is just as well as there are no real rests.

Captaine Flamme . . . . . 7b+

Cheese de Luxe . . . . . 8a+

15 Unknown. 8a

16 Les Maîtres du Monde 6c
1) **6c.** Use some aid to get to a steep juggy crack.
2) **6c.** Move out left from the belay and follow the excellent wall.
3) **6c.** Climb the wall above using a point of aid where the bolts
get very close - can be freed at a very bouldery **7b**.
4) **6b+.** The wall to the top.

17 Axiome d'Euclide 6c
1) **6c.** Use aid to start then climb to the base of the groove.
2) **5+.** Follow the groove. 3) **6a+.** The wall the top.

18 Les Gros Trous . . . . 6a+
A hard start, and not a good warm-up.

19 Mémoire. . . . . 6a+
Shares the start with *Les Gros Trous*.

20 La Diagonale. 6a

Sisteron

South - Right
Page 57

South - Centre
Right   Page 56

South - Centre
Left   Page 55

South - Left
Page 54

La Faille
Page 52

Cétele
Sisteron
Volx
Orpierre
Bellecombe
Baume Rousse
Ubrieux
Saint Julien
Saint Léger
Malaucène
Combe Obscure
Les Dentelles
Venasque
Buoux

	No star	☆	☆☆	☆☆☆
Up to 4+	2	-	3	-
5 to 6a+	4	12	12	4
6b to 7a	2	9	12	4
7a+ and up	-	3	7	1

Sisteron is a compact and approachable crag, consisting of a large but narrow fin of rock, with slabby, sunny routes on one side, and a few shady, steep routes on the other. The rock quality is excellent, though the slabby routes tend to have cleaner rock than the steep ones. As a destination, it's not extensive enough for a base, but makes a good alternative to Céüse if you're feeling like having an easy day and can't face the walk-in.

Sisteron has a small climbing shop which also offers shoe resoles. If you look hard, you will find it at 12 Rue du Grand Couvert - tourist information should be able to offer a map and directions as it's well hidden.

Approach

Sisteron can be easily accessed from the A51 by exiting either at junction 22 (from the south) or 23 (from the north). The crag is clearly visible from the town; head north on the N85 to the first roundabout, and take the first exit onto the D951, this crosses the river, once on the other side, turn right and drive below the crag until you can reach parking places on the side of the road. Please don't park in the village.

Conditions

The crag mostly faces south although there are a few north-facing hard routes on La Faille. It is exposed to the wind and on cold, windy days can be quite unpleasant. If you're looking to climb on the sunny side, it would be wise to avoid hot days when the place turns into an oven.

If you're killing some time waiting for the sun to go down before you can get on the rock, there is an extensive and popular summer lido in the town.

If you're looking to climb on the steep, shady side, then any time except winter should provide reasonable conditions. It is also worth noting that early in the season, the north-facing wall may be a bit dirty.

Caption, anyone?

Céüse

Sisteron

Volx

Orpierre

Belleombe

Baume Rousse

Ubrieux

Saint Julien

Saint Leger

Malaucène

Combe Obscure

Les Dentelles

Venasque

Buoux

Nicolas Le Baut on *L'Arapède* (6c) - *page 56* - on the South Face at Sisteron.

La Faille - South Face

A highly unusual place consisting of two walls that largely face each other. The south-facing wall gets sun on the routes on the left and shade on the routes further right.

Routes 13 to 22 on the continuation of the slabby side

Main South Face

Routes 23 to 32 are on the opposite steep side

2 min | Sun and shade | Slabby

---

1 Pinocchio . . . . 4+

2 Les Trois Marches . . . . 4+

3 Les Petites Lèvres . . . . 5+

4 Les Grandes Lèvres 5

5 Chichou 5
Photo opposite.

6 Mario Brousse 5

7 La Peinarde 6a

8 Géant Jaune 6a

9 Tête en l'Air . . . . 5+

10 Sur Prise Partie . . . . 6b+
Can be climbed at 5+ with a point of aid.

11 Tétine Fétiche 5
Start up a short flake then move up and right to follow a crack.

12 Starsky . . . . 5+
Start 3m to the right at a crack and follow a series of cracks.

The next routes are on the slabby wall in the gap.

13 Lovy 6b
A metal name plate and line of expansion bolts point the way.

---

14 Le Compilateur . . . . 5+
A big rubbly crack moving right towards the top.

15 Débris du Cosmos 7b
1) **6b.** Start 1m right of the start of the raised ground and follow thin crack and shiny bolts to a belay.
2) **7b.** The steep crack above leads to the top.

16 Mascotte 6c
1) **6a+.** Climb hairline cracks up the slab to the optional belay.
2) **6c.** Follow steep cracks up the headwall.

17 La Traversée des Amonites 6a
Start as for *Mascotte*, tip-toe along the thin flakes with interest. Continue to a belay at the top of a layback flake.

18 La Salsa des Démons . . . . . 6c+
1) **6c+.** 2m right of *Mascott* (metal name plate) climb a featureless wall, moving right to a belay.
2) **6c.** The right-hand line of bolts to the top of the wall.

19 Poussières d'Étoiles . . . . 6a+
1) **6a+.** Follow a line of expansion bolts to the belay of *La Salsa*
2) **6a.** The left-hand line of bolts.

20 A Tatons les Tétons . . . . 6a+
8m to the right, a featureless line leads to a low belay.

21 Shinobie . . . . 5+
3m to the right, a crack leads to the same belay as *A Tatons.*

22 Les Vertiges de la Souris 7a
3m to the right is a thin crack. Climb this up the wall, ignoring the belay of *La Traversée des Amonites* on your right.

La Faille - North Face

he north-facing wall is a distinctly cold and intimidating
eature, the lines are very impressive but you will want to
y them on a hot day when the shade is welcome.

❸ Voyage **7b**
art 1m right of the end wall, at the left-hand side of the north-
cing wall, and follow the striking crack to a mid-height belay.

he next line to the right is presumably a project.

❹ La Vie à Deux **8a**
0m right of *Voyage*, a series of thin cracks and good blocks
ads up to a cave and the belay.

❺ Shimoda **7c**
e dyke starting 1m to the right of *La Vie* and finishing as for
at route.

❻ 2001 . . . . **7c**
e next crack along, with a metal name plate pointing the way.

❼ Présence **8b**
e dyke 3m to the right soon turns into an thin crack which
es nearly all the way to the top.

e line of expansion bolts to the right is a project.

❽ Pulsion . . . . **8a+**
art just left of the big step in the ground and follow a
ectacular thin crack all the way.

❾ Unknown . . . . **?**
art as for *Pulsion* then move out right to follow a parallel line
bolts.

❿ L'Autoroute de l'Enfer . . . . . **8a+**
e last big crackline before the end of the wall. Take the right-
nd line of bolts to the belay. No details on the left-hand line.

⓫ Super Crack **7a**
e last of the cracks isn't very super. Follow the crack for 4m
d the belay on the ledge.

⓬ Crack . . . . **6a+**
boulder-problem-sized route just to the right.

Davina Borrow-Jones on *Chichou* (5) - *opposite* on the South Face of
La Faille. The steep North Face can be seen on the left of the photo.

Cédise · Sisteron · Voix · Orpierre · Bellecombe · Baume Rousse · Ubrieux · Saint Julien · Saint Léger · Malaucène · Combe Obscure · Les Dentelles · Venasque · Buoux

Céüse

Sisteron

Voix

Orpierre

Bellecombe

Baume Rousse

Ubrieux

Saint Julien

Saint Léger

Malaucène

Combe Obscure

Les Dentelles

Venasque

Buoux

South Face

An impressive steep slab with excellent rock and an array of compelling lines - not one for a hot day though since you will fry!

2 min | Lots of sun | Slabby

La Faille

30m

25m

20m

25m

1 Le Belvédère des Amoureux		6c+
2 Le Fronton		6c
3 Carnage		7a+
4 Viol de Nuit		6a+
5 Véga		4+
6 Merlin l'Enchanteur		5
7 Les Mesons		5
8 L'Épée de Damocles		5+
9 Au Nom de la Rose		6b+
10 Excalibur		7a
11 Les Doigts de Fée		6a
12 Le Dièdre		5+

2 min | Lots of sun | Slabby

32m

28m

25m

20m

Bambinette - next page

Quatsup Mon Œil . . . . 6a+

L'Etreinte du Pilier 6b

Clog . . . . 5+

Les Sous Doués Passent le Crux . . 5+

Mégalomaniaque 6c

Altaïr . . . . 4+

19 Deux et Demi . . . . 5+

20 Deux Trois Quarts 6a

21 Marthe, Jusque'Au Bout de Tes Rêves
. . . . 5

22 Denèbe . . . . 4+

Céüse · Sisteron · Voix · Orpierre · Bellecombe · Baume Rousse · Ubrieux · Saint Julien · Saint Léger · Malaucène · Combe Obscure · Les Dentelles · Venasque · Buoux

23 Bambinette . . . . 6b+
1) 5+, 2) 6b+

24 Bambino 6c
1) 6b+, 2) 6c

25 Le Braqueur de Poubelles 6b
1) 6b, 2) 6b

26 Le Messie Récalcitrant 6c
1) 6c, 2) 6c

27 L'Arapède 6c
1) 6c, 2) 6b+. *See photo on page 51.*

4 min | Lots of sun | Slabby

28 L'Arapèdissime . . . . 6b+

29 Les Cannelures . . . . 6b+

30 Isa-Véga . . . . 6c+

31 Un Pavillon d'Or 7a

32 Je Vous Salue Marie . . 7a+

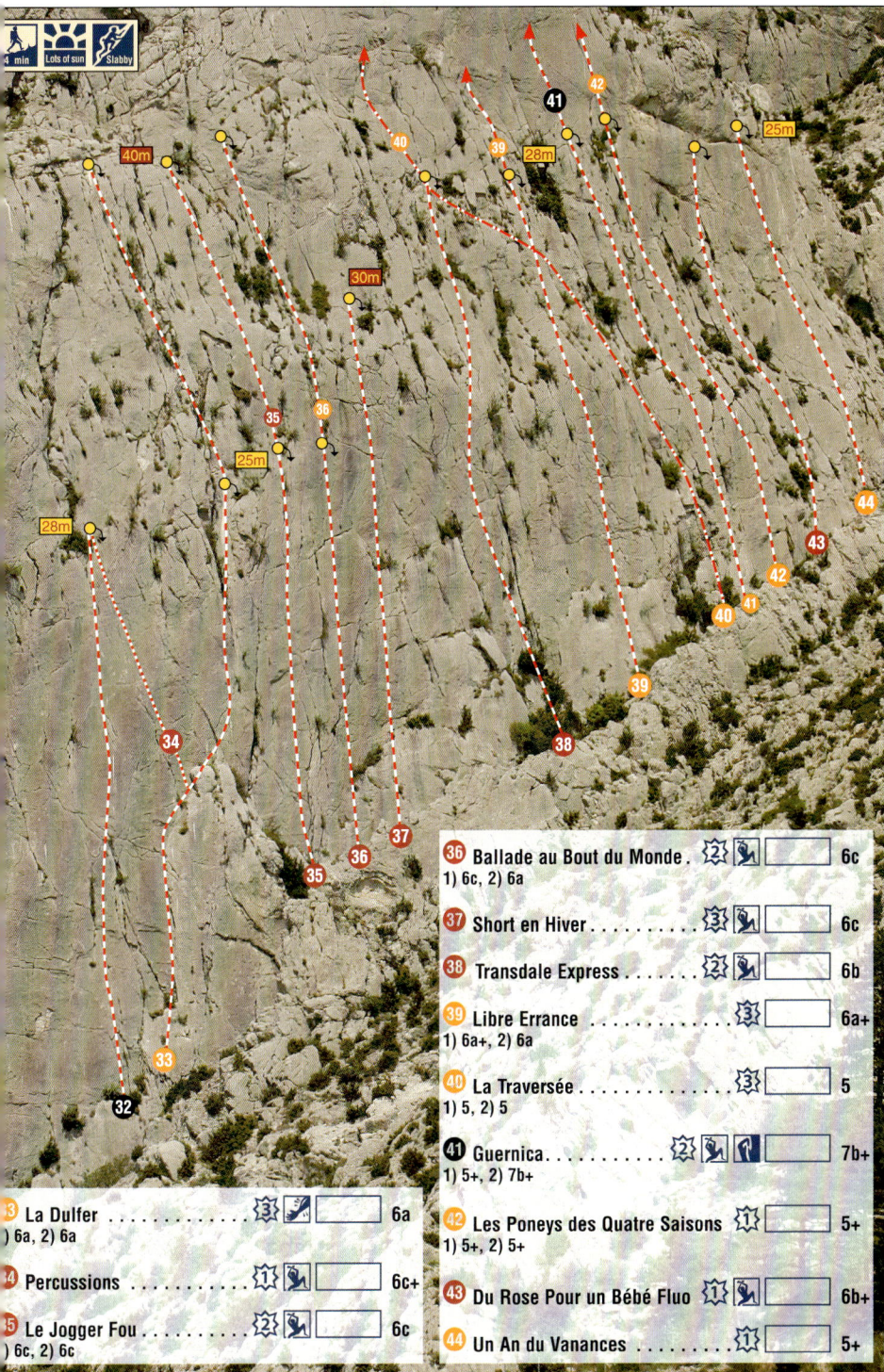

4 min | Lots of sun | Slabby

40m

30m

35

36

25m

28m

34

35

36

37

32

33

40

39

28m

42

41

25m

44

43

42

41

40

39

38

Céüse
Sisteron
Volx
Orpierre
Bellecombe
Baume Rousse
Ubrieux
Saint Julien
Saint Léger
Malaucène
Combe Obscure
Les Dentelles
Venasque
Buoux

36 Ballade au Bout du Monde 6c
1) 6c, 2) 6a

37 Short en Hiver 6c

38 Transdale Express 6b

39 Libre Errance . . . . 6a+
1) 6a+, 2) 6a

40 La Traversée 5
1) 5, 2) 5

41 Guernica . . . . 7b+
1) 5+, 2) 7b+

42 Les Poneys des Quatre Saisons 5+
1) 5+, 2) 5+

43 Du Rose Pour un Bébé Fluo 6b+

44 Un An du Vanances . . . . . . 5+

33 La Dulfer 6a
1) 6a, 2) 6a

34 Percussions . . . . 6c+

35 Le Jogger Fou 6c
1) 6c, 2) 6c

Volx

La Grotte
Page 62

Céüse

Sisteron

Volx

Orpierre

Bellecombe

Baume Rousse

Ubrieux

Saint Julien

Saint Léger

Malaucène

Combe Obscure

Les Dentelles

Venasque

Buoux

La Petite Grotte
Page 65

Céüse
Sisteron
Voix
Orpierre
Bellecombe
Baume Rousse
Ubrieux
Saint Julien
Saint Léger
Malaucène
Combe Obscure
Les Dentelles
Venasque
Buoux

	No star	⚙	⚙⚙	⚙
Up to 4+	-	-	-	
5 to 6a+	-	3	1	-
6b to 7a	-	2	3	-
7a+ and up	6	13	16	5

Volx isn't up to the quality of the other crags in this guidebook, but when it's raining and everything else is soaking, you'll be glad of Volx as it is one of the few places where you can be sure to find something dry. There are a number of slabby sectors to the right of the Grottes, but they are not protected from the rain.

Approach

Volx lies above the village of the same name, just off the D4096. At some lights, head up through the town then around to the right past the church and the mini fountain (drinking water). Turn right at the sign 'site d'escalade' and continue until you come to a second sign. Don't turn right up the hill as there is no parking, instead continue briefly and take a left into a car park. From here, return to the 'site d'escalade' sign and follow the road steeply up the hill for five minutes until you reach the crag. There's a toilet on site.

Conditions

As mentioned, much of Volx is impervious to rain, so it's a popular spot on a wet day. You'll get plenty of sun too, though in the winter months you'll need to stick around on the right side of the Grotte to get the most rays. During the summer, Volx isn't as much as a sun trap as you might expect, the steepness of the rock acts as an excellent sun-shade and you can expect to find plenty of shade on the rock in the afternoon and the evening.

Despite its limitations, Volx has seen some heavy traffic over the years. The result of this is some impressive polish. This is less of an issue on the steeper, juggy routes than it is on the slabbier ones, L'arche de Nausée in particular is now so polished that it is worth climbing to see just how polished it is.

There has been some stability work carried out on the cliff to protect the local buildings. As yet this has not impacted on any of the routes listed although it is not known what future plans there are.

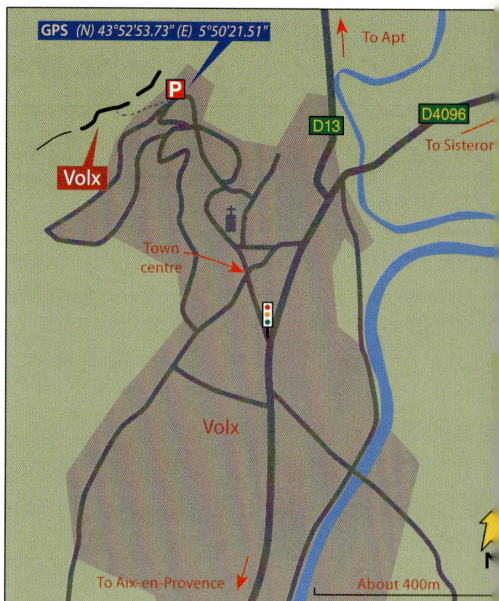

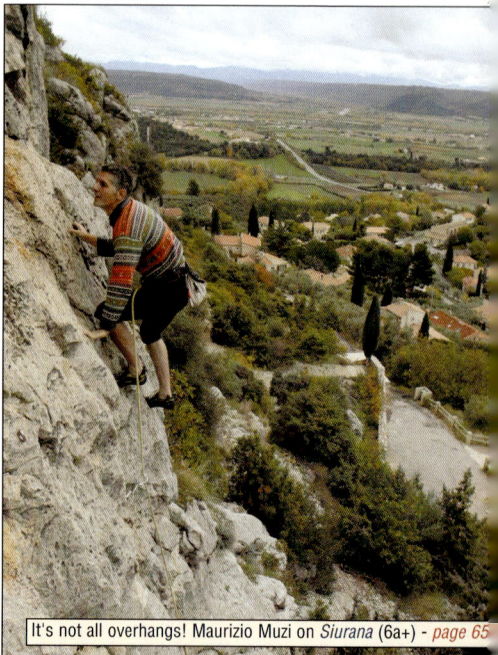

GPS (N) 43°52'53.73" (E) 5°50'21.51"

To Apt
P
D13
D4096
To Sisteron
Volx
Town centre
Volx
To Aix-en-Provence
About 400m

It's not all overhangs! Maurizio Muzi on *Siurana* (6a+) - *page 65*

Céüse

Sisteron

Volx

Orpierre

Bellecombe

Baume Rousse

Ubrieux

Saint Julien

Saint Léger

Malaucène

Combe Obscure

Les Dentelles

Venasque

Buoux

Steve McClure climbing *Gradiva* (8a+) - *page 64* - in the main cave at Volx. Photo: Stuart Littlefair

La Grotte - Left
Some great steep all-weather jug pulling, and some more
fingery offerings at the far left end. The first five routes
can be a bit damp towards the top after rain.

1 Génération Écologie... 7a+

2 Safe Sex.......... 7b+
A few hard pulls towards the end.

3 Scandale 8a

4 Youpala .... 8a+

5 Bienvenue au Club.... 7c+

6 Zarbie 7b
A good ledge to rest on, but then things get tough.

7 Hot Spot 6b
A popular warm-up. When you're done you can move your clip
onto...

8 Indulgence 7a
A hard pull on the reinforced flake, but plenty of bolts.

9 Traquenard 7b
An impressive line through some steep ground.

10 Conan le Barbare..... 7a
The steep rightwards trending line with a tricky finale. Long
quickdraws are worth taking or improvising to reduce drag.

11 Le Clown Entre les Dents 7c

12 L'Inversée Satanique 8a

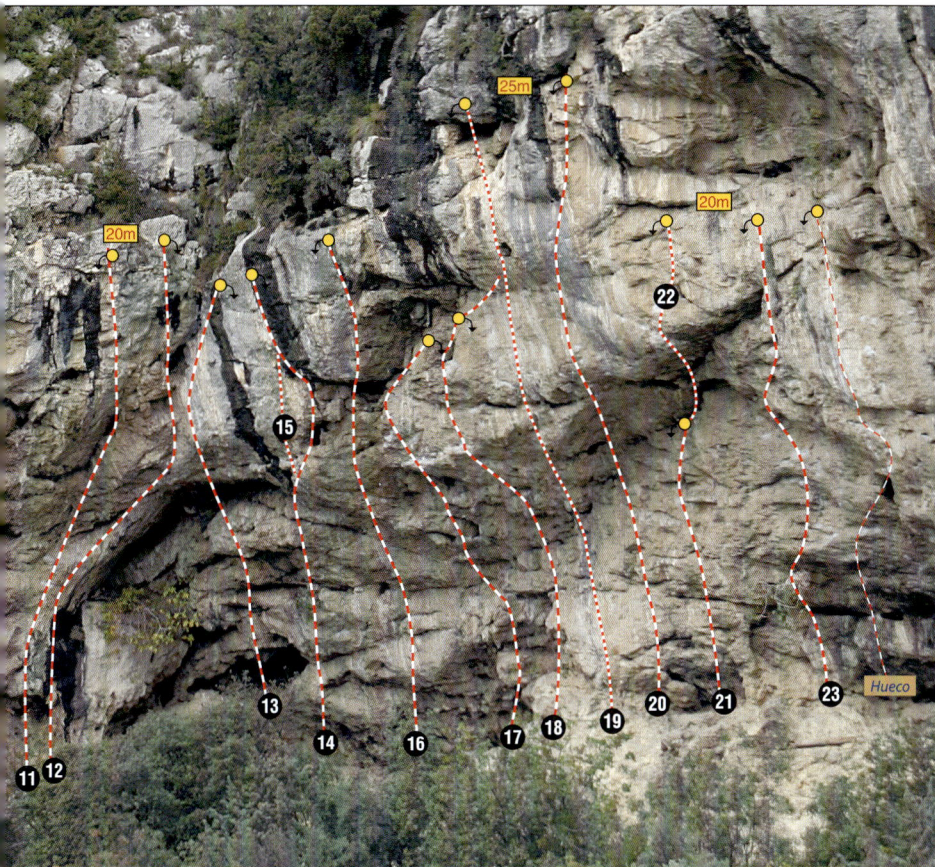

Céüse

Sisteron

Volx

Orpierre

Bellecombe

Baume Rousse

Ubrieux

Saint Julien

Saint Léger

Malaucène

Combe Obscure

Les Dentelles

Venasque

Buoux

20 Ans Après . . . . 7c+

Oxygène 7c

Oxygène Directe 7c

100% De Matière Grasse 7c+

Charles de Goal 7b
eep, jug-ridden micro route. Worth a go regardless of what
e you climb. Mind the pigeons.

Zovirax . . . . 7c+
be extended into the next route at 8b.

L'Empire des Sens . . . . 8a+
e a popular 8b.

Vague 8b

㉑ Spinoza . . . . 7b+

㉒ Spinoza Direct 8a
This short extension looks like an easy tick but certainly packs a
punch, especially if you get the sequence wrong.

㉓ L'Invitation au Voyage . . . . 7c+

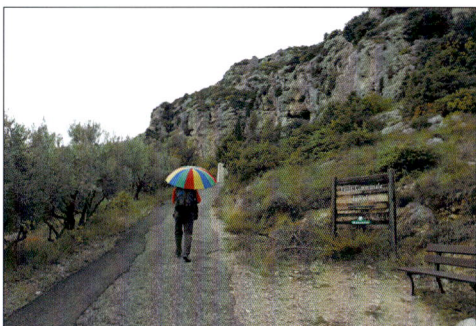

The usual conditions that necessitate a visit to Volx.

Céüse

Sisteron

Volx

Orpierre

Bellecombe

Baume Rousse

Ubrieux

Saint Julien

Saint Léger

Malaucène

Combe Obscure

Les Dentelles

Venasque

Buoux

❶ Hueco . . . . 　　　　7b+
A Volx classic, the final tufa is the scene of many a fright.

❷ Shaoshing . . . . . . 　　　　8a
One of the best routes at Volx. A hard boulder problem with some painful holds leads to easier but more sustained climbing. Inevitably, at this grade, the last moves are where you'll fall off!

❸ Théorème . . . . 　　　　8b
Short and hard, a harder, more direct version of *Shaoshing*.

❹ Gradiva . . . . 　　　　8a+
A manufactured route. Follow the line of stuck-on crimps up the otherwise blank section of rock. Enjoyment is directly proportional to finger strength, move on if you're weak in this department!
Photo on page 61.

❺ L'Arche de Nausée . . . . 　　　　7a+
Tough at both ends. A great line, but the polish removes the stars.

❻ La Nausée de l'Aube . . . . 　　　　7b

❼ Terminator . . . . 　　　　8b

❽ Le Super Plafond . . . . 　　　　8c+

❾ Le Plafond de la Ligne Maginot
. . . . 　　　　8c

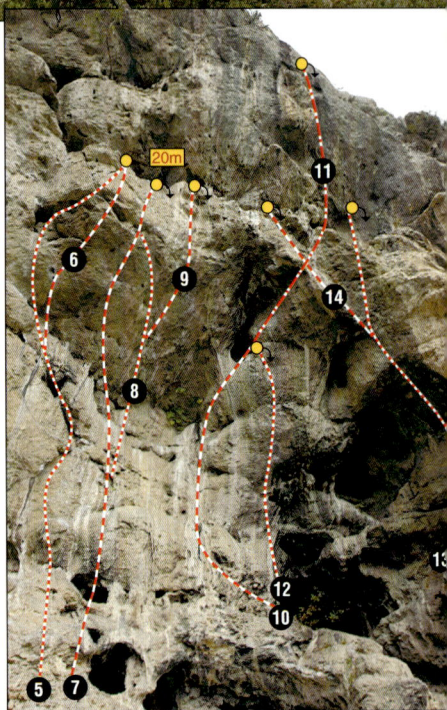

Céüse

Sisteron

Volx

Orpierre

Bellecombe

Baume Rousse

Ubrieux

Saint Julien

Saint Léger

Malaucène

Combe Obscure

Les Dentelles

Venasque

Buoux

Zig Zag . . . . 7c+

Zig Zag Extension 8a
tinue to the top of the crag.

0% Matière Grise. 7c
ort bouldery offering.

Zelig 8a

Zelig Crac Bottin 8b

Zorro . . . . 6c+
od little route with a well-placed belay.

Cajolynn 6a
od little warm-up.

Siurana . . . . 6a+
easant route that has a few ancient pegs still in place.
o on page 60.

La Clara . . . . 5+
can also be started from higher.

La Petite Grotte
A very small, but tough sector to the right of the main
cave. The routes aren't much more than big boulder
problems, and require very careful belaying. A bouldering
mat is worth carrying up, if you happen to have one.

19 Newlook 7b

20 Grottesque . . . . 8a+
This little gem sees less attention than the other hard routes
though is well worth the effort.

21 Petit Test 8a

22 Samourai . . . . 7c+

23 Riders on the Storm 7b

24 Consolidation . . . . 6b+

25 Les Estagnots 6b

26 Bascule 6a

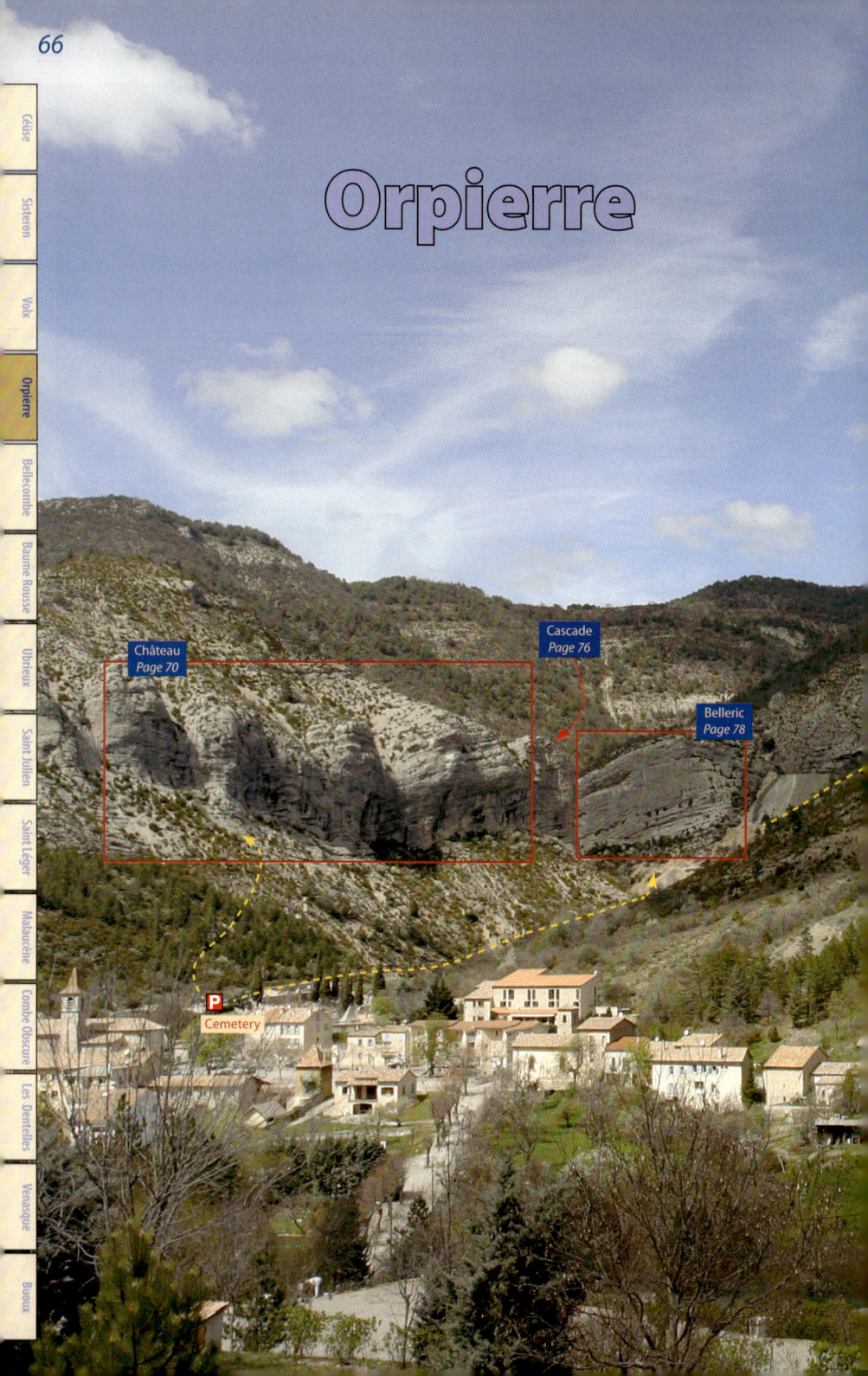

Céüse

Sisteron

Volx

Orpierre

Bellecombe

Baume Rousse

Ubrieux

Saint Julien

Saint Léger

Malaucène

Combe Obscure

Les Dentelles

Venasque

Buoux

Orpierre

Château
Page 70

Cascade
Page 76

Belleric
Page 78

P

Cemetery

Quiquillon
Page 82

Mur Chamois
Page 86

P
'l'Adrech'

Céüse

Sisteron

Volx

Orpierre

Bellecombe

Baume Rousse

Ubrieux

Saint Julien

Saint Léger

Malaucène

Combe Obscure

Les Dentelles

Venasque

Buoux

	No star	✸	✸✸	✸
Up to 4+	1	11	1	
5 to 6a+	12	41	28	1
6b to 7a	5	18	22	
7a+ and up	4	3	19	1

Orpierre is a convenient and popular destination. With sectors ranging from single pitch to long routes, all well equipped and within walking distance of the campsite, it's no wonder that Orpierre is ever-popular, even if some of the routes are starting to feel more than a little polished. Its location allows climbing on the crags around Buis-les-Baronnies or Céüse to be reached, making it either a good place to base yourself to explore a number of areas, or a place to visit for a day if you fancy a change of scenery. The town has a climbing shop, a mini-market, and plenty of gîtes.

Approaches

The climbing areas are all found a short walk from the town. If you're staying in Orpierre, there's no need to drive anywhere. The crags are very well signposted, and finding them is mostly a matter of starting in the right place and following the signs.

Château (left side): The best approach is from the upper car park next to the cemetery (there are two cemetery car parks). A path leads off from the corner of the car park, and zig-zags to the left side of Château.

Château (right side) Cascade and Belleric: From the lower of the two car parks next to the cemetery, follow the path next to the river. This path zig-zags its way in the direction of Belleric, eventually splitting with one path leading to the right side of Belleric, and one leading to the left. The left split is also used to gain access to Cascade and the right side of Belleric.

Quiquillon: There are a few options, it can be approached by skirting a path along the bas⋯ from Belleric, there are a few steep sections with some via ferrata. Alternatively follow a signed path up from Paradis parking area. Finally, it is possible to park at l'Adrech and follo⋯ a path from there.

Conditions

The area is generally cooler than the crags around Buis further west. During warm weather expect to be chasing the shade. Most wait until early afternoon before heading out to the east-facing areas. After rain, much of the area seeps badly, but Le Puy stays wonderfully dr⋯

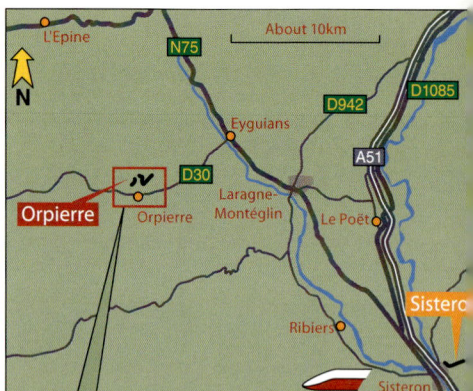

Cêüse

Sisteron

Volx

Orpierre

Bellecombe

Baume Rousse

Ubrieux

Saint Julien

Saint Léger

Malaucène

Combe Obscure

Les Dentelles

Venasque

Buoux

Daniel Moore on *Je T'Aime Moi Non Plus* (7a) - *page 73* - on the Château.

Château - Left

A varied and popular wall that gets the shade in the early afternoon. The left side of Château is well populated with routes in the 4s and 5s and is very popular with novice groups. The best approach is to take the direct path from the village-end of the upper car park, next to the cemetery, and walk along the base until you're at your chosen sector.

1 Ciao Emile 5

2 L'Éloge de la Fruit . . . . 4+

3 Paris-Texas 4

4 Le Serpent d'Étoile . . . . 4+

5 Ini 4

6 Tiation . . . . 4+

7 Traffic 4

8 Canardo 5

9 Palmer 5

10 Les Clochards Célestes . . . . 5+

11 Le Ficelou de Miss Waïkiki . . . . 5+

12 Think Punk 5

13 Cachou Pour un Lézard . . . . 5+

14 Les Racines du Ciel 6a

15 Maudit Manège 6b
It is only **5+** to the first lower-off.

16 Sax, Éponge et Rodéo . . . . 5+

17 Dernière Prise Avant le Relais . 5+

18 Le Ventre Plein 5

19 Les Rescapés de la Côte d'Azur 5

20 Lent Dehors 5

21 Le Fou d'Amérique 5

22 Le Fou Direct . . . . 5+

23 L'Apprentie . . . . 5+

24 Banane Molle . . . . 5+

25 Chatozaure 6a

26 Fifi Bras d'Acier . . . . 5+

27 Sonic 6a

28 Au Boulot Nico 6a

Céüse | Sisteron | Voix | Orpierre | Bellecombe | Baume Rousse | Ubrieux | Saint Julien | Saint Léger | Malaucène | Combe Obscure | Les Dentelles | Venasque | Buoux

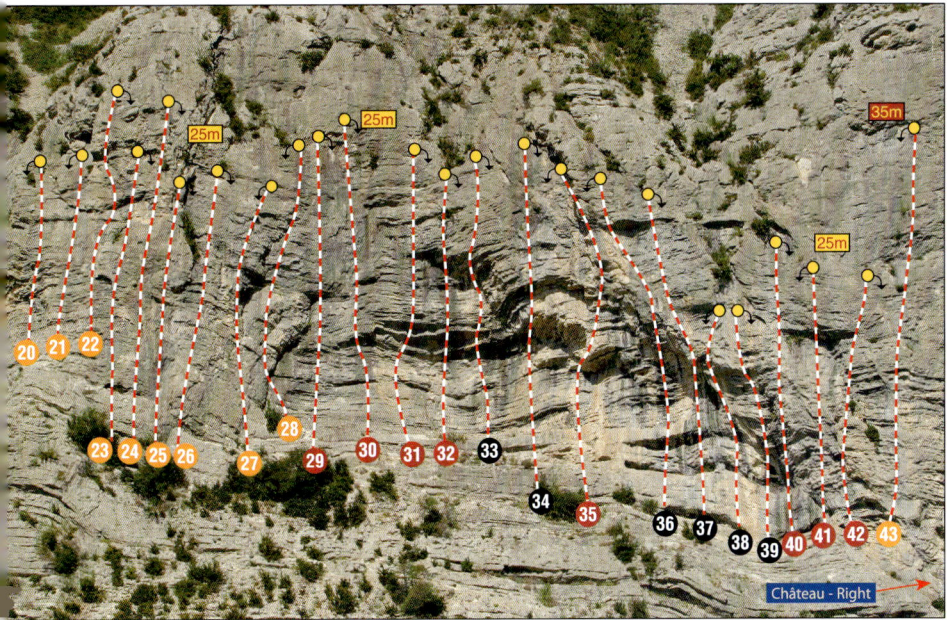

Céüse

Sisteron

Voix

Orpierre

Bellecombe

Baume Rousse

Ubrieux

Saint Julien

Saint Leger

Malaucène

Combe Obscure

Les Dentelles

Venasque

Buoux

Les Blessures de L'Âme . . .	🔟 🧗		7a
Evitons d'Importuner l'Étrangleur	🔢 🧗		7a
Les Copains d'Abord	🔢 💪		6c+
Golum	🔢 💪		7a
Travailler Moins	🔢 💪		7a+
Les Vindages du Diable . . .	📷 💪		7a+
Mon Ami Bart	🔢 💪		6c+
Pas de Bras, Pas du Chocolat	🔺 💪 🔧		7b
Essaie Encore	🔺 💪 🔧		7a+
Tombe et Tais-Toi.	🔺 🧗 💪		7b
7 Mai 1995, Désillusion	🔺 🧗 💪		7b
Les Kilos Vont en Enfer .	🔺 🔧 💪		7a
Ça C'est Fait			6b
Unknown.	🔢		6b
La Moulinette Endimanchée . . .	🔺		6a

Orpierre, the village with rocks on the brain.

1 Poupoupidou ou le Chant des Étoiles
. . . . 🔲 6a+

2 C Saké Bon 6b

3 Purge Ta Peine 6c

4 Ohm 7b

5 Ca Va Couiner 7c

6 Je Suis une Hyène . . . . 8b+

7 Mission Impossible . . . 8c

8 Pourquoi tant de Haine? 7b+

9 Toutes les Chances plus Une
. . . . 7b

10 L'Ange Gardien 7b

11 Les Ailes du Désir . . . . 6c+
Sustained climbing leads to technical final slab.

12 Pour un Bébé Robot . . . 7b

13 La Couronne d'Épines 6b

Terrains de montagne : risque de chutes de pierres.
Restez vigilants. Port du casque conseillé. Ne stationnez pas inutilement au pied des voies.

Mountaineering grounds : risks of rockfalls. Watch out for falling rocks. Wearing of helmet is advisable. Don't linger on at the foot of the routes for undue reason.

Bergterrain : Achtung Steinschlag. Bleiben sie umsichtig. Das Tragen eines Helmes wird angeraten. Parken sie nicht unnötigerweise am Fusse der Kletterrouten.

Château Right

The character of the right-end of the crag is defined by a number of steep, sustained lines. There are still a range of lower-grade routes that are well-placed as warm-ups, but expect these to be quite polished.

Y'a Plus de Limites

Céüse | Sisteron | Voix | **Orpierre** | Bellecombe | Baume Rousse | Ubrieux | Saint Julien | Saint Léger | Malaucène | Combe Obscure | Les Dentelles | Venasque | Buoux

Le Vol d'Icare 6b

Costaud Lulu . . . . 6a+

Amélie Mélodie 6a

Fais-Toi Plaisir 6a

Destruction . . . . 7b+

Bookaro Banzaï 8a

Hurlement . . . . 8a+

N'Oubliez Jamais 8b

Heureusement il y a la Bière
. . . . 7c+

Game Over 8a

Maman, Je Vais Mourir 7c

Même Pas Mal 7c

Reste Avec Moi 7c
care on the top runout section.

Pourquoi t'es Malheureux . 7c

28 Dur, Dur d'être un Mutant . . 7c+

29 Jusque lá, Ça Va 6b
The extension is **7c**.

30 La Semaine Prochaine, j'Enlève la Haut
. . . . 6b
A popular route therefore a little polished.

31 L'Exterminateur d'Écailles . . . . . 6a+

32 Consommez-moi Nature 6c
Hard for the grade. Crossing the bulge on slopers proves to be the main challenge.

33 N Comme Cornichon . . . 7a+

34 Duo d'Amour Pour Vélo et Trottinette
. . . . 7b
It has a bolt-on hold. **8a** if you avoid it.

35 Shoot Again . . . . 7a+

36 Le Guerrier Pacifique . . . . . 7b+

37 Je T'Aime Moi Non Plus 7a
See photo on page 69.

Je T'Aime Moi
Non Plus

Cascade

38 **Y'a Plus de Limites** 6b
Photo opposite.

39 **Le Chant des Baleines** . . . . . . 5+

40 **Sauve qui Peut la Vie** . . . . 5+

41 **Le Cimetière des Éléphants** 6a
1) 5, 2) 6a

42 **H$_2$O** 5

43 **Le Piton Inconnu** . . . . 5+
1) 5, 2) 5+

44 **Poil Dans la Main** 6a
1) 5+, 2) 6a+

45 **Raoul Petite** . . . . 5+

Further right are a number of short routes, each starting with a point of aid to cross a roof. Their grades range from 4 to 6a. The routes further right again are part of Cascade.

Orpierre

Sisteron

Veynes

Orpierre

Bellecombe

Baume Rousse

Ubrieux

Saint Julien

Saint Léger

Malaucène

Combe Obscure

Les Dentelles

Venasque

Buoux

Cèüse

Sisteron

Volx

Orpierre

Bellecombe

Baume Rousse

Ubrieux

Saint Julien

Saint Léger

Malaucène

Combe Obscure

Les Dentelles

Venasque

Buoux

Davina Borrow-Jones on *Y'a Plus de Limites* (6b) - *opposite*.

Géise
Sisteron
Volx
Orpierre
Bellecombe
Baume Rousse
Ubrieux
Saint Julien
Saint Léger
Malaucène
Combe Obscure
Les Dentelles
Venasque
Buoux

❶	Special Mammouth			6b
❷	La où il y a une Volonté, il y a un Chemin			
	. . . .			7a+
❸	Gaine ton Corps			6b+
❹	C'est où qu'c'est dur?			6c
❺	Chérie, Fais-moi Mal			6c+
❻	Tais-toi, Tais-toi			6b+
❼	What's Up?			6a
❽	Yen en Péplou			6b
❾	L'Homme Débloque			6a+
❿	2000 Bains, la Baignore de l'Espace			
	. . . .			5+
⑪	État d'Urgence			5+
⑫	Rivière de Pastis			6a+
⑬	Gourmandise			6a
⑭	Envie			5+

15 min | Morning | Slabby

Cascade

A popular sector at the right-hand side of Château with short, friendly routes mostly inhabiting the lower grades. The routes at the far right-hand side have a stream at their base and may be unreachable when the stream has more than normal volume.

Orgueil	1	5+	22 Mael First	1	4+

Orgueil . . . . 1 ☐ 5+
Avarice . . . . 1 ☐ 5
Colère . . . . 1 ☐ 5+
Paresse . . . . 1 🧗 ☐ 6a
Luxure . . . . 1 ☐ 5+

Tout sur les Pieds, Rien dans la Tête
. . . . 1 ☐ 5+
Coupe-Doigts . . . . 1 ☐ 5

22 Mael First . . . . 1 ☐ 4+
23 Calvaire One . . . . 2 ☐ 5+
24 Babouin Land . . . . 2 ☐ 5+
25 Œuf Dur . . . . 2 ☐ 5+
26 Eclectik Electrik . . . . 1 🧗 ☐ 6a
27 Capharnaum . . . . 1 🧗 ☐ 6a
28 Chutes de Pierres . . . . 1 ☐ 5
29 La Plage . . . . 1 ☐ 3+

Balleric

15 min | Morning | Slabby

25m 20m 10m

Céüse · Sisteron · Volx · Orpierre · Bellecombe · Baume Rousse · Ubrieux · Saint Julien · Saint Léger · Malaucène · Combe Obscure · Les Dentelles · Venasque · Buoux

Céüse

Sisteron

Volx

Orpierre

Bellecombe

Baume Rousse

Ubrieux

Saint Julien

Saint Léger

Malaucène

Combe Obscure

Les Dentelles

Venasque

Buoux

From mid morning

25m

30m

25m

35m

1 2 3 4 5 6 7 8 9

Belleric

A good sunny wall with lots to go at in the 5s and 6
It is a popular spot for practising multi-pitch climbin
For these longer routes it is possible to descend by
abseil down the routes, or by walking down around
the right side of the crag.

15 min   Lots of sun   Vertical

50m

24

35r

23

30m

23

24

22

17

30m

15

30m

13

12m

22

23

17   18   19   20   21

15   16

13   14

12

9   10   11

Céüse
Sisteron
Voix
Orpierre
Bellecombe
Baume Rousse
Ubrieux
Saint Julien
Saint Léger
Malaucène
Combe Obscure
Les Dentelles
Venasque
Buoux

...eat rock on the Cascade wall.

Trop Bon Trop Con 6b

Va Chercher Bonheur au Relais 6a+

Avec Vue Sur Ta Mère . . . . 5+

Zone Érogène 6b

Unknown. . . . . ?

Steph . . . . 6b+

Parcours Santé . . . . 6c+

Régime Sans Sel 6c

Régime de Bananes 6c

Regards Complices . . . . . . 6b+

Échine . . . . 6a+

Quatre Kilos 170 Plus Tard, Mélodie
. . . . 6b

Le Petit Toit 6a
6a, 2) 5+

14 Un Soir le Téléphone 6a

15 Jour de Transes 6c
1) 6b, 2) 6c

16 Amours Toujours . . . . 6a+

17 Le Grand Toit . . . . 6b+
1) 6a, 2) 6b+. Better approached via *Amours Toujours*.

18 Eh, Super Jules, Tu Craques . . . 6a+

19 La Voie de Son Maître 6a

20 Unknown. . . . . ?
Unknown but probably not that hard.

21 Le Foc et L'Enfant . . . . 5+

22 Les Bijoux de Spaggiari . . . . . . 5+
1) 5+, 2) 5+

23 Plus Fort Que Moi, Tu Meurs . . . 6b
1) 5+, 2) 5+, 3) 6b

24 Rogntudju 6b
1) 5, 2) 6a+, 3) 6b

25 min | Lots of sun | Slabby | Multi-pitch

Ceüse
Sisteron
Volx
Orpierre
Bellecombe
Baume Rousse
Ubreux
Saint Julien
Saint Léger
Malaucène
Combe Obscure
Les Dentelles
Venasque
Buoux

Descent

50m

50m

25m

25m

25m

1
2
3
4
5
6
7
8
9
10
11
12
13
14
15
16

● Rinocéphale . . . . 6b+
5+, 2) 6b+

❍ Ca Roule Ma Poule 6a
5, 2) 6a

❍ Ironie du Sport 6a
5, 2) 6a

❍ André-Aline Shoot . . . . 5+
5, 2) 5+

❍ Violence et Passion 6a
5, 2) 6a

● Moins Quarante àl'Ombre . 6b
5, 2) 6b

❍ SOS.com 5

❍ Tropique du Capricorne. 5
5, 2) 5, 3) 5

❍ Balai Brosse 5
4+, 2) 5

❍ Radio Lucien. . . . . 4+
noto this page.

❍ Les Branchés 5
4, 2) 5

❷ Greenpeace. 5
4, 2) 5

❸ Les P'tits Loups. 3
n be continued to a ledge and then walk-off.

❹ Mimi Cracra 3
n be continued to a ledge and then walk-off.

❺ Merlin l'Enchanteur 3
*n be continued to the walk-off. A line of bolts also continues
the top of the crag - details unknown.*

❻ Mary Poppins 3

Céüse
Sisteron
Volx
Orpierre
Bellecombe
Baume Rousse
Ubrieux
Saint Julien
Saint Léger
Malaucène
Combe Obscure
Les Dentelles
Venasque
Buoux

ne slab climbing on Radio Lucien *(4+) - this page - on Belleric.*

Left margin tabs: Céüse, Sisteron, Volx, Orpierre, Bellecombe, Baume Rousse, Ubrieux, Saint Julien, Saint Léger, Malaucene, Combe Obscure, Les Dentelles, Venasque, Buoux

120m
90m
60m
30m
Southe...

Quiquillon - West Face

An array of good, long routes up some very impressive ground, combined with morning shade, make these good objectives for those wanting a mini 'big day out'. A word of caution - the multi-pitches are toughly graded and using a spot or two of aid on these routes is common.
Approach - See page 68.
Descent - Abseil back down the routes or down the Southeast Face.

❶ Mine de Rien . . . . 7c+
1) 7a, 2) 7b+, 3) 7c+, 4) 7c

❷ Ave Maria 6c
1) 5+, 2) 6b+, 3) 6c, 4) 6b+, 5) 4+

❸ Tout Rouge 7b
1) 5+, 2) 6c+, 3) 7a, 4) 7b. Can be done at 6c with a bit of aid.

❹ Promenade Digestive 7b
1) 6c, 2) 6c+, 3) 7b, 4) 6c, 5) 6a

❺ La Terreur du Chien Fou . . . 6b
1) 5+, 2) 6b, 3) 5. Aid is used to start the pitch. 4) 5, 5) 6a, 5...

❻ Voyage 6a
1) 5+, 2) 5+, 3) 5, 4) 6a. Can be done at 5+ with some aid.

Southeast Face (Shorter Routes) *Page 84*

Quiquillon - Southeast Face (Long Routes)

n impressive wall with a number of big routes that go all the ay. Descent is possible either by abseil, or by walking off to e east (right on the photo). There are a number of shorter utes that go no further than the mid-way ledges - these are tailed on the following pages.

pproach - See page 68.

Le Dièdre Sud . . . . 5+
Orpierre classic following strong features all the way to the o of the crag. Use a pair of ropes or a single 70m to get down.
5+, 2) 5, 3) 5, 4) 5+, 5) 5, 6) 5, 7) 5

La Grotte . . . . 5+
5, 2) 5+, 3) 5, 4) 5+, 5) 5, 6) 5

N'Important où Hors du Monde . 6a+
5+, 2) 6a, 3) 4+, 4) 5+, 5) 6a+, 6) 5+, 7) 5

4 La Jungle en Folie . . . . 6a+
1) 5+, 2) 5, 3) 5, 4) 4+, 5) 4+, 6) 5+, 7) 6a+, 8) 5

5 Brazil . . . . 5+
1) 5, 2) 5, 3) 5, 4) 5, 5) 5, 6) 5, 7) 5+

6 Fleur de Lotus 6b
1) 6a+, 2) 6a+, 3) 5b, 4) 6b, 5) 6a. Long pitches on this one.

Célèse · Sisteron · Volx · Orpierre · Bellecombe · Baume Rousse · Ubrieux · Saint Julien · Saint Léger · Malaucène · Combe Obscure · Les Dentelles · Venasque · Buoux

Gélise

Sisteron

Volx

Orpierre

Bellecombe

Baume Rousse

Ubrieux

Saint Julien

Saint Léger

Malaucène

Combe Obscure

Les Dentelles

Venasque

Buoux

60m
40m
40m
38m
35m
30m
25m
25m
25m

Quiquillon - Southeast Face
There are a number of shorter routes that
go no further than the mid-way ledges.
Approach - See page 68.

1 Le Dièdre Sud . . . . 5+
See page 83 for the full topo.

2 Adieu Gary Cooper 6c

3 Le Mur Bleu 6b

4 Mistral Gagnant . . . . 6a+

5 Les Héros Sont Fatigués 6a

6 Le Cimetière des Nains . . . . . . 6a+

7 Où est Passée la Noce 6a

8 Cauchemars de Roudoudou 6a
1) 6a, 2) 6a

9 Le Blues de la Métropole . . 6b

10 J'ai Oublié le Jour 6c

11 Beau Dommage 6b
1) 6b, 2) 6b

12 Si t'Assures, C'est Pas Dur . . . . 6b+

13 Vivement la Bombe 7a
1) 7a, 2) 7a

14 Heureusement il y a la Mer 7a
1) 7a, 2) 7a

15 Maman, Regarde Je Vole 6b
1) 6b, 2) 6b

Mur Chamois

Plus Dure Sera la Chute . . . 🧗📋 [ ] **7a**
, 2) **7a**

Soleil Cherche Futur. . . . . . 📋🧗 [ ] **6b**
+, 2) **6b**

Des Fleurs Pour Algernon . . 📋🧗 [ ] **6b**

Du Cidre Pour Les Étoiles . . . . . 📋 [ ] **6a**
+, 2) **6a**

Le Ramier. . . . . 📋 [ ] **5+**
+, 2) **5.** Can be climbed at **6a** to the right.

Bas les Pattes . . . . 📋 [ ] **5+**

Le Bal des Puces Maudites 📋🧗 [ ] **6c**
a, 2) **5,** 3) **6c**

Laissez Passer les Clowns . 📋🧗 [ ] **6c**
a, 2) **6c**

Les Épinards Radioactifs . . . . . 📋 [ ] **6a+**

25 La Grotte (P1) . . . . 📋 [ ] **5**
See page 83 for the rest of the route to the top of the wall.

26 N'Important oú Hors du Monde (P1)
. . . . 📋 [ ] **5+**
See page 83 for the rest of the route to the top of the wall.

27 La Jungle en Folie (P1) . . . . . . 📋 [ ] **5**
See page 83 for the rest of the route to the top of the wall.

28 La Chaînon Manquant. . . . . . . 📋 [ ] **5+**

29 Le Choc du Primitif . . . . 📋 [ ] **5+**

30 Brazil (P1) . . . . 📋 [ ] **5**
See page 83 for the rest of the route to the top of the wall.

31 L'Horlage Portative . . . . 📋 [ ] **5**

32 Fleur de Lotus (P1) . . . . 📋 [ ] **6a+**
See page 83 for the rest of the route to the top of the wall.

Cédise
Sisteron
Volx
Orpierre
Bellecombe
Baume Rousse
Ubrieux
Saint Julien
Saint Léger
Malaucène
Combe Obscure
Les Dentelles
Venasque
Buoux

Géise
Sisteron
Volx
Orpierre
Bellecombe
Baume Rousse
Ubrieux
Saint Julien
Saint Léger
Malaucène
Combe Obscure
Les Dentelles
Venasque
Buoux

Mur Chamois

This shorter clean wall lies on the lower right-hand side of the main Southeast Face and it gives fingery and runout wall climbing. **Approach -** See page 68.

1 Tartine de Clous . . . . 🔲 🔲 🔲 **6c**
1) 5+, 2) 6c

2 Le Paradis . . . . 🔲 🔲 **6a+**

3 On Achève Bien les Chevaux 🔲 🔲 🔲 **6c+**

5 Directe du Chamois . . . . . . 🔲 🔲 🔲 **7a**

4 Panique en Ouganda . . 🔲 🔲 🔲 🔲 **6c+**

6 Sueur aux Tripes . . . . 🔲 🔲 **7a**

7 Terreur en Antarctique . . . . 🔲 🔲 **7a**

Further Areas

There are a number of other crags to the right of Mur Chamois, and new routes are being added every year. Details for these areas are in the local guidebook.

4 Heures
A wide range of single pitch routes from 3 to 6b+, fifteen minutes from the Adrech car park.

Ascle
A small number of multi-pitch routes with a remote feel to them, but only thirty minutes from the Adrech car park.

Adrech
A range of routes from 5 to 6c up to five pitches in length, fifteen minutes from the Adrech car park. La Face Cachée has hard, east-facing single pitch routes up to 7c+.

Blaches
A range of areas from low grade single and multi-pitch routes to hard single pitch routes fifteen minutes from Adrech parking.

Le Puy

This isolated sector gets the afternoom shade and is remarkably sheltered during rain which makes it a good place to know about if the weather's unsettled. Generally, the extensions are better than their pre-ambles, and the symbols are given for going all the way. Look out for the odd loose hold.

Approach - See page 68.

Cross the river from the town via a wide wooden bridge and take a footpath off to the right after about 100m.

Approach - See page 68.

Cétise

Sisteron

Voix

Orpierre

Bellecombe

Baume Rousse

Ubrieux

Saint Julien

Saint Léger

Malaucène

Combe Obscure

Les Dentelles

Venasque

Buoux

1 Comme un Oiseau sans Ailes 7a+
6b, 2) 7a+

2 Seul au Monde . . . . 7b+
6b+, 2) 7b+

3 Il est où le Gros 7b
6c, 2) 7b

4 Gravé dans la Roche 7b
6b, 2) 7a+

5 Mille Millards de Mille Cailloux
. . . . 7b+
1) 6b+, 2) 7c

6 Le Meilleur du Pire 7c
1) 6a, 2) 7b+

7 La Gib's . . . . 7c+
1) 6b, 2) 7c

8 La Poisse 8a
1) 6c+, 2) 7c+

Céüse

Sisteron

Volx

Orpierre

Bellecombe

Baume Rousse

Ubrieux

Saint Julien

Saint Léger

Malaucène

Combe Obscure

Les Dentelles

Venasque

Buoux

Often mistaken for being a crag itself, Buis-les-Baronnies is a charming town surrounded by excellent crags, and with a lot more within a half hour drive. It is a great destination for climbers wanting to sample a number of areas without having to move too far.

Getting there and getting around

A good way to get to Buis is by taking the TGV direct to Avignon. You can pick up a hire car at the station, and it's about an hour by car from Avignon to Buis. If you are coming by air, the major airports are Nimes, Marseille, and Toulon, but there are also flights to Avignon. The roads around Buis are not particularly fast, the nearest autoroute is the A7 to the west, if you're arriving from the east, a number of small roads link Buis to the N75 and the N96, though avoid the route via Orpierre if you don't wish to drive over a mountain (it can be closed in the winter). The only realistic non-car option is to get to Avignon, then catch a bus to Orange then another onto Buis, stay at the Municipal campsite, climb at Saint Julien and Ubrieux and get lifts from other climbers.

Where to stay

There are a number of campsites in Buis, and in the surrounding area. The municipal campsite is well-situated a couple of minutes walk from the centre of town, and lies within easy walking distance of the amazing fin of Saint Julien. There are a number of gites available to rent, the most convenient accommodation for Saint Léger is La Bergerie des Salamandres, a couple of minutes walk from the crag.

Local guidebooks

At that moment there are separate mini guidebooks to each of the main areas surrounding Buis, though a more comprehensive local guidebook is currently in production and when it comes out it should be available in the tourist information office in the town. **Escalades Autour du Ventoux** (2008, €20) gives more comprehensive coverage of Saint Léger, Malaucène and Combe Obscure and is available at La Bergerie at Saint Léger. For an alternative point of view, Jingo Wobbly's **Avignon Soleil** covers many of the areas featured here, plus a couple that aren't.

Web links

www.bergerie-des-salamandres.com
www.buislesbaronnies.com

Buis-les-Baronnies

Bellecombe - Baume Rousse - Ubrieux
Saint Julien - Saint Léger - Malaucène
Combe Obscure

Céüse
Sisteron
Volx
Orpierre
Bellecombe
Baume Rousse
Ubrieux
Saint Julien
Saint Léger
Malaucène
Combe Obscure
Les Dentelles
Venasque
Buoux

s Singer on *Libertine* (6c+) - *page 96* - Bellecombe.

Grande Arete
Page 94

Upper Tier
Page 97

Libertine Wa
Page 96

Dulf

Grande Arete

Céüse

Sisteron

Volx

Orpierre

Bellecombe

Baume Rousse

Ubrieux

Saint Julien

Saint Léger

Malaucène

Combe Obscure

Les Dentelles

Venasque

Buoux

Bellecombe

Céüse

Sisteron

Volx

Orpierre

Bellecombe

Baume Rousse

Ubrieux

Saint Julien

Saint Leger

Malaucène

Combe Obscure

Les Dentelles

Venasque

Buoux

Bellecombe

Packed with quality routes, and with a sense of scale often lacking in roadside sport climbing, Bellecombe is a gem of a crag that has something for everyone. The three pitch *Grande Arete* is an obvious line to go at, and if you're up for some run-out 6b+ crack climbing, have a go at *Dulf* while you're at it.

	No star	☼	☼☼	
Up to 4+	-	-	-	
5 to 6a+	1	11	1	
6b to 7a	-	5	4	
7a+ and up	-	-	8	

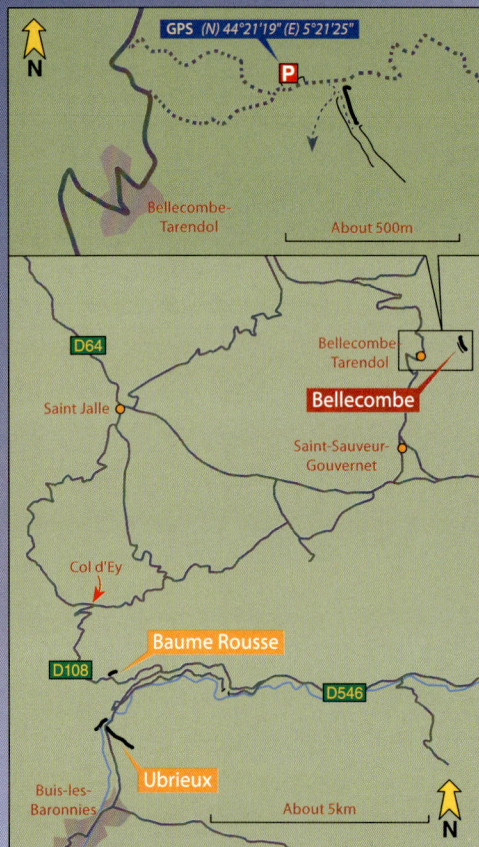

Approach

From Bellecombe-Tarendol, take the second unmarked unsurfaced track on the right whe leaving the town in a northerly direction. So the crag is in full view. Park at a small layby on the left, opposite a track leading down to a river crossing. Follow this to the start of *Grande Arete*. For the rest of the routes, a maintained path leads up along the base. To get the Upper Tier, follow the steep path pa all the lower sectors, then follow fixed ropes left across the face.

Conditions

The crag faces south, and gets plenty of su though the starts are shady when the sun is low. Due to its exposed position, it's not an ideal venue when it's cold and the wind is blowing.

The crag and the parking from the approach tra

Céüse · Sisteron · Volx · Orpierre · Bellecombe · Baume Rousse · Ubrieux · Saint Julien · Saint Léger · Malaucène · Combe Obscure · Les Dentelles · Venasque · Buoux

Céüse

Sisteron

Volx

Orpierre

Bellecombe

Baume Rousse

Ubrieux

Saint Julien

Saint Léger

Malaucène

Combe Obscure

Les Dentelles

Venasque

Buoux

Chris Singer and Ollie Ryall on the final pitch of *Grande Arete* (6b+) - *page 95* - Bellecombe.

From mid morning
5 min

Upper Tier

70m

60m

60m

35m

50m

Libert

28m

25m

25m

30m

Céüse

Sisteron

Volx

Orpierre

Bellecombe

Baume Rousse

Ubrieux

Saint Julien

Saint Léger

Malaucene

Combe Obscure

Les Dentelles

Venasque

Buoux

Grande Arete

election of brilliant wall climbs. *Grande Arete* and *Dulf*
the classics of the crag, following strong features in
ctacular positions.

Grande Arete . . . . 6b+
+, 2) 6b+, 3) 6b, 4) 6a. *Photo on page 93.*

Convoi Exceptionelle . . . . . 7b+
e up the 'back' side of the crag. Start at the third belay of
de Arete and continue to the top.

*next two routes lead to a ledge from where one of the walls
routes starts.*

Le Sas . . . . 5+
eful pitch for reaching the ledge where *Dulf* starts.

L'Eau de Là . . . . 6b+
rder way of getting to the *Dulf* ledge.

Maravilla 7c
wall climbing.

Dulf . . . . 6b+
sic jamming and laybacking. The bolts are very widely
ed but it takes trad gear if you want to reduce the runouts,
if this is your limit, you definitely do! The second pitch takes
to the top at **6a**. *Photo on this page.*

L'Onde Verte . . . . 7a+
up *Dulf*, then head right (belay possible - **6a** this far). Then
nd the thin wall to rejoin *Dulf* at the belay.

Ascenseur Pour le Plasir . . . 7b
first half of a great climb.

L'Haut de Là . . . . 7a+
brilliant continuation to the top. The final section is less
quality but well-situated - **6c**. *Photo on page 3.*

Hard Saga 7c

Petit Roque 7a
the mid-height belay is **Mat** - the grade is the same, so you
as well carry on to the top.

Rêve de Crémallière 7a

Ultime Limite 7a

Nouvelles Données 7a

Trinquille 7b

Pièce Montée . . . . 7b+

Singer climbing *Dulf* (6b+) - *this page.*

Céüse

Sisteron

Volx

Orpierre

Bellecombe

Baume Rousse

Ubrieux

Saint Julien

Saint Léger

Malaucène

Combe Obscure

Les Dentelles

Venasque

Buoux

Céüse

Sisteron

Volx

Orpierre

Bellecombe

Baume Rousse

Ubrieux

Saint Julien

Saint Léger

Malaucène

Combe Obscure

Les Dentelles

Venasque

Buoux

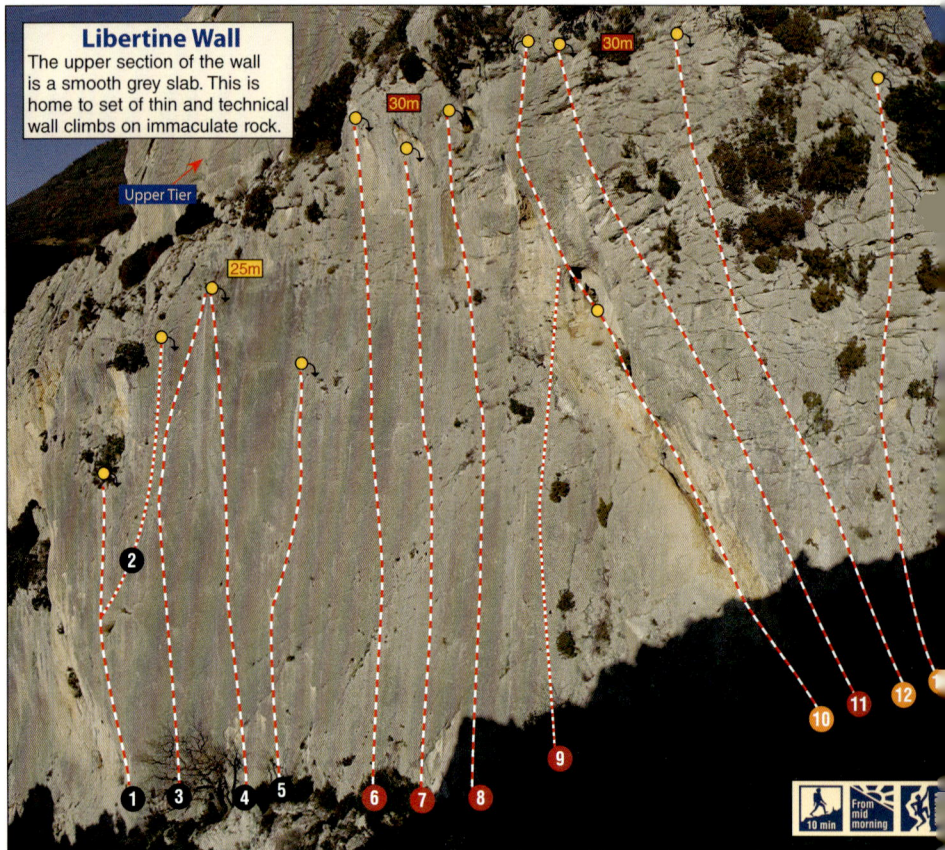

Libertine Wall
The upper section of the wall is a smooth grey slab. This is home to set of thin and technical wall climbs on immaculate rock.

Upper Tier

30m

30m

25m

❶ Picolina 7b

❷ Coquillages et Crustacés 7b+

❸ Du Vent Plein les Doigts 8a

❹ Panettone 7c

❺ Court Message 7b

❻ Libertine. . . . . 6c+
See photo on page 89.

❼ Passage aux Aveux 6c

❽ Elle est Douce 7a

❾ Passage a Tabac . . . . 6b+

❿ Diagonale 6a

⓫ La Buchrie . . . . 6b+

⓬ Les Trois Sœurs . . . . 6a+

⓭ Arostiche . . . . 5+

Upper Tier

⓮ Rataillon. 6b

⓯ Quignan 6a

⓰ Désaccord Mineur 6b

⓱ Sulmona 6a
Photo opposite.

⓲ Des Bourgeons Plein les Poches . . 6a

⓳ Vol d'Autochtone 6a

⓴ Pas Si Tranquille 5

㉑ L'Heure Folle . . . . 5+

㉒ Relance et Croise 6a

㉓ La Cerise . . . . 5+

㉔ Local Roc 5

Ollie Ryall on *Sulmona* (6a+) - *opposite*.

Upper Tier

A fine, featured grey slab that can be approached either by climbing one of the routes on the lower tier, or by following the path in from the right. There are a series of fixed ropes to protect the traverse in.

15 min | From mid morning | Slabby

20m

20m

12m

24

23

22

21

20

19

18

17

16

15

14

10

Libertine Wall

Céüse
Sisteron
Volx
Orpierre
Bellecombe
Baume Rousse
Ubrieux
Saint Julien
Saint Léger
Malaucène
Combe Obscure
Les Dentelles
Venasque
Buoux

Baume Rousse

Céüse

Sisteron

Orpierre

Bellecombe

Baume Rousse

Ubrieux

Saint Julien

Saint Léger

Malaucène

Combe Obscure

Les Dentelles

Venasque

Buoux

Back Wall
Page 105

Gauche Compétition
Page 104

Gauche Facile
Page 102

Droite Compétition
Page 106

Droite Initiation
Page 108

Célise

Sisteron

Volx

Orpierre

Bellecombe

Baume Rousse

Ubrieux

Saint Julien

Saint Léger

Malaucène

Combe Obscure

Les Dentelles

Venasque

Buoux

	No star	⭐	⭐⭐	
Up to 4+	1	6	2	
5 to 6a+	6	17	6	
6b to 7a	3	5	7	
7a+ and up	7	4	10	

Baume Rousse has an amazing spread of quality routes across the grade spectrum, and no climber could fail to have at least one good day here. It also has some of the most agreeable bolting you will ever encounter, and the crag is the perfect place to hone single or multi-pitch climbing skills.

Approach

The crag lies about 2km north of Buis-les-Baronnies. From Buis, follow the D546 north past the Gorge d'Ubrieux, over the bridge, and take a left onto the D108. Follow this for about 2km, (avoiding turning off onto the D108a at a sharp bend) until you're under the crag on the right. There is a parking area on the right. A pair of parallel paths lead up from the climbing sign at the roadside, the left goes to Gauche Facile, the right leads to the Central 'Competition' section, alternatively you may branch off right to get to Droite Initiation.

Col d'Ey

Baume Rousse

D108

D546

GPS *(N) 44°18'07" (E) 5°16'50"*

Ubrieux

Buis-les-Baronnies

About 5km

Conditions

While it's mainly south facing, Baume Rousse also offers sun or shade throughout the day, so you can chase the sun in the winter, or the shade whe it's hot. The left-hand east-facing wall gets the most shade, and can take a couple of weeks to dry out after rain.

Competition routes

An interesting feature of many of the climbs at Baume Rousse is th fact that they were established for a climbing competition back in the days when competitions were held outdoors on rock. The res of this is you can see how you compare with the elite French youth of 1995 - if you can do every route set for the junior gir you're doing pretty well.

Céüse

Sisteron

Volx

Orpierre

Bellecombe

Baume Rousse

Ubrieux

Saint Julien

Saint Léger

Malaucène

Combe Obscure

Les Dentelles

Venasque

Buoux

Carrie Cojocari on *Sikaraté* (5+) - *page*

Céüse

Sisteron

Volx

Orpierre

Bellecombe

Baume Rousse

Ubrieux

Saint Julien

Saint Leger

Malaucène

Combe Obscure

Les Dentelles

Venasque

Buoux

Sam Hamer on *Rigpa ou la Nature de l'esprit* (8a) - *page 106.*

Céüse

Sisteron

Volx

Orpierre

Bellecombe

Baume Rousse

Ubrieux

Saint Julien

Saint Léger

Malaucène

Combe Obscure

Les Dentelles

Venasque

Buoux

5 min | Lots of sun | Slabby

35m
30m
30m
25m

1 2 3 4 5 6 7 8 9 10 11 12 13 14 15 16 17

Gauche Facile

A nice friendly place to start off. Though many of the routes stretch to the full length of a 70m rope to lower off, The longest routes have mid-way belays to allow easy retreats for those with shorter ropes.

Au Bout . . . . ☼ 🪢 [____] **6a+**
…eresting face climbing, keep left on the crux. It can be split at
…elay, above this it is only **4+**. *Photo on this page.*

Coin Coin . . . . ☼ [____] **5+**
… climbing up a natural line. Mid-way belay possible.

Murmuroa . . . . ☼ [____] **4+**
…fect holds on perfect rock.

La Bavette Spatiale . . . . . . ☼ 🪢 [____] **6a**
…ugh to get started - bridge up between the tree and the rock.
… a bit hairy getting to the first bolt - though you can protect
…s section by lassoing a tree stump with your rope, or placing
…ig nut.

Milky Way . . . . ☼ 🪢 [____] **6b+**
…ood long pitch. Once you've got to the first bolt, step left. It's
…eally good **5+** to the first belay, but even better above.

Étoile Fuyante . . . . 🪢 🪢 [____] **7b+**
…rrific crimping - one for a very cold day, better still go climb
…mething that isn't on grey rock at this grade.

Couleur d'Embruns . . . . ☼ [____] **6a+**
…e brown groove starts a long pitch that gets very close to
…ky Way towards the top.

Unnamed . . . . [____] **5+**
…ong pitch with a slightly scrappy start up a broken groove.

À Suivre . . . . [____] **3**
…mb the rib - you can start from the base or from the big ledge
…ttle higher.

La Cigale et la Fourmi . . . . . . ☼ [____] **3**
… flake. It doesn't get much easier than this.

Concombre Masqué . . . . ☼ [____] **4**
… last section and belay are shared with the next route.

L'Émile et Une Nuit . . . . ☼ [____] **4**
…rt in a short groove to the left of a tree.

Soleil Levante . . . . ☼ 🪢 [____] **6b+**
…ne thin moves and polished holds.

Étoile des Neiges . . . . ☼ 🪢 [____] **6c+**
…ugh one! Technical and a bit polished.

Pleine Lune . . . . ☼ [____] **6a**
…y close to the next route in places.

Le Dièdre . . . . ☼ [____] **5**
…ood line and a long pitch. The route may continue further but
… bolts run out.

Le Pilier . . . . ☼ [____] **5**
… be continued as for *Le Dièdre*.

Céüse
Sisteron
Volx
Orpierre
Bellecombe
Baume Rousse
Ubrieux
Saint Julien
Saint Léger
Malaucène
Combe Obscure
Les Dentelles
Venasque
Buoux

Chris Singer on *Au Bout* (6a+) - *this page*.

Céüse
Sisteron
Volx
Orpierre
Bellecombe
Baume Rousse
Ubrieux
Saint Julien
Saint Léger
Malaucène
Combe Obscure
Les Dentelles
Venasque
Buoux

Gauche Compétition

The left-hand wall gets the shade in the afternoon. Further to the right, routes on the upper tier are accessed via a fixed cable than runs most of the width of the cliff.

20m from ledge
35m from ground

20m from ledge

30m

20m

15m

① **Qualif á la Place du Kalife**
. . . . 6a+
Offwidth to start, then excellent face climbing. Second qualifier for the Junior Girls.

② **Les Ailes du Vizir.** . 7a
A hard, fingery and reachy crux which may be impossible for the short. Junior Girls' Final.

③ **Les Mille-et-Unes Buis** . . . . 6a+
A technical start - climb the groove to the right to bring the grade down to **5**.

④ **La Cicane** 6b
An enyoyable introduction to the harder routes here.

⑤ **Les Bellecombaises** . . . 7a+
Follow the brown streak - one short hard section only, so be prepared to pull on some small holds.

⑥ **O.K.** 7a
There is a poor start to the right but it is better to scramble up the ledge. The grade is the same for the whole route.

⑦ **Gnocchi on Heaven's Door** 6b
A great pitch, much better than it looks.

⑧ **Clash** 7a
A boulder problem with bolts.

⑨ **Les Macaronis de la Mort** . . 7a
A powerful start leads to a technical and sustained outing.

⑩ **Le Mythe** 7b
Another boulder problem with bolts.

⑪ **Les Raviolis de L'Enfer** 7b
A great route that keeps you on your toes throughout.

12 min · Morning · Steep

20m from ledge
35m from ground

15m

20 22 24 25 26 27 28 29 23 21 23

Traverse protected by cable

The Back Wall

Some good sustained hard routes at are to be found above the cable-protected catwalk that runs most of the width of the back wall. It's worth bringing a couple of slings and screwgates to use as cow's tails to protect the traverse. Even if you leave your partner on the ground, long slings are useful to reduce rope-drag.

Céüse · Sisteron · Volx · Orpierre · Bellecombe · **Baume Rousse** · Ubrieux · Saint Julien · Saint Léger · Malaucène · Combe Obscure · Les Dentelles · Venasque · Buoux

Cheloup Plage 6a
rappy little route - useful as an approach though.

Les Spaghettis des Ténèbres. . . 8a
7b to the first belay. Semi-final for junior boys.

Pasta de l'Éléphant . . . . 6a+
be dirty after rain. The fun starts above the ledge.

Al Dente 6a
n route that includes some tufas at the overhang.

Les Nouilles de l'Obscur . . . 7b+

Piano 6a

La Cicciolina . . . . 6b+

Barilla Sound System 7c
uldery little route that packs it in.

Pasta à Shout 7b
uple of tough moves, but good rests.

No Slibards Today . . . . 6a+
dy pulling on jugs to a hard crux, then back to the pulling.

22 La Giclette du Graou . . . . 7a+

23 La Caraille 6b
Can link into the next route, but it is worthwhile in its own right. The right-hand variation is **6a** and links well into the *La Racaille* and *Aband Fils de Crapaud* - bring slings to extend.

24 La Voie des Abeilles . . . . . 7a+
The crux lies in the grey rock at the top. Often with a bees' nest.

25 La Racaille 7a
Steep 'orange' leads to thin 'grey' - great positions. Second qualifier for junior boys.

26 Aband Fils de Crapaud 7a
Big holds lead to a thin traverse, then easier to the top. First qualifier for junior boys.

27 Jimmy Petit Fils de Crao, Père de Rahan
. . . . 7b+

28 Unnamed . . . . 6c+

29 Pipouze Line . . . . 7b+
Harder than when first climbed due to losing a hold. It is not very pleasant.

❶ Unnamed . . . . 🗝1 [ ] 8b+
Starting in the depths of the cave, climb horizontally to finish on more vertical ground.

❷ Unnamed . . . . 🗝2 [ ] 8a
Slow to dry.

❸ 6662 . . . . 🗝2 [ ] 7c+

❹ Tout Court Tout Dur . . . 🗝2 [ ] 7b
A hard, fingery crux. High in the grade.

❺ L'Ecolo Net . . . . 🗝2 [ ] 7a
Another one that is hard for the grade.

Start up L'Ecolo Net for the next three routes.

❻ Le Samsara. . . . . 🗝2 [ ] 8a+

❼ J'aurais Voulu être un Artiste
. . . . 🗝2 [ ] 8a
Good holds soon lead to some technical moves.

❽ Pipouille la Fripouille. . . . . . . 🗝1 [ ] 8a

❾ Rigpa ou la Nature de l'esprit 🗝3 [ ] 8a
A popular route, with a tricky finish. *Photo on page 101.*

❿ Les Secrets de Régine . . . . 🗝3 [ ] 8a
The obvious line to move your clips onto when you've done *Rigpa...*

⓫ Saga Corsica . . . . 🗝2 [ ] 8b
There's a bolt to get you on the ledge, but it's probably best to belay from the ledge. Follow the cave roof, then move right and take the roof direct.

Droite Compétition

A collection of top-class hard routes to go at ensures that Baume Rousse has something for everyone. If you're looking for shade in which to finish your project, get here early.

Routes 15 to 17 around the corner

Rahan, fils de Crao . . . . . . 🎵 📷 ☐ **7b+**
enyoyable route with a good rest possible before the traverse
. No particularly hard moves. *Photo this page*.

Si t'as Rien d'Autre à Faire . 🔧 🔧 ☐ **7c**
st qualification route for junior boys.

Haschisch B . . . . 🎵 🔧 🔧 ☐ **6b**
owerful start, a leisurely middle and a technical end.

Rigni, Rignette et Rignoulou . . . 🎵 ☐ **6b+**

Babaat Connection . . . . 🎵 ☐ **6a**

La Sirène en Pyjama . . . . 🎵 ☐ **6b**

Dévers et des Pas Mürs . . . 🎵 🔧 ☐ **6c**
interesting route that avoids the nasty starts of the next
ple of routes.

Go Up. . . . . 🎵 ☐ **7a**

Vindiou. . . . . 🎵 ☐ **7a+**

2002 L'Épicier de l'Espace . . . . 🎵 ☐ **(6b+)**
s route used to have some bolt-on holds for the start but
se have now gone and it is impossible in its current state.
t qualifier for junior girls.

Toby Dunn on *Rahan, Fils de Crao* (7b+) - *this page*.

Céüse
Sisteron
Volx
Orpierre
Bellecombe
Baume Rousse
Ubrieux
Saint Julien
Saint Léger
Malaucène
Combe Obscure
Les Dentelles
Venasque
Buoux

These routes can be split at mid-height belays and the difficulty level tends to be sustained over the two pitches.

Sector Droite Initiation

It's hard to imagine a better place for taking novice climbers - the bolts are plentiful, the rock good and the angle allows plenty of time to take in the view. Just one thing to bear in mind, there are some loose bits lying around on the ledges, so it's worth bringing a helmet, especially if the crag is busy.

1 La Reine des Bouses 4
The first route follows the ridge.

2 Tilt 4

3 Unnamed 4
Start just right of a tree and then follow a grooveline, continuing to the top. A midway belay is possible.

4 Unnamed 5
Pass a small block overhang on the left, then follow the bolts to the top.

5 Tartivore 5
Aim to the right side of the block overhang to start. The second pitch has some interest.

6 Fleur Bleue . . . . 5+
The first pitch offers a belay under the (small) block overhang, then continue to the top.

7 Handy-Cap Repos 5
Start just to the right of a tree. There is a midway belay possible, just right of the belay on the previous route.

8 Julie Quensand . . . . 5+
Start at the painted number '6', just left of a bush. The first few metres are considerably harder than the remainder of the route.

Cédise
Sisteron
Volx
Orpierre
Bellecombe
Baume Rousse
Ubrieux
Saint Julien
Saint Léger
Malaucène
Combe Obscure
Les Dentelles
Venasque
Buoux

Unnamed . . . . 5+
crappy route that will take a while to clean up.

Lolotte Glaciaire 5
ew metres of tricky slab climbing need to be addressed before
e easy climbing leads to the top.

Les Bandits 5
ig letter '8' is painted at the start.

Pile Poil . . . . 5+
ne thin moves to contend with. Start at the big painted '9'.

Les Lézards 5

Vieille Chernille 5

Unnamed 5
* to be confused with the following route.

Chou Roi Pour Léa . . . . 5+
longest route here, taking the corner all the way.

17 L'Éperon 1 . . . . 6b+
An odd line following a diagonal crack, but never really climbing
it. Steady until the last few metres.

18 L'Éperon 2 . . . . 5+

19 L'Éperon 3 . . . . 5+

*Around the pillar to the right is a collection of good routes which
take clean lines up an impressive slab. Some routes have more
bolts than holds, and there are plenty of holds!*

20 Thorodin 5

21 Sikaraté . . . . 5+
Photo on page 100.

22 Le Tyrex . . . . 6b+

23 Douce Colère 3
Photo this page.

24 Dou Dou 5

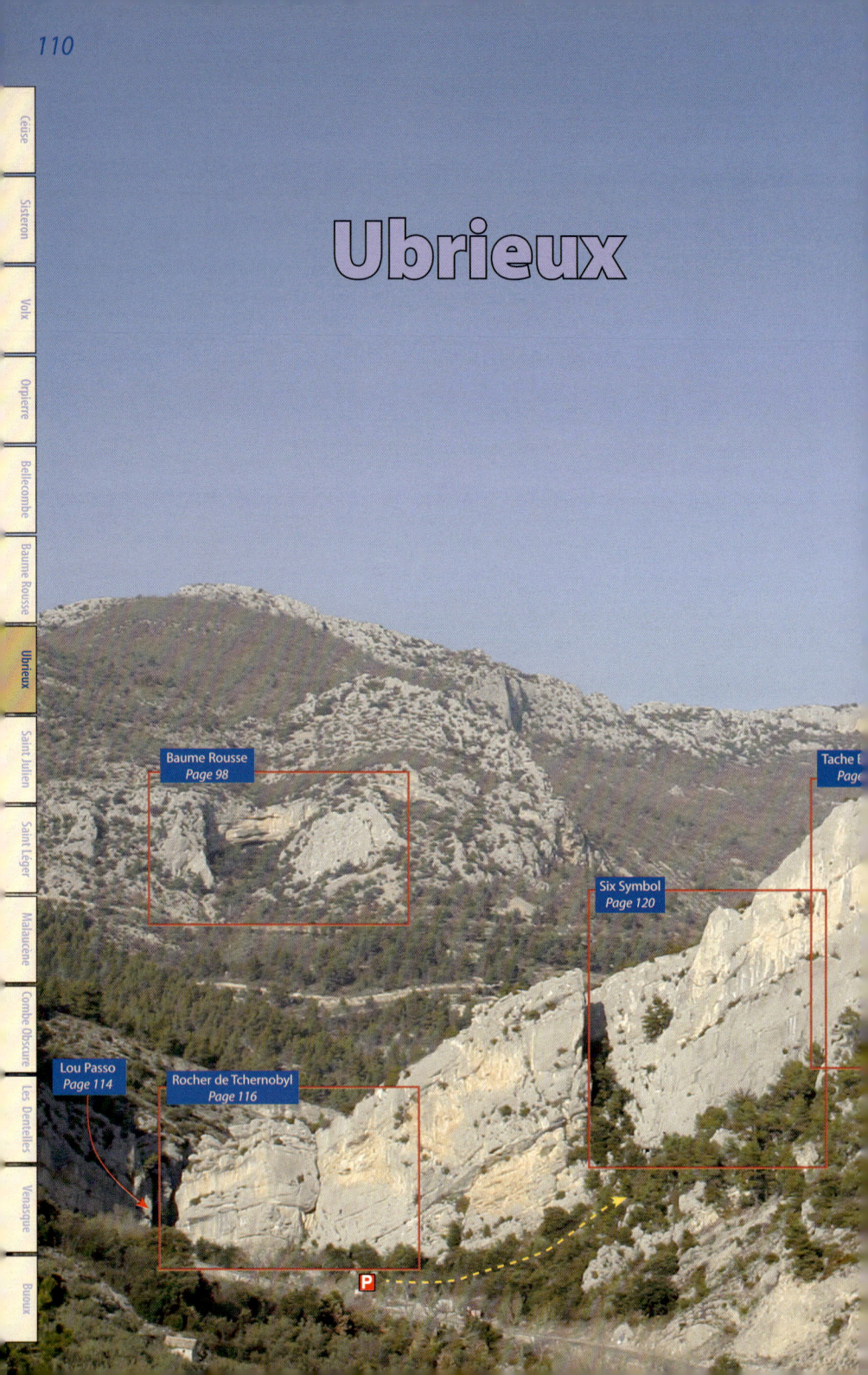

Ubrieux

Géise

Sisteron

Volx

Orpierre

Bellecombe

Baume Rousse

Ubrieux

Saint Julien

Saint Léger

Malaucène

Combe Obscure

Les Dentelles

Vénasque

Buoux

Baume Rousse
Page 98

Tache E
Pag

Six Symbol
Page 120

Lou Passo
Page 114

Rocher de Tchernobyl
Page 116

P

Le Bout du
Monde
Page 124

Frisson Pour
Une Jeune Fille

Céüse

Sisteron

Volx

Orpierre

Bellecombe

Baume Rousse

Ubrieux

Saint Julien

Saint Léger

Malaucène

Combe Obscure

Les Dentelles

Venasque

Buoux

	No star	☼	☼☼	☼
Up to 4+	7	10	-	
5 to 6a+	4	20	10	2
6b to 7a	3	16	12	8
7a+ and up	4	4	9	3

Céüse · Sisteron · Volx · Orpierre · Bellecombe · Baume Rousse · Ubrieux · Saint Julien · Saint Léger · Malaucène · Combe Obscure · Les Dentelles · Venasque · Buoux

With a few exceptions, Ubrieux is a crag for those wanting mid-grade routes consisting of technical climbing. The generally-slabby walls naturally offer many different lines up the same piece of rock, and a 6a can easily feel like a 7a if you're as much as a metre off - we've described the easiest lines, and the reader is invited to discover the hard variations at their leisure.

Approach

Head north from Buis-les-Baronnies on the D646 and you can't miss the extensive limestone crag that runs up the hill on the right. Where the crag meets the road there is a parking area with picnic tables. A path follows the base of the cliff. This is an extensive cliff, and there are more routes than described here. Once away from the popular areas the quality of the rock and of the approach path deteriorate noticeable. To get to Lou Passo, walk (or drive) up the road and cross the river at the bridge, take a path left immediately after the bridge and follow this down-river until a short section of via ferrata leads down to the riverside, follow the river for a short distance (past the *beginners' initiation slab*) until you arrive at the routes shown.

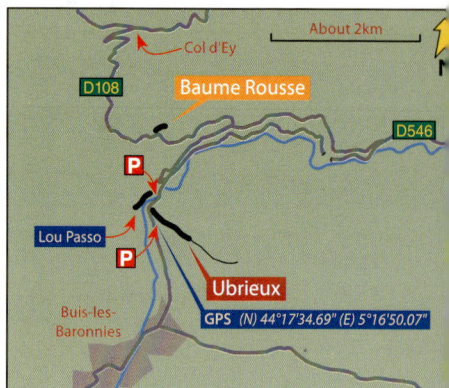

About 2km
Col d'Ey
D108
Baume Rousse
D546
P
Lou Passo
P
Ubrieux
GPS (N) 44°17'34.69" (E) 5°16'50.07"
Buis-les-Baronnies

Conditions

The crag faces south-west, and gets plenty of sun from mid-day onwards. The rock dries very quickly after rain, and plentiful tree cover allows some shade for those on belay duty. Lou Passo gets the morning sun and seeps after rain. After heavy rain the river may swell to make the base of routes unreachable.

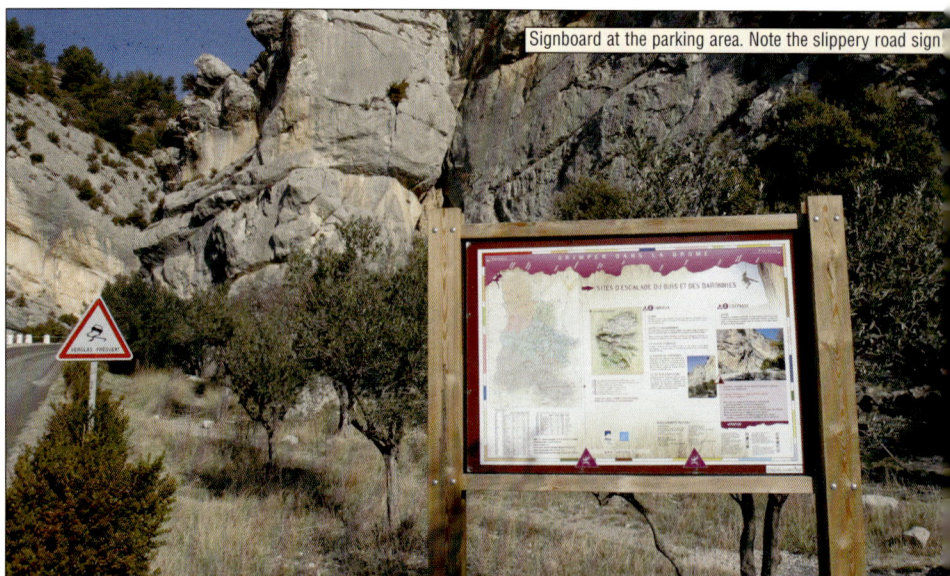

Signboard at the parking area. Note the slippery road sign

Craig Entwistle on *Faille Qui Maille* (6c) - *page 120* - Six Symbol Wall, Ubrieux.

Célise
Sisteron
Volx
Orpierre
Bellecombe
Baume Rousse
Ubrieux
Saint Julien
Saint Léger
Malaucène
Combe Obscure
Les Dentelles
Venasque
Roux

Lou Passo

Technically not actually a part of Ubrieux, Lou Passo is just the other side of the road and the river that cuts through the gorge. The harder routes are excellent, and there are plenty of very easy routes here too, but not much in the middle. It is a great spot for a bit of swimming in hot weather.

Bolted VERY easy routes

More routes above the water which can be rigged for exciting top-roping

Routes 12 to 20 obscured by trees

❶ **Ms Colombe** 8b

❷ **Doux Souvenir** . . . . 8a+

❸ **Cétacé** . . . . 7c+

❹ **Nico** 7c

❺ **Psychose** 7b

❻ **Hardcore** . . . . 7b+
A super line continuing all the way up the crumbly corner.

❼ **Ciao Bella** 7c

❽ **Flashdance** . . . . 7a+
Chipped but still good, and with spaced bolts. Start up the groove (high first bolt), alternatively climb the tufas to the left and add a grade. *Photo opposite.*

❾ **Mito** 7c

❿ **Beurk** 7b

⓫ **Bloody Hill** . . . . 5+

The routes further right are hidden by the trees. They are short and difficult to distinguish from each other. The routes across the river at Ubrieux are better but also more exposed to the sun.

⓬ **Eclipse** . . . . 6a+

⓭ **Cana** . . . . 4+

⓮ **Fonctionnaire** 5
The longest of these routes continues up the slabby groove above the trees.

⓯ **Calament** 4

⓰ **Toit ou Moi** . . . . 4+

⓱ **Cro Magnon** 4

⓲ **La Voie Souple** . . . . 5+

⓳ **20 Cents** . . . . 4+

⓴ **Poussin** . . . . 4+

⓴ **Le Tas** 5

⓴ **Abigail** 6b

The routes continue further right, with a number of routes at the very lowest grades. It is arguable whether the via ferrata approach is harder than some of them.

Céüse
Sisteron
Voix
Orpierre
Bellecombe
Baume Rousse
Ubrieux
Saint Julien
Saint Léger
Malaucène
Combe Obscure
Les Dentelles
Venasque
Buoux

Cédise
Sisteron
Voix
Orpierre
Bellecombe
Baume Rousse
Ubrieux
Saint Julien
Saint Léger
Malaucène
Combe Obscure
Les Dentelles
Venasque
Buoux

Rocher de Tchernobyl - Left
Walk-ins don't get much shorter than this!
A good variety of routes from technical grey
face climbs to some bouldery test-pieces.

Ceüse

Sisteron

Volx

Orpierre

Bellecombe

Baume Rousse

Ubrieux

Saint Julien

Saint Léger

Malaucène

Combe Obscure

Les Dentelles

Venasque

Buoux

Franck Debon on the *Hésitation* (4+) - *this page*.

Cédise
Sisteron
Volx
Orpierre
Bellecombe
Baume Rousse
Ubrieux
Saint Julien
Saint Léger
Malaucène
Combe Obscure
Les Dentelles
Venasque
Buoux

Toit Robi. . . . . 6c+
n micro-route through the roof at its widest - getting to the
s easy...

Ça Cartoon . . . . 6b+
nuous move at the roof gains a drilled slot, you're supposed
gnore the good holds on the right and turn the lip directly at
but this way makes far more sense.

Sensation 6b
e fun at the lip of the roof, basically using the same holds as
he previous route. The extension is a bouldery **6c**.

Oh! Con! / Serre Les Fesses 6b
ow the brown streak - the paint at the base describes this as
routes, but there is only one line of bolts, resulting in much
fusion. The extension is **6c**.

Ira de la Lune 6b
rect line up the grey rock.

Au Taquet Bouboul 6b
e left at the top to avoid the roof.

Planète Rock. 6b
th doing for the mantelshelf finish, ... just!

Les Sauc' d'Italia . . . . 6a+
ther mantel, but at least there's a crack to help.

Ecolo Man. . . . . 6b+
ld topo gave this 4+ - a bit harsh!

Aphrodite 5

11 Hésitation . . . . 4+
The extension is a fierce **7a+**. *Photo this page.*

12 Ulala 5
The extension is a thin **6b**.

13 L'XYZ. . . . . 5+

14 L'ABC. . . . . 4+

15 La Casse Dalle 6b
Not as good as its neighbours.

16 Tchernobyl 6c
Some very thin climbing.

17 Le Grand Chaos. . . . . 6b+
Good sustained climbing - big holds where it's steep, small ones
where it's not.

18 Oraison Funèbre 7b
Some tough pulls on small holds through the steep section
entirely justify the grade, though interesting climbing remains.

19 Passeport Pour l'Enfer. 7b+
Very bouldery - the crux is like a Fontainebleau boulder problem,
without the friction.

20 Dernier Soupir. 6b
Start up the following route.

21 Mammouth Cave . . . . 5+
A big, ugly, compelling chimney.

Roadside

From mid morning

Slabby

Rocher de Tchernobyl - Right

This is a good spot for getting plenty of routes in the green and orange spot range. The length of the routes is restricted by poor quality rock higher up - the four routes that do go all the way are all excellent, but tougher.

30m

15m

1 2 3 4 5 6 7 8 9 10 11 12 13 14 15 16

Ceüse

Sisteron

Volx

Orpierre

Bellecombe

Baume Rousse

Ubrieux

Saint Julien

Saint Léger

Malaucène

Combe Obscure

Les Dentelles

Venasque

Buoux

Cérise
Sisteron
Volx
Orpierre
Bellecombe
Baume Rousse
Ubrieux
Saint Julien
Saint Léger
Malaucène
Combe Obscure
Les Dentelles
Venasque
Buoux

Le Paradis . . . . 6b+
in slab leads to fun overhanging moves to gain the headwall.

Le Mythe 6c
grey wall has some reachy moves to small holds.

Le K d'Annibal. . . . . . 6c+
in slab and a technical finish.

Nuage . . . . 6b+
ood contrasting pitch.

Le Clou Foireux 5

Samiby. 6a
nical moves leading from break to break. *Photo this page.*

Andropose . . . . 5+

8 Maybe . . . . 5+

9 Mikado. . . . . 4+

10 Rambo Varrior. 5

11 Beaux Parleurs . . . . 5+

12 Mercure . . . . 5+

13 Jupiter . . . . 4+

14 Kipertou . . . . 4+

15 Splach . . . . 4+

16 Perfo / Clero . . . . 4+

The first routes are up the gully to the left of the face.

1 Crache tes Tripes pour l'Enfer
. . . . 7b
The thin wall 2m right of the end of the gully.

2 La Finesse des Doigtés 7b
Start about 4m from the end of the gully.

3 Climbing Show 7c
Start just to the right of a hollybush. Ultra thin.

4 Climbing Showbiz 7b
Start up *Climbing Show* then break left (a solitary bolt between the routes shows the way) to finish up *La Finesse des Doigtés*.

5 Rock Toi de Là . . . . 6c+
Take a line past a big vegetated scoop.

6 Cheminement 3
Starting halfway up the gully, a bolted scramble leads up to a big ledge. From here you can access the belays on the next few routes by scrambling, handy if you want to set up some top-ropes.

7 Le Reymonde 5
A left-hand version is possible at **4+**.

8 Le Grand Jo 5
Aim for the big layback flake.

9 Le Gégène . . . . 4+
A right shocker at the grade! Popular and polished.

10 Post Natal . . . . 6a+

11 L'Enfance de l'Art 6a
First clip is a bit high.

12 Psychose 5
Another high first bolt.

13 Déséquilibre . . . . 6b★
Straightforward climbing to an overhang for some fun moves then cruise to the finish.

14 Subtilité Tactile . . . . 6a+

15 Faille qui Maille 6c
Aim for a black runnel high up. *Photo on page 113.*

16 Turpitude 7b
Some fierce and thin climbing on the grey rock.

17 Symphonie du Graton . . . . . 6c+
Fun and varied climbing with excellent flowing movement.

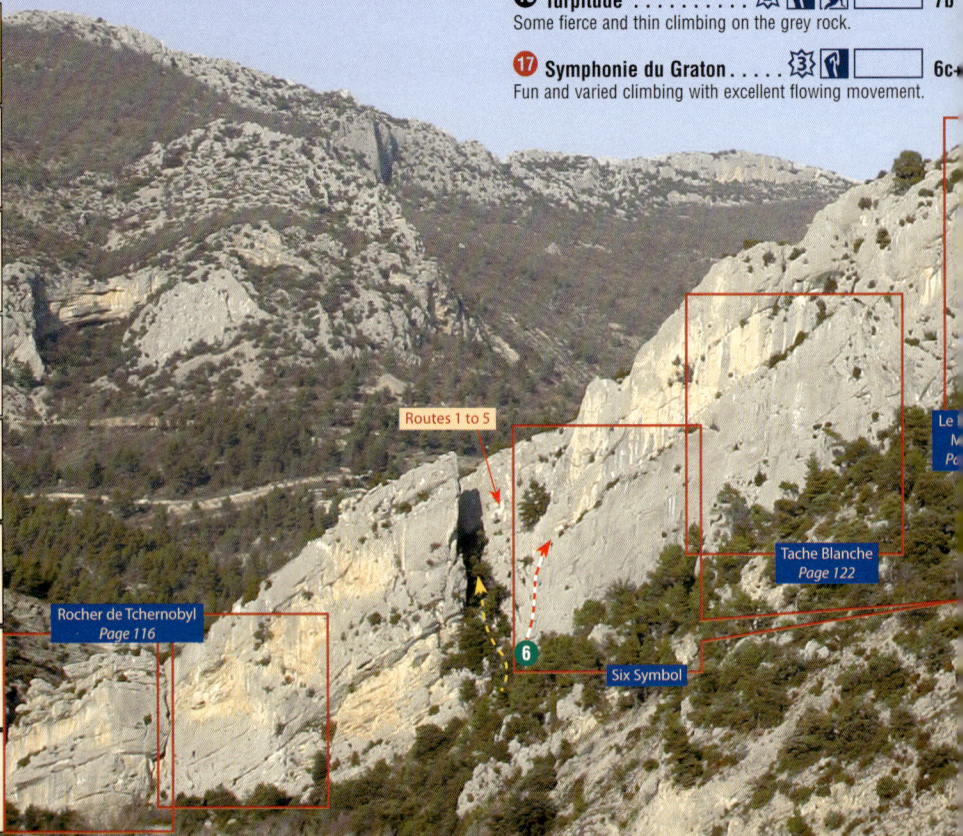

Routes 1 to 5

6

Six Symbol

Tache Blanche
Page 122

Rocher de Tchernobyl
Page 116

Céüse
Sisteron
Volx
Orpierre
Bellecombe
Baume Rousse
Ubrieux
Saint Julien
Saint Léger
Malaucène
Combe Obscure
Les Dentelles
Venasque
Buoux

Six Symbol

Not that different from Rocher de Tchernobyl, but a notch harder. The upper wall has poor rock and is not climbed on.

High first bolts - A few of the routes here have very high first bolts, and a clip-stick could be of use. Alternatively, with some of the routes, you can scramble up an easier line and pre-clip the first or second bolts.

⑱ Sublimation **6c**
Good sustained climbing with nice body position and foot work.

⑲ Kesako . . . . **6c+**
Start to the left of the tree. A great route with unique moves that leave a smile on your face.

⑳ Six Symbol . . . . **7a+**
Start to the right of the tree. The route the sector was named after isn't actually the best route here.

㉑ Pointe Limite Zero . . . . **7a+**

㉒ Flagrant Délire . . . . **7c+**

Céüse
Sisteron
Volx
Orpierre
Bellecombe
Baume Rousse
Ubrieux
Saint Julien
Saint Leger
Malaucène
Combe Obscure
Les Dentelles
Venasque
Buoux

Tache Blanche

More perfect grey slabs. At the top end are some long pitches that make the walk up the hill worthwhile, though you will need to take care even with a 70m rope.

Céüse

Sisteron

Volx

Orpierre

Bellecombe

Baume Rousse

Ubrieux

Saint Julien

Saint Léger

Malaucène

Combe Obscure

Les Dentelles

Venasque

Buoux

40m
35m
30m
30m

10

19 20 21

18

17

16
15

14

13
12

11

9
8
7
6
5

4

3 2 1

1 Des Doigts et des Orteils ⚐⚐ 🧗 🧗 ☐ 7a
Some very thin moves, probably a lot harder for those of less than average height.

2 Entrechat . . . . ⚐⚐ 🧗 ☐ 6c
One steep section provides the difficulty.

3 Le Pas Décisif . . . . ⚐ 🧗 ☐ 6c

4 Le Bal à Jo . . . . ⚐ 🧗 ☐ 6b

5 Paradoxe . . . . ⚐ 🧗 ☐ 6b
Start a couple of metres left of a corner, then trend right.

Le Repos du Grimpeur . . . . 5+

rt behind a large boulder and follow cracks up the centre of pillar.

Déverse-Gondage . . . . 5+

H.S . . . . 5+

Sudation Excessive . . . . . . 6c+

ne really thin moves, but the difficulties are short-lived.

Bébé S'Amuse . . . . 6a+

Symphonie Inachevée 6a

Éléphant Girl . . . . 6a+

oto on this page.

Ciao l'Enfoiré ! . . . . 5+

s possible to lower off from the lower belays (two to choose m) but not much harder to continue to the top.

Les Flambeurs . . . . 6b+

ightful climbing throughout.

Cupidos . . . . 6a+

Embraces-toi . . . . 6b+

Ripoux . . . . 5+

her polished, but still good.

Les Pieds Dans les Poches 4

Vendredi 13 4

Le Diagonal du Fou . . . . . . 6a+

absorbing, technical treat. Short people might find the belay tle high.

Désir 6c

u can get down with a 70m rope - just!

Surprise Sur Prise 7a

reat pitch which saves the best until the very last. You can get wn with a 70m rope - just!

Adam Gill on *Éléphant Girl* (6a+) - *this page.*

Cédise

Sisteron

Volx

Orpierre

Bellecombe

Baume Rousse

Ubrieux

Saint Julien

Saint Léger

Malaucène

Combe Obscure

Les Dentelles

Venasque

Buoux

Le Bout du Monde

Long pitches with the odd bit of vegetation. If you're feeling confident, you can just about get away with a 70m rope, but an 80m is more useful and safer. Whatever you do, take great care when lowering!

15 min | From mid morning | Slabby

40m

40m

15m

1 2 3 4 4 5 6

Céüse
Sisteron
Volx
Orpierre
Bellecombe
Baume Rousse
Ubrieux
Saint Julien
Saint Léger
Malaucène
Combe Obscure
Les Dentelles
Venasque
Buoux

Caresses-la . . . . ☆2 ☐ **6b**
be linked into the next route if you fancy a different finish.

Frau Petra . . . . ☆3 ☐ **6b**
uperb sustained adventure up the grey rock - the finale into
groove is over all too soon.

Volupté . . . . ☆1 ☐ **6b**
tle dirty climbing at the bottom leads to nice rock and fun
ves at the top.

Sadam . . . . ☐ **6a/b**
options soon present themselves, the left line is **6b**, the
t, **6a**. On the upper section, the left-hand line is **6a+** (better
bing) and the right-hand line is **6a**.

Morphée . . . . ☆3 ☐ **6a+**
d clean rock makes this route stand out.

Le 7ème Ciel . . . . ☐ **7a**
roof provides an interesting boulder problem, but it's best
to carry on past the single ring bolt, the dark upper wall is
y and the only holds are drilled slots - yuk!

p hiking up to hill and eventually you will get to this three
h route. There are other routes on this section, but this
ws a good line and should have less loose rock.

Frisson Pour une Jeune Fille . . . ☆2 ☐ **5+**
+, 2) **6a**, 3) **5+/6b**. There are three possible finishes for the
pitch: left for **6b**, right for **6a**, and a little further right at **5+**.

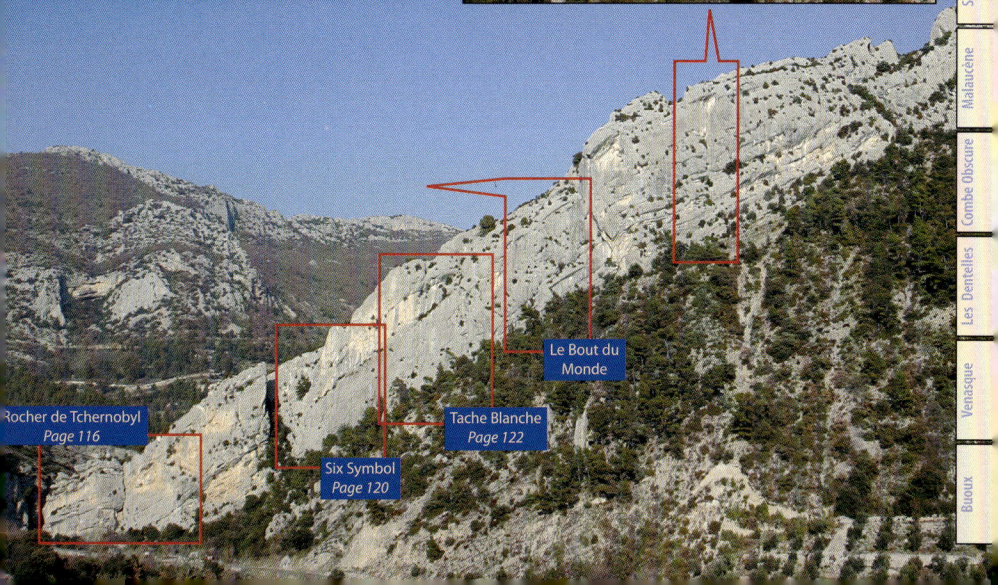

70m

30m

Le Bout du
Monde

Tache Blanche
Page 122

Six Symbol
Page 120

Rocher de Tchernobyl
Page 116

Célise

Sisteron

Voix

Orpierre

Bellecombe

Baume Rousse

Ubrieux

Saint Julien

Saint Léger

Malaucène

Combe Obscure

Les Dentelles

Venasque

Buoux

Le Rocher de Saint Julien

Les Lames
Page 136

Le Nez
Page 134

Des Guêpes
Page 132

Gastronome
Page 130

Céüse

Sisteron

Volx

Orpierre

Bellecombe

Baume Rousse

Ubrieux

Saint Julien

Saint Léger

Malaucène

Combe Obscure

Les Dentelles

Venasque

Buoux

127

Hibou
Page 138

Clocher
Page 140

Céüse

Sisteron

Volx

Orpierre

Bellecombe

Baume Rousse

Ubrieux

Saint Julien

Saint Léger

Malaucène

Combe Obscure

Les Dentelles

Venasque

Buoux

Saint Julien

	No star	☆	☆☆	☆
Up to 4+	2	-	-	
5 to 6a+	1	19	10	9
6b to 7a	3	15	11	★
7a+ and up	-	1	6	

Dominating the skyline above Buis-les-Baronnies, Saint Julien is an enormous fin of rock that simply begs to be climbed. The routes are, with a few exceptions, brilliant, often taking strong natural lines in two or more pitches, to reach the ridge. Saint Julien is particularly appealing to climbers operating between 5 and 6b, though there are a number of excellent harder routes that pick their way up to smooth vertical faces.

Approach

The crag is approached from Buis-les-Baronnies. At the north end of the town, cross the green bridge over the river and turn left, then take the first right past the campground and swimming pool. Follow the road towards the crag, the north face of which is in plain view. There is a small parking area with a climbing information board on the right-hand side of the road just before a sharp turn. From here, cross the road and follow a trail up towards the crag. Occasionally the trail joins a much larger track, but it soon leads off again on the left. All areas can be accessed by following vague trails at the base of the cliff. Although there are big tracks that also make th[eir] way to the base, there is no access right to them, so please stick to the trail.

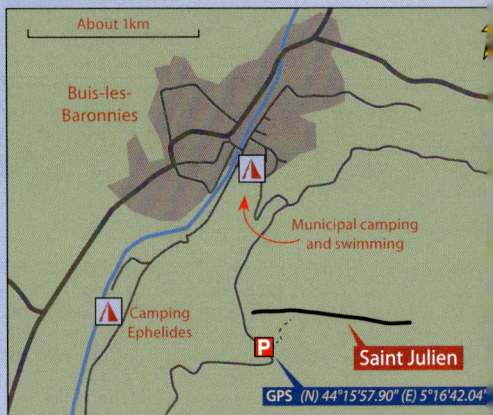

About 1km

Buis-les-Baronnies

Municipal camping and swimming

Camping Ephelides

P

Saint Julien

GPS (N) 44°15'57.90" (E) 5°16'42.04'

Conditions

The cliff is south-facing, and gets plenty of sun. On windy days being on the top of the cliff can feel like you're in the middle of a hurricane, even though the base may be quite shelter[ed]

Gear

There are plenty of pitches here longer than 35m, so a pair of half ropes is a good idea, or better still, one very very long one (80m+). The crag is known for having a bit of loose rock, so on a busy day when there are parties above you - be particularly aware. A helmet is a good idea.

The spectacular fin of Saint Julien. Photo: Alan Ja[mes]

Céüse

Sisteron

Volx

Orpierre

Beaucombe

Baume Rousse

Ubrieux

Saint Julien

Saint Léger

Malaucène

Combe Obscure

Les Dentelles

Venasque

Buoux

Chris Singer on the second pitch of *La Grotte* (6a) - *page 130* - Sector Gastronome.

Gastronome

Some great long routes to go at - it's worth topping out as the view from the crest is stunning. Getting down is simply a matter of abseiling, a 70m rope works, but using two ropes is much quicker than one. There are a number of short, low-grade routes left of the routes described.

1 Eric à Pic . . . . ☐ 4

2 Le Petit Cheval . . . . ☐ 4+

3 La Plante à Scion. . . . . ⚙ ☐ 5+
A line left of the bush. It's **4+** to the intermediate belay,

4 Trop de Vin Rouge . . . . ⚙ ⛏ ☐ 6a

5 Prise de Tête . . . . ⚙ ⛏ ☐ 6a

20 min · Lots of sun · Slabby · Vertical · Multi-pitch

Céüse
Sisteron
Volx
Orpierre
Bellecombe
Baume Rousse
Ubrieux
Saint Julien
Saint Léger
Malaucène
Combe Obscure
Les Dentelles
Venasque
Buoux

La Grotte . . . . 🔲 6a
. Follow the slab into the cave, then through the hole into the
er cave, walk left to the belay.
a. A great pitch, follow the big flake/crack to the tree (belay
sible over to the left) then out right taking the line of least
stance to belay at the tree.
. Follow the slab in a superb position.
o this page and page 129.

Love on the Bite . . . . . 🔲 6c+
xcellent long single pitch.

L'Espadon . . . . 🔲 5+
. Past the white rock scar, on broken rock.
+. The wall above - stay in the flakes.
+. Move down and traverse to the good flakes - ignore the
line of bolts you come to (or follow it at about **6b+**).
+. A well-positioned pitch.
. Three bolts leads to a belay at the top.

9 Équinoxe . . . . 🔲 6c
1) 6b, 2) 6c.

10 Électrochoc . . . . . . 🔲 7a
A long pitch that looks impossibly hard even when you're on top
of it, but it's all there if you look. It would feel a fair bit easier if
the right holds are chalked.

11 La Gastronome . . . . 🔲 5+
1) 5+, 2) 5+, 3) 5. Join and finish up *L'Espadon*, or abseil off.

12 Le Gastonome de Gris . . . . 🔲 6a

Ollie Ryall and Chris Singer negotiating the tunnel
on the first pitch of *La Grotte* (5) - *this page*

Des Guêpes

Some striking lines that weave their way to the summit ridge make this a great spot. The harder wall climbs are also well worth seeking out but expect a tough time.

25 min | Lots of sun | Slabby | Vertical

Céüse
Sisteron
Volx
Orpierre
Bellecombe
Baume Rousse
Ubrieux
Saint Julien
Saint Léger
Malaucène
Combe Obscure
Les Dentelles
Venasque
Buoux

1 Ça Va Saigner . . . . 🗓1 ▢ **6c**
1) **6a+.** A huge first pitch. 2) **6c**

2 L'Aéroplane Blindé. . . . 🗓2 🧗 ▢ **7a**
1) **6a.** A poor approach pitch. 2) **7a.** The cracked grey wall is the first of a trio of hard 'grey' wall climbs.

3 Le Bandar Fou . . . . 🗓3 ▢ **6c**
1) **6a**, 2) **6c.** The fantastic big corner, and as good as it looks.

4 Planéité . . . . 🗓2 🧗 ▢ **7a+**
1) **6a**, 2) **7a+**

5 Le Salaire de la Peur . . 🗓2 🧗 ▢ **7b+**
1) **6a**, 2) **7b+**

6 L'Aéroplane . . . . 🗓2 ▢ **6b**
1) **4+**, 2) **5**. The right-hand variation is **6a**.
3) **6b**. Can be aided to bring the overall grade down to **5**. 4) **3**

7 L'Aéroplane Direct . . . . . . 🗓2 🧗 ▢ **6b**
1) **5**, 2) **6b.** The corner crack with interest.

8 Xinibition . . . . 🗓2 🧗 ▢ **6a**

9 L'Univers des Rêves . . . 🗓2 🧗 ▢ **6b+**
1) **6b**, 2) **6b+.** A wild excursion across the headwall.

10 Tao . . . . 🗓1 ▢ **6a**
1) **6a+**, 2) **5+**

11 Y Mao . . . . 🗓1 🧗 ▢ **6a**

12 Le Pillier Gris . . . . 🗓3 ▢ **5+**
1) **5**, 2) **5 / 5+.** Left line is **5**, the right **5+**.

13 Les Initiateurs . . . . 🗓1 ▢ **6a**
1) **6a**, 2) **6a**

14 Les Guêpes (Normale) . . . . 🗓2 ▢ **5**
1) **5.** Avoid following the bolts into the orange gully at the end of this pitch. 2) **5**, 3) **5**

15 La Directe des Guêpes . . . . . . 🗓1 ▢ **6a**
1) **5+**, 2) **5+.** Two variations both the same grade. 3) **6a**

16 Les Trois Mousquetons . . . . 🗓3 ▢ **6b**
1) **5**, 2) **6b.** *Photo on this page.*

17 La Zaza . . . . 🗓1 ▢ **6b**
1) **6a+**, 2) **6b**, 3) **6a+.** There are three options for the final pitch - all the same grade. The left line splits offering a fine corner crack, or an alternative line further left. The right-hand split joins the belay of *Les Trois Mousquetons.*

Céüse
Sisteron
Volx
Orpierre
Bellecombe
Baume Rousse
Ubrieux
Saint Julien
Saint Léger
Malaucène
Combe Obscure
Les Dentelles
Venasque
Buoux

Le Nez

Some good, technical slabby routes with worthwhile second pitches. A 70m rope or longer is recommended for this sector if you're not using double ropes.

75m

70m

12

40m

7

6

1

2

4

3

30m

1

8

9

30m

Bibus

2 3 4 5 6 8 9 10 11 12

Céüse

Sisteron

Volx

Orpierre

Bellecombe

Baume Rousse

Ubrieux

Saint Julien

Saint Léger

Malaucène

Combe Obscure

Les Dentelles

Venasque

Buoux

Shanti . . . . 6a+
6a, 2) 6a+, 3) 6a

La Madelon. . . . . 6a+
6a+, 2) 6a

Hypercubitus . . . . 6c+
6c, 2) 6c+

Le Nez 6a
6a, 2) 6a

Force Majeure. 7a
nd your way around *Le Nez* to take in the least featured rock.

Des Pieds, Des Mains 6a
6a, 2) 6a

7 Des Pieds, Des Mains Direct 7a
The alternative finish up the headwall.

8 Le Barbarin Fourchu . . . . 6c+
1) 6c+, 2) 6c

9 Les Deux Vivants . . . . . 6c+
1) 6b, 2) 6c+. A good couple of pitches, the first works your feet, the second your fingers. *Photo on this page*.

10 Clash . . . . 6b+

11 La Gouttière . . . . 6a+

12 Les Cigales . . . . 6a+
1) 6a+, 2) 5, 2) 5+

Céüse

Sisteron

Volx

Orpierre

Bellecombe

Baume Rousse

Ubrieux

Saint Julien

Saint Leger

Malaucene

Combe Obscure

Les Dentelles

Venasque

Buoux

e Ryall on *Les Deux Vivants* (6c+) - *this page*.

Les Lames

The area for some brilliant sustained wall climbing. Bring lots of quickdraws and miss the mid-station belays to get the full experience.

Céüse
Sisteron
Volx
Orpierre
Bellecombe
Baume Rousse
Ubrieux
Saint Julien
Saint Léger
Malaucène
Combe Obscure
Les Dentelles
Venasque
Buoux

1 Bibus . . . . 5+
1) 5+, 2) 5+, 3) 5+, 4) 5. Getting very polished.

2 Ubick . . . . 7a+
1) 6c+, 2) 7a+

3 Bibus Directe . . . . 6a+
1) 5+, 2) 6a+. *Photo this page.*

4 Désir . . . . 6c+

5 Les Lames 6b
1) 6a+, 2) 6b

6 Pandémonium 6c
Brilliant wall climbing. A grade **5** to the intermediate belay.

7 Tango Funèbre . . . . 7a+
A grade **5** to the intermediate belay.

8 Tango Panaché 7a
A grade **5** to the intermediate belay.

9 La Directissime 6b
1) 6b, 2) 6a+, 3) 5+

10 Éclair d'Absurdité . . . . 7a+
6b to the first belay.

11 Charter pour l'Enfer . . . 7b+
6b+ to the first belay.

12 La Parat-Paris 7a
1) 6b, 2) 7a, 3) 6b

13 Tannhäuser . . . . 6b+
1) 6b, 2) 6b+

14 La Rampe . . . . 6a+
1) 6a+, 2) 6a+, 3) 6a

15 Osiris 6b

16 Horus 6c
Can be split at the mid-height lower-off. The second half is **6b+**.

17 La Tournyaire . . . . 5+
1) 5+, 2) 5, 3) 5

18 La Xafred . . . . 6a+
1) 5, 2) 6a+, 3) 6a+

19 La Bouscaude Direct . . . . 5+
1) 4+, 2) 5+, 3) 5+

20 La Bouscaude Normale . . . . 5+
1) 4+, 2) 4+, 3) 5

Céüse
Sisteron
Voix
Orpierre
Bellecombe
Baume Rousse
Ubrieux
Saint Julien
Saint Léger
Malaucène
Combe Obscure
Les Dentelles
Venasque
Buoux

Craig Entwistle on the superb second pitch of *Bibus Directe* (6a+) - *this page.*

Céüse
Sisteron
Volx
Orpierre
Bellecombe
Baume Rousse
Ubrieux
Saint Julien
Saint Léger
Malaucène
Combe Obscure
Les Dentelles
Venasque
Buoux

Hibou

The *via ferrata* is a fun way of getting down from
some of the routes. You can continue along the
ferrata as far as the summit cross. If you intend
take the *via ferrata* down, it's worth rememberin
to take a couple of slings and some screwgates

1 La Mésange 6c

2 Urgence d'Vivre . . . . 5+
1) 5, 2) 3, 3) 5+, 4) 4+

3 Unnamed 6c

4 L'Œuf de Pâques 6c
1) 6a, 2) 5+, 3) 6a, 4) 3, 5) 6c

5 Fleur de Rêves 6c
1) 6b, 2) 6b+, 3) 6c

6 Les Dalles 6c
1) 6c. Two starts: 6b on left, 6c on right. 2) 5, 3) 5

7 Les 3 P. 6a
1) 5+, 2) 6a, 3) 5+

8 La Directe du Bastion 6a
1) 5+, 2) 6a, 3) 5+

9 O l'Oubliée 6a

10 Le Pilier des Trous . . . . 6a+
1) 6a+, 2) 6a+, 3) 6a

11 La Voie des Trous . . . . 5+
1) 4+. Right-hand variant is **5**. 2) 5, 3) 5+. As for *Les 3 P.*

12 Via Ferrata . . . . Fun
Great fun and great exposure with two starts. Descend back
down it, or see the next page for a walking/abseil descent.

13 La Cour des Miracles 7a
1) 6a+, 2) 7a

14 Le Rouge et le Noir 7a
1) 7a, 2) 6b+

15 Le Hibou. 6c
1) 6c. Nasty sharp rock. 2) 6b+

16 Alian . . . . 5+

Gastronome
Page 130

Des Guêpes
Page 132

Le Nez
Page 134

Les Lames
Page 136

Hibou

Clocher
Page 140

Céüse

Sisteron

Volx

Orpierre

Bellecombe

Baume Rousse

Ubrieux

Saint Julien

Saint Léger

Malaucène

Combe Obscure

Les Dentelles

Venasque

Buoux

35 min | Lots of sun | Slabby | Vertical | Multi-pitch

Descent from the Via Ferrata
Traverse the ridge for a while before descending gulleys to rea[ch] belay of *Ramonage Guaranti*. A 3[5m] abseil gets you to the path belo[w]

Céüse
Sisteron
Volx
Orpierre
Bellcombe
Baume Rousse
Ubrieux
Saint Julien
Saint Léger
Malaucène
Combe Obscura
Les Dentelles
Venasque
Buoux

70m
65m
50m
50m
45m
35m
30m

Clocher
An impressive-looking sector that allows a descent usin[g] the via ferrata if you so choose. The first pitches are a b[it] rambling, and the tops, though impressively situated ten[d] to be on little-frequented sharp rock.

1 Anaxagore **7b**
1) 6b, 2) 6b, 3) 7b

2 La Françoise . . . . **6a+**
1) 6a. Start at the crack/fluting. **2) 5+, 3) 6a+**

3 L'Éperon de la Croix . . . . **5+**
1) 5+, 2) 6a. Great climbing on perfect rock.

4 Super Phoenix **7a**
1) 6b. A rambling yet bouldery approach pitch. **2) 7a.** Not quite as good as it looks, though in a great position, the rock is sharp.

5 La Directe du Clocher . . **7b**
1) 6b, 2) 6a+. The right-hand variant is the same grade. **3) 7b**

6 Les Grands Boulevards **6b**
1) 6b, 2) 6b, 3) 6b

7 Nick Jo **6b**
1) 6a+. A poor pitch. The right-hand variant is **6c+** and better.
2) 6b. A fine line up the crack and dyke with interesting climbing and a very definite crux.

8 Tranquille Coucounet . . . . **5+**

9 Ramonage Guaranti . . . . **6a+**

10 Prends-la Comme Elle Vient . . . **6c**
1) 5. At this grade, follow the chimney. Following the bolts up the arete is more like **6b+**. **2) 6c.** Brilliant face climbing.

11 La Momie "Libérée **6b**
1) 5+, 2) 6b. Follow the prominent corner.

Céüse
Sisteron
Voix
Orpierre
Bellecombe
Baume Rousse
Ubrieux
Saint Julien
Saint Léger
Malaucène
Combe Obscure
Les Dentelles
Venasque
Buoux

North Face
Page 166

Céüse

Sisteron

Voix

Orpierre

Bellecombe

Baume Rousse

Ubrieux

Saint Julien

Saint Léger

Malaucène

Combe Obscure

Les Dentelles

Venasque

Buoux

Saint Léger

Andalouse *Page 148*

La Démocraie du Plus Fort *Page 150*

Praniania *Page 152*

L'Œil du Loup *Page 159*

Le Voleur de Pésanteur *Page 160*

La Farce Tranquille *Page 162*

Slip Bouse and Milési *Page 164*

Céüse

Sisteron

Volx

Orpierre

Bellecombe

Baume Rousse

Ubrieux

Saint Julien

Saint Léger

Malaucène

Combe Obscure

Les Dentelles

Venasque

Buoux

	No star	☆	☆☆	☆
Up to 4+	-	-	-	-
5 to 6a+	6	1	1	-
6b to 7a	24	26	16	8
7a+ and up	54	54	73	2

While still a 'work in progress', Saint Léger is undoubtedly already up there with the other great masterpieces of French sport climbing. There's no hiding the fact that this is a hard crag, but there are enough gems in the mid 6s to justify a visit if you're not quite up to the 7s and 8s.

Approach

Saint Léger lies just off the D40 that runs east from Mollans-sur-Ouvèze. The turning off the D40 lies between the 9km and 10km marker stones, and when travelling from Mollans, is indicated by a sign for 'La Bergerie 1km'. Park outside La Bergerie at a small parking area - if this is full, park considerably near by as access is *delicate*. **DO NOT CAMP HERE.** There is a lovely (and popular) swimming spot by the bridge. There are two approach paths:

1) Above the parking area, the GR footpath (marked in red and white) leads up the hill around La Bergerie, keep your eyes open for the left turn and follow it back down to the river.

2) A more direct and less strenuous route is to follow the river itself which is fine in hot weather when you can paddle, but more awkward in cooler weather or when the level is up. **Do not go anywhere near the grounds of La Bergerie since this is likely to cause access problems.**

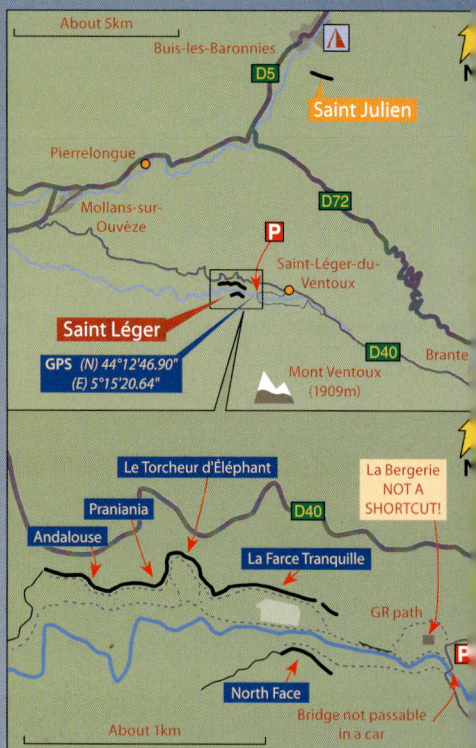

About 5km

Buis-les-Baronnies

D5

Saint Julien

Pierrelongue

D72

Mollans-sur-Ouvèze

P

Saint-Léger-du-Ventoux

Saint Léger

GPS (N) 44°12'46.90"
(E) 5°15'20.64"

D40

Brante

Mont Ventoux
(1909m)

Le Torcheur d'Éléphant

La Bergerie
NOT A
SHORTCUT!

Praniania

D40

Andalouse

La Farce Tranquille

GR path

P

North Face

Bridge not passable
in a car

About 1km

Conditions

The main, largely south-facing crags get plenty of sun, through shade can be found around the East Face. The North Face gets the shade, welcome in the summer months, but in the winter, you'll freeze.

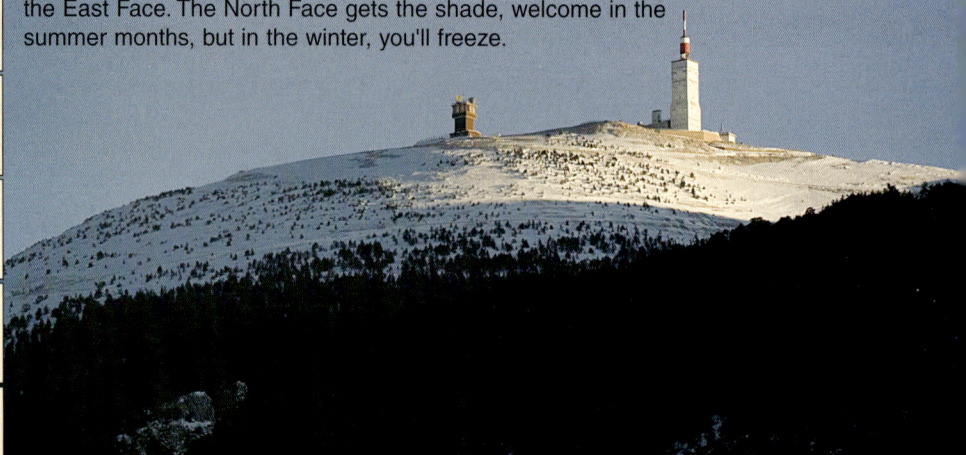

The magnificent Mont Ventoux towers over Saint Léger. Photo: Simon Richardson/DarkPeakImages

non Richardson on the *Arquée Pieds Tendu* (7b+) - *see page 147*.

Céüse

Sisteron

Voix

Orpierre

Bellecombe

Baume Rousse

Ubrieux

Saint Julien

Saint Léger

Malaucène

Combe Obscure

Les Dentelles

Venasque

Buoux

Céüse

Sisteron

Volx

Orpierre

Bellecombe

Baume Rousse

Ubrieux

Saint Julien

Saint Léger

Malaucène

Combe Obscure

Les Dentelles

Venasque

Buoux

❶ Extremadura 7c

❷ Don Quichotte 7c

❸ Pas du Bras Pas du Chocolat . . . 7c+

❹ Le Mollahs de la Molasse Me Lassent
. . . . 7b

❺ Un Jour Mon Prince Viendra Me Délivrer
. . . . 7a

❻ Haka Nerveux . . . . 6c+

❼ Mes Vacances à Honolulu 6c

❽ Vent d'Ouest 7b-

❾ Cap au Large 7c

❿ Le Syndrome de Plombier . . . 8a
The steep direct start is **Radioactive man** - grade unknown.

⓫ Avec Vue sur Mémerere . . . 7c-
The upper bulge has some particularly tough moves.

⓬ Sous l'Œil de la Baleine 7c-

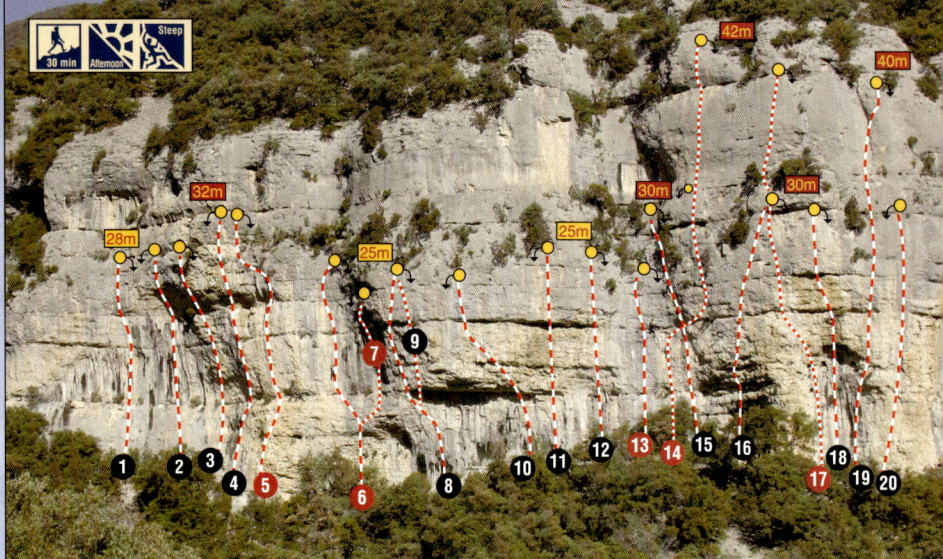

Fi, Flo, Floty and Andalouse

Praniania
Page 152

Piedra Salvage
Page 154

L'Œil du Loup
Page 159

Le Voleur de Pésanteur
Page 160

Other sectors are
hidden from view

La Farce Tran
Page 162

Fi, Flo, Floty

The furthest described section sets the theme
of steep starts leading to vertical headwalls. The
rock continues further left with some impressive
walls which are in the process of being developed.
Consult the local guides for more information.

Vivre Libre . . . . 6b+
d rock, with some tricky moves.

Là Bas . . . . 6c+
eriously long pitch.

Ouest . . . . 7a+
oulder problem to an easier, pleasant groove.

Joe's Ballade . . . . 7a+
teep start where route-finding skills come in handy. It is so
ep that it is a real pain to strip.

Les Colonnes d'Hercules 6c+
ellent, even with the short section of dodgy rock where it
ds up and left. Can be extended, though it's not worth it.

Name Unknown 7b
irect line through the roofs.

La Porte des Champs-Élysées
. . . . 7a+
assic up the tufas and the long wall and slab above. Never
sically desperate, but a bit engaging at the top.

Crescendo . . . . 7a+
rux section almost entirely on drilled pockets, and even a bolt
hold. Bizarre, yet still enjoyable.

21 La Temple de la Méduse . . . 7b
Classic steep tufas, a rest and a brilliant exposed crimpy bulge
to follow. The grade is for the left-hand start, the right-hand start
is **7b+**.

22 Conciliabule avec le Diable 7c

23 Isao 6c
A short pitch with some sharp crimping. The extension through
the tufa-streaked bulge is **7c**.

24 Fi, Flo, Floty . . . . . 7c+
An awesome huge pitch up the steep orange wall. Only a short
hard section but the rest is not a path, and very runout in places.

25 Arquée Pieds Tendre . . . . . 7b+
The beautiful streaky wall. A great climb, and worth getting that
80m rope for - and you'll need it as there's no mid-station.
Photo on page 145.

26 La Belle Andalouse . . . . . . 7b+
Follow some sika'd holds through the lower bulge, and keep
pulling on the 'enhanced' pockets above.

27 C'est Comme un Rêve 7a
Superb, some steep ground to get to the ledge, the grey wall
above is sustained but only has one tricky move.

28 Et Derrière Coule une Rivière 6c+
A few hard pulls through the bulge, then steady, but take plenty of
clips for this one.

Cécle · Sisteron · Volx · Orpierre · Bellecombe · Baume Rousse · Ubreux · Saint Julien · **Saint Léger** · Malaucene · Combe Obscure · Les Dentelles · Venasque · Buoux

Fi, Fo, Floty

Andalouse

The domain of big smooth face climbing. This sector has a refreshing supply of routes in the mid grades ensuring its popularity.

❶ Je Ne Fais Que Passer Ma Route

.... 6c
Varied and interesting movement with excellent rock after an indifferent start.

❷ Passer Entre les Gouttes ..... 7a+
A short intense section.

❸ Moby Dick. 7c
'Plastic style' pulls on good holds lead to a final sequence which is tricky to read onsight. Low in the grade.

❹ Al Andalouse. 8a
Thin physical and dynamic all the way. Two good shakeouts, one with occasional in-situ beer. *Photo opposite.*

❺ Esméralda 7c
An alternative, easier finish to *Al Andalouse*.

❻ Mano Negra .... 7a+
The beautiful vertical groove gives unusually balancy climbing.

❼ La Gourmandises. 6c
Heave over the initial roof, then enjoy the *gouttes d'eau*.

❽ La Gourmandises du Vautour. .. 6c+
This can also be reached from *Maître Vautour*.

❾ Maître Vautour .... 6b+
A juggy start and a delicate finish.

❿ Le Deux Beaufs en Vacances. ... 6b+
A nice piece of tufa precedes another pleasant grey slab.

⓫ La Maître et son Disciple 6b
A tricky start and a long, enjoyable slab.

⓬ Le Vautour est Là. 6b

⓭ Un Truc de Passage 6c
Start just left of a low roof, climb right of the grey streak, then move left and continue up the streak.

⓮ Pensées Afghanes .... 6b+
Pull through the right-hand end of the overhang to start, then wind up the red wall, past some (usually chalky) flakes.

⓯ Trafic de Bouses Chez les Vautours

.... 6a-
Climb the groove, then out right onto the big grey shield that offers some tricky moves.

⓰ Sécheresse Intellectuelle .... 7c+
Take a line left of the dark grey rock.

Céüse

Sisteron

Volx

Orpierre

Bellecombe

Baume Rousse

Ubrieux

Saint Julien

Saint Léger

Malaucène

Combe Obscure

Les Dentelles

Venasque

Buoux

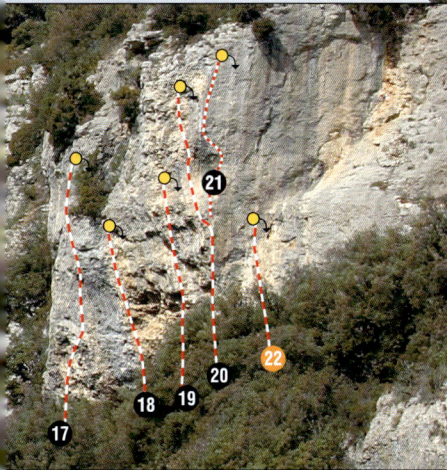

...ht of the previous routes is a small, isolated sector with the
...owing routes. The most obvious feature is a roof that runs the
...gth of the bottom of the wall.

Life Maker . . . . □ **7b+**
...ghtward-trending line at the far left side of the wall.

Le Désespoir du Naxos . . . . . . 🔄 □ **7c+**
...eep line through the middle of the roof.

Gageure . . . . 🔄 □ **8b**
...ery steep line a few metres before the right end of the wall.

Relation Virtuelle . . . . 🔄 □ **8a**
...ts as for *Kiwisi...* then moves out left.

Kiwasi ou la Maison Qui Chante 🔄 □ **7c+**
...tufa-covered arete at the right end of the wall.

Nina . . . . □ **5+**
...slab right of the big corner.

...or Estrangin on *Al Andalouse* (8a) - *opposite.*

Céüse

Sisteron

Volx

Orpierre

Bellecombe

Baume Rousse

Ubrieux

Saint Julien

Saint Léger

Mabucène

Combe Obscure

Les Dentelles

Venasque

Buoux

La Démocraie du Plus Fort

A smaller wall than its neighbours but what it lacks in height, it makes up for in difficulty. It is mostly black spot climbing here on smooth and steep rock.

Victime d'un Non Nœud (7a+) - *opposite*

Praniania

20m
25m

30 min | Lots of sun | Vertical | Steep

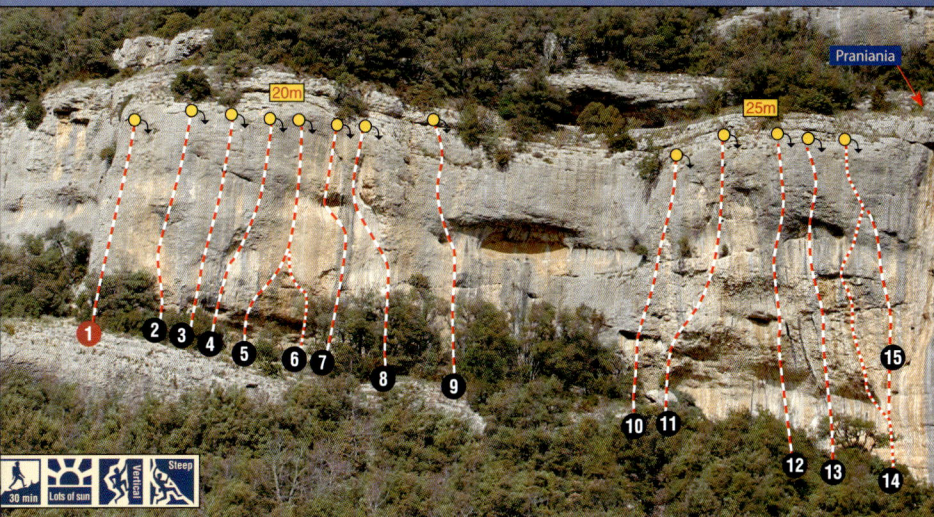

❶	Unknown.	6b+
❷	Adoigtracourcix	8a+
❸	Oh! St-Léger Fais-Nous au Relais	8a+
❹	La Thérapie du Mal par le Mâle	8a+
❺	Toutes les 20 Minutes, Je Suis Miné	8b
❻	La Barre à un Million d'Années	8b
❼	Unknown.	7b+
❽	Le Pouvoir Destructeur des Bruits de Chiottes	7a+
❾	Le Pouvoir Consitutif	7b
❿	Victime d'un Non Nœud . . . *Photo this page*.	7a+
⓫	La Démocraie du Plus Fort.	7c+
⓬	La Ligne Claire	8c
�13	La Tournée du Patron	8c
⓮	Lézard d'École.	8a
⓯	L'Homme en Bleu	8a

Céüse
Sisteron
Volx
Orpierre
Bellecombe
Baume Rousse
Ubrieux
Saint Julien
Saint Léger
Malaucène
Combe Obscure
Les Dentelles
Venasque
Buoux

La Démocraie du Plus Fort

Praniania

An impressive sector with some incredible hard wall climbs and a number of awe-inspiring projects.

1 Crunch 7b
The corner. **6b+** to the first belay

2 More Moy . . . . 8b+

3 En Verve et Contre Tous . . . 8b+

4 Project . . . .
The working title is *La Théorie des Cordes*.

5 Praniania 8b
The classic of the sector.

6 La Tounga . . . . 7c+
The striking orange wall.

7 Mamba les Couilles 7b

8 Project . . . . ?
The working title is *Surchauffe Pondérale*, and it should be somewhere in the region of 8c when it's done.

9 Mélodie Pour un Ami Ardéchois 8a+

10 Project . . . . ?

11 Project . . . . ?
The working title is *Retour Gagnant*.

12 En Attendant Ernest 8c
A hold has broken, so the grade may be inaccurate.

13 King Kong 8b
An impressive line featuring hard, fingery climbing.

14 Mythoplastique 6c-

15 Franco de Porc 7b

16 L'Écume des Pierres 7c

17 Les Lectures d'Anne Alphabéte. 8a
L'Écume leads off to the left, and *Princessa* leads off to the rig

18 Princessa 7c-

19 Autant Suspend Mon Vol 8b

20 Project . . . . ?

21 Crackinette (project) . . . . ?
Just don't expect too many finger-locks.

22 Sault Qui Peut 8a
Photo on page 7.

23 Project . . . . ?
The working title is *Les Petits Chefs du Néan*

30m
35m
20m
40m

18
16
14
15
17
19
20
21
22
23
24
25
26
27

Piedra
Salvage

Éole Maître des Vents 8a
r a tough start, sustained wall climbing keeps on going.

Le Foudre de Zeus 7a
prominent diagonal corner. Burly laybacking and bridging

Thierry Comme une Baleine 7c
r a bouldery crux, sustained wall climbing remains. Excellent
:tions, but some awful rock and big runouts; may clean up
me.

Le Linceul de Pénélope . . . 7b
n below the ledge that the previous route starts on.
edible positions with climbing and rock to match. Some good
s, but keeps going all the way to the belay! *Photo this page.*

Céüse
Sisteron
Voix
Orpierre
Bellecombe
Baume Rousse
Ubrieux
Saint Julien
Saint Léger
Malaucène
Combe Obscure
Les Dentelles
Venasque
Buoux

Linceul de Pénélope (7b) - this page.

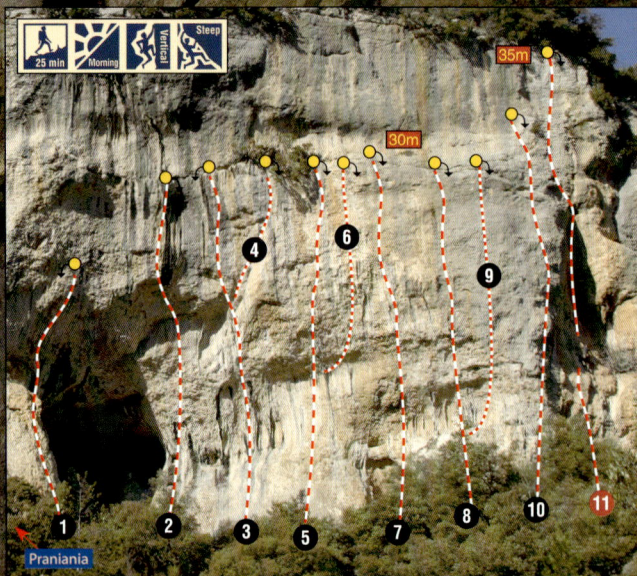

Piedra Salvage

Unlike the other crags on the south side of the river, you can get plenty of afternoon shade here - which is often very welcome!

Gedise

Sisteron

Volx

Orpierre

Bellecombe

Baume Rousse

Ubrieux

Saint Julien

Saint Léger

Malaucène

Combe Obscure

Les Dentelles

Venasque

Buoux

25 min | Morning | Steep

35m

30m

4

6

9

1

2

3

5

7

8

10

11

Praniania

Le Mari de la Baleine (8a) - *opposite*.
Photo: Simon Richardson/DarkPeakIma

Céüse
Sisteron
Volx
Orpierre
Bellecombe
Baume Rousse
Ubrieux
Saint Julien
Saint Léger
Malaucène
Combe Obscure
Les Dentelles
Venasque
Buoux

Le Bataille de Marathon . . . 8b

Le Concept . . . . 8b+
of the classics of the crag.

Le Nabab . . . . 8b+
:her classic.

Dis Moi Qui Tu Haïs, Je Te Diral Qui Tu Suis
. . . . 8a

Le Placard . . . . 8a+
top is often the scene of some big airtime.

Stiquel Man . . . . 8a+
dery.

Abrège Nief. 8b
illiant route.

Le Mari de la Baleine . . 8a
ort and bouldery crux, then much easier. *Photo opposite*.

Baleine Sous Galet . . . 7c
ird start leads to a finish similar to the next route.

Le Short Dans le Trou 7b
start is a bit scrappy, but it gets much better.

11 **Piedra Salvage** . . . . . . 6b+
A steep start leads to a technical corner, and it's not over until you're at the tree-belay. Never desperate but there's a lot of it. *Photo on page 5*.

12 **Bas Rési et Haut Coton** . . . . 7a+

13 **75 La Totale** 7a

14 **Rencontre du Troisième Slip** . . . 7a
Feels a bit exposed at the top, especially onsight.

15 **Un Treuil Pour JB** 7b
Some tough tufa climbing to finish.

16 **La Machine à Remonter le Pan**
. . . . 7b+
Start up *Un Treuil Pour JB* then break out right.

17 **Project** . . . .
The working title is *Thermique la Grenouille*.

18 **L'Écornifleur** 6b
Interesting and steady climbing leads to a steep finish.

19 **Un Voyage à Nanard** . . . . 6b+
Bridge up to a couple of steeper pulls.

20 **Tchatchounette** . . . . 6c+
Steep tufa pulling, and a deceptive bulge.

21 **Belle Laurette** 7b

Céüse

Sisteron

Volx

Orpierre

Bellecombe

Baume Rousse

Ubrieux

Saint Julien

Saint Léger

Malaucène

Combe Obscure

Les Dentelles

Venasque

Buoux

Le Mythomane

The mega-steep back wall is the home to some ultra-hard routes - the steepness alone provides some shade throughout the day when the sun is high in the sky.

1 **Magne Ma Voie, Touche Ton Cul**

. . . . 7b

Grapple with the slippery tufa to finish. It can be finished via the perched flake on the left at a more balanced **7a**.

2 **Qi Cuit** 7b

The right-hand line to the same belay as *Magne Ma Voie,...*

3 **Lachez le Troupeau** . . . 8a

4 **Indigo Galinacé** . . . . . . 8a+

Tackle a prominent grey tufa at half-height.

5 **FFM Meuh** . . . . 7c+

6 **Cool Frénésie** . . . . 7c+

7 **Le Fluide Glacial** . . . . . 8b+

8 **Les Abodominables** . . . 8b+

9 **Les Intermutants du Spectacle**

. . . . 8b+

10 **En Dépit du Bon Sens** . . 8c

10 **L'idéal Chimérique** 8c

Rarely repeated, even by 8c standards. Could be 8c+!

11 **Fiphigénie et Gaga Même Nom**

. . . . 8b

12 **Le Mur des Six Clopes** . . 8b

May be 8b.

13 **Les Épinards aux Violettes**

. . . . 8a

May be 8a.

14 **Le Mythomane** 7c

Powerful moves lead to a long, juggy mid section with good rests. The finish is glorious but potentially frustrating!

15 **Du Miel Entre Tes Seins** . . . 7b

A great route, a 'top end of the grade' start leads to a sneaky no-hands rest, but by then it's steady to the top.

16 **Express Surmarqée** . . . 8a

17 **Magne Ton Cul, Pas Ma Voie**

. . . . 7b

Brilliant technical moves and a very tricky onsight.

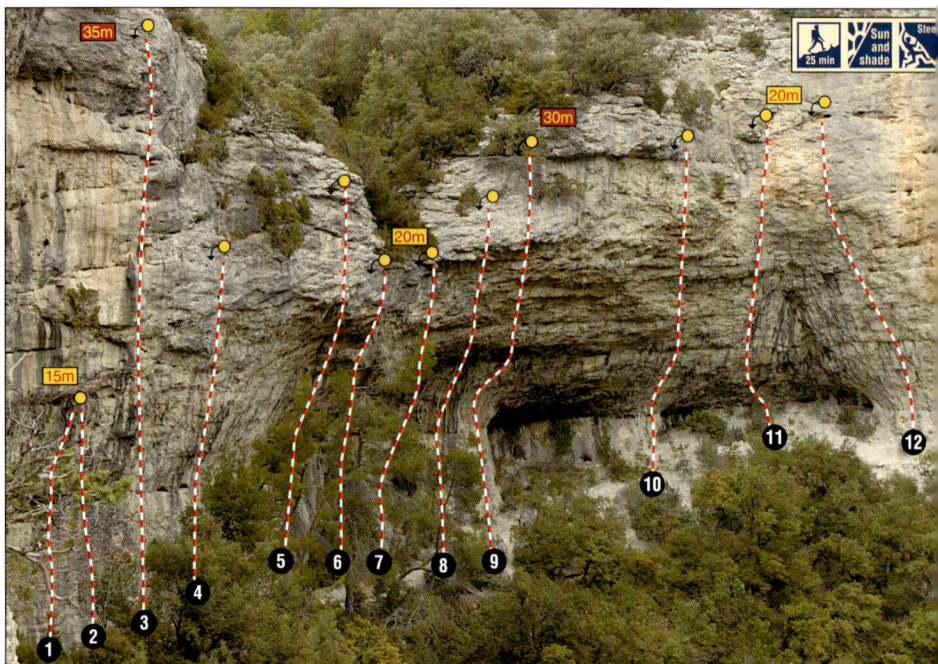

Magne Ton Cul...extension

. . . . 🔲🔲🔲 7c+
big burly prow to the top of the crag. It's an extension - so
esting at the belay!

Clément Comme Il Respire

. . . . 🔲🔲🔲 7a+
d climbing, soft at this grade, though run-out.

Le Torcheur d'Éléphant . . . . 🔲🔲🔲 6c+
eat route, with good holds - it gets harder as you get higher.

Face à Face . . . . 🔲🔲 6b+

Hassan Bush, Georges Hussein; clonage...

. . . . 🔲🔲🔲 7b
asy first half isn't much of a warm up for the pumpy
wall.

23 Une Épineuse Opération . . . . . . 🔲🔲 7a+
Steep, positive and low in the grade.

24 Les Mysteries de L'Ouest . . 🔲🔲🔲 7b

25 Les Jardins d'Hiver de Groucho 🔲🔲 6c

26 La Verge de Moïse . . . . 🔲🔲 7a

27 Je Mange Diététique et Je Pète Bio

. . . . 🔲🔲 6c+

28 Impression Primaire d'une Joie Profonde

. . . . 🔲🔲 7a+

Le Torcheur d'Éléphant

s west-facing wall gives a bit of shade for those who
e early morning starts. *Un Torcheur* is in fact one
's position in life is to clean the derrière of another,
nflict pain, so pity not the elephant.

Va Comme le Vent

Céüse

Sisteron

Volx

Orpierre

Bellecombe

Baume Rousse

Ubrieux

Saint Julien

Saint Léger

Malaucène

Combe Obscure

Les Dentelles

Venasque

Buoux

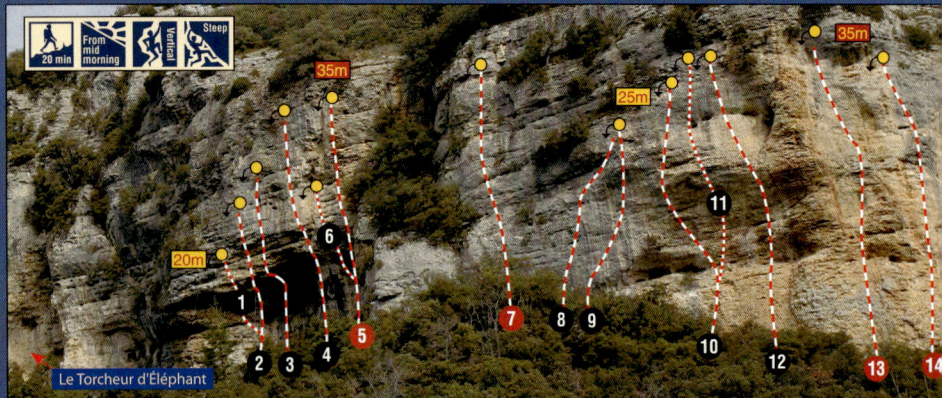

20 min | From mid morning | Vertical | Steep

35m

25m

20m

Le Torcheur d'Éléphant

Va Comme le Vent

This west-facing wall has little of interest except for the routes on its far right-hand side, near the arete.

❶ **Où Sont Vos Tablettes de Chocolat** . 　　7b

❷ **Du 24 Carats** . . . . 　　7b

❸ **Baume au Cœur** . . . . 　　7▶

❹ **Sol y Sombra** . . . . 　　7◀

❺ **Rien Que du Ciel Ordinaire** . . . 　　6

❻ **Ecoutes les Oiseaux** . . . . 　　7b

❼ **La Cavale du Géomètre** . . . . 　　6c

❽ **M est son Emblème** . . . . 　　7b

❾ **A Ma Belle Étoile** . . . . 　　8a

❿ **Illustrator Effets Spéciaux** . . . . 　　7b

⓫ **Les Ruines de l'Âme** . . . . 　　7b

⓬ **Promenade Massaï** . . . . 　　7a

⓭ **Va Comme le Vent** . . . . 　　6c
A long, intricate pitch requiring sharp route-finding skills despite the bolts. The belay is just a little too high! *Photo this page.*

⓮ **Qui Court Dans le Prairie** . . . . . 　　6c

Chris Singer heading off up *Va Comme le Vent* (6c) - *this pa*

L'Œil du Loup		6c+
Psikanalyse d'Un Égo Atrophié .		7c+
Le Bonheur en Suspension		7b+
extension is **7c+**.		
Lou Ravi.		7c
Ca Va Chémar		7c+
Un Égo Superdimensionné		8a+
Quadra Club		8b

22 Saphira		7b+
23 Tout est Chaos.		7b
24 Les Rois du Pétrole		7a+
25 Divine Idylle		7a
26 Femmes, Je Vous Aime		6b
27 Tu Montes Chérie.		6b
28 La Violence Éternelle		6c
Crumbly at present, it may clean up.		

L'Œil du Loup

...aried sector, the routes around here have been ...eloped more recently than most, and so will feel a little ...s well-travelled than average.

30m

30m

Va Comme le Vent

35m

35m

25m

17

16 17

18

19

20

21 22

23 24

25

Le Voleur de Pésanteur

26

27 28

15

Céüse

Sisteron

Volx

Orpierre

Bellecombe

Baume Rousse

Ubrieux

Saint Julien

Saint Léger

Malaucène

Combe Obscure

Les Dentelles

Venasque

Buoux

1 S.O.eScalade . . . . [   ] 6a+
A poor start, but a pleasant slab after that.

2 A Deux Pas d'Ici . . . . 🎌🧗 [   ] 6b
Tricky finishing moves.

3 Mélancolique et Désabuse . . . . . . [   ] 6b+
Good rock and moves.

4 Didoudibouda . . . . 🎌🧗 [   ] 6c+
A thin start, followed by some fun moves through the bulge.

5 L'Affreux Jojo . . . . [   ] 7a

6 Esthète Éthique et Toc . . . . [   ] 7b

7 Moitié Quiche, Moitié Pizza . . 🧗 [   ] 7c+

8 Du Vent Dans les Coffres en Bambou
. . . . 🎌🧗 [   ] 7a+
Pumpy moves on big holds and tufas lead to a good rest, and
some thin crimping to reach the easier upper section.

9 La Lévrotte . . . . 🎌🪚 [   ] 7a
A steep mid section with a cheeky drilled pocket.

10 Un Monde à Refaire . . . . . . 🎌🧗 [   ] 7a
Move left after the beefy mid-height crux.

11 Sale Fée Mal Brossée . 🎌🪚🧗 [   ] 7b
A series of jugs through the steepness allow you to hang arou
long enough to get nicely pumped before the thin finish.

12 Quand Je Vois Tes Yeux . . . . . . 🎌 [   ] 7b

13 Le Voleur de Pésanteur 🎌🧗🪚 [   ] 7c
The lower wall has awesome crimping, then slopy moves to g
a resting spot on the tufas. The top bulge is a brilliant finale w
some powerful yarding. *Photo opposite*.

14 Seins Légers Couilles Plombées 🧗 [   ] 7b

15 Star'nac . . . . [   ] 7b

16 Les Mots Bleus . . . . [   ] 7a

[icons: 20 min | From mid morning | Vertical]

Le Voleur de Pésanteur
A popular spot with mixed groups due to the
close proximity of the steep, sustained routes
in the 7s and slabby routes in the 6s.

L'Œil du Loup

La Farce Tranc

(side tabs: Céüse, Sisteron, Volx, Orpierre, Bellecombe, Baume Rousse, Ubrieux, Saint Julien, Saint Léger, Malaucène, Combe Obscure, Les Dentelles, Venasque, Buoux)

Cëüse

Sisteron

Volx

Orpierre

Bellecombe

Baume Rousse

Ubrieux

Saint Julien

Saint Léger

Malaucène

Combe Obscure

Les Dentelles

Venasque

Buoux

Toby Dunn on *Le Voleur de Pésanteur* (7c) - *opposite.*

30m

25m

35m

Le Voleur de Pésanteur

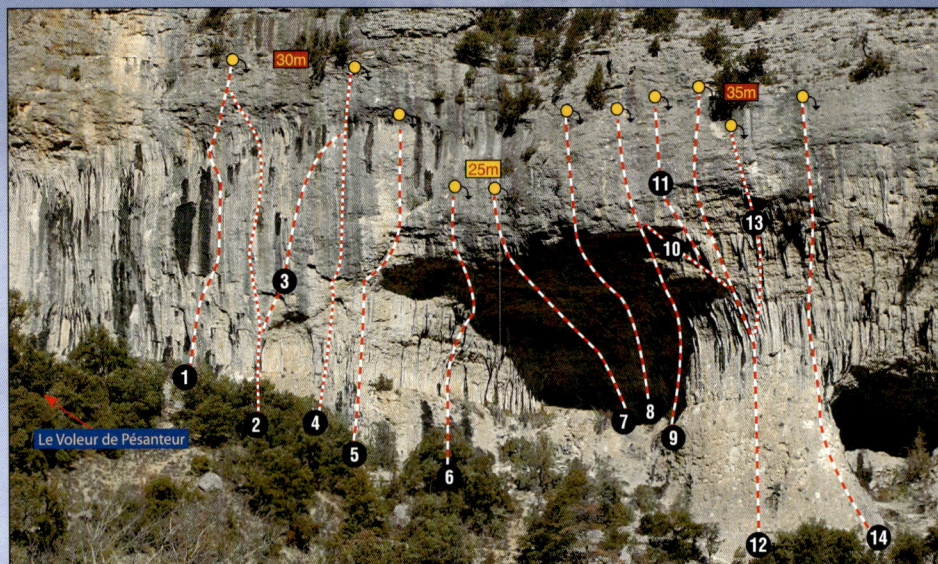

1 Ni Nire, Ni Pleurer, Ni Maudire…Comprendre
. . . . 7b

2 Ah Tu Verras, Tu Verras 7b

3 Azimut . . . . 7b+

4 Bush d'Égout 7c

5 Oussama l'Air Explosif 7c

6 Project . . . . ?

7 Project . . . . ?

8 Foetus Trou du Cus . . . 8b+

9 Chipolatas et Jakusi . . . 8b

10 Le Diagonale Duboc . . . 8b
Start up *La Farce Tranquille* then traverse out left to finish for
Chipolatas et Jakusi. A classic exercise in power endurance
crossing extremely steep terrain with little in the way of rests.

11 Project . . . . ?
The working title is *C'est Clair et Nief*. Head up from midway
along the traverse of *Le Diagonale Duboc*.

12 La Farce Tranquille . . . 8a

13 Barbule 8a
Start up *La Farce Tranquille* then move right. May be 7c+.

Praniania
Page 152

Piedra Salvage
Page 154

L'Œil du Loup
Page 159

Le Voleur de Pésanteur
Page 160

La Farce Tranquille

The main event at Saint Léger when it comes to
steep, sustained tufa climbs. A sector for the strong
only. The projects should provide some of the
hardest routes at the crag when they are completed.

Céüse

Sisteron

Volx

Orpierre

Bellecombe

Baume Rousse

Ubrieux

Saint Julien

Saint Léger

Malaucène

Combe Obscure

Les Dentelles

Venasque

Buoux

Slip Bouse

La Farce Tranquille

Slip Bouse and Milési
Page 164

Tant Que J'aurais une Ombre. . . 8a

T'as pas Pissé Là. . . . . 8a+
bulging wall only succumbs to a very determined effort.
tively bouldery considering the length of rope required!

En Voie Dure Simone . . 8c

Le Zèle du Poulet. . . . . 8b+

La Réserve 8b

Légitime Démence. . . . 8a+

Cétacé . . . . 8b+

21 Ousama L'air Dur. . . . . 8b+

22 La Hyène . . . . 8b+

23 J'Sais Pas. 8b

24 A.O.C. La Baleine 8b

25 Le Prince du Lactique. . 8a+

26 Quelques Instants au Bord du Monde
. . . . 8a

27 Project . . . . ?

28 La Lutte Décrasse . . . . 7c+

29 L'ame de Mon Slam. . . . . . 7b+

Side tabs:
Céüse
Sisteron
Volx
Orpierre
Bellecombe
Baume Rousse
Ubrieux
Saint Julien
Saint Léger
Malaucène
Combe Obscure
Les Dentelles
Venasque
Buoux

Célise · Sisteron · Volx · Orpierre · Bellecombe · Baume Rousse · Ubrieux · Saint Julien · **Saint Léger** · Malaucène · Combe Obscure · Les Dentelles · Venasque · Buoux

Slip Bouse and Milési

After passing the initial overhanging sector, this is the first developed part of the crag you reach when walking-in. Its closeness combined with the wide selection of difficulties on offer ensures popularity.

The name plates are not to be used as footholds!

1 L'Assiette C+ 7c
A satisfying bouldery route. Careful with the rock on the final few metres. Shared belay with Slip Bouse.

2 Slip Bouse 8a
A good 'starter for eight'.

3 Spit Bull . . . . 8a+

4 Spit Bouse . . . . 8a+
Very bouldery and powerful at the mid-height niche.

5 Hilti Blues 8a

6 Des Colos pour Échapper au Blues
. . . . 8a

7 Le Psikapathe . . . . 7b+

8 L'Œil du Cyclope . . . . . 8a+

9 Contrat Pour Escalade . 8a

10 Attrape Gentiment le Lapin Garou
. . . . 8a+

11 Le Bijou . . . . 8a+

12 Mort au Petit Chef Alpiniste
. . . . 7c
Sustained tufa climbing, to a good rest, and a disappointingly desperate finishing move.

13 Sumos Joueurs d'Épée 7b
Unique: desperate insecure back and footing or layback and squeeze? Think 'slate off-width' and you're close.

14 Jamais Deux Sans Trois 7a

15 Ictophage 7c

16 En Chaussons sur la Tête de Kojak
. . . . 7b

17 Mon Cœur est Rempli d'Elles 7b
Blind and tricky through the bulge

18 Jean Sébastien sur Chiurer . . . 6c
A short, technical pitch.

19 Slam Calme Grave, Frère 6c
A technical slabby start leads to some powerful pulls at the to

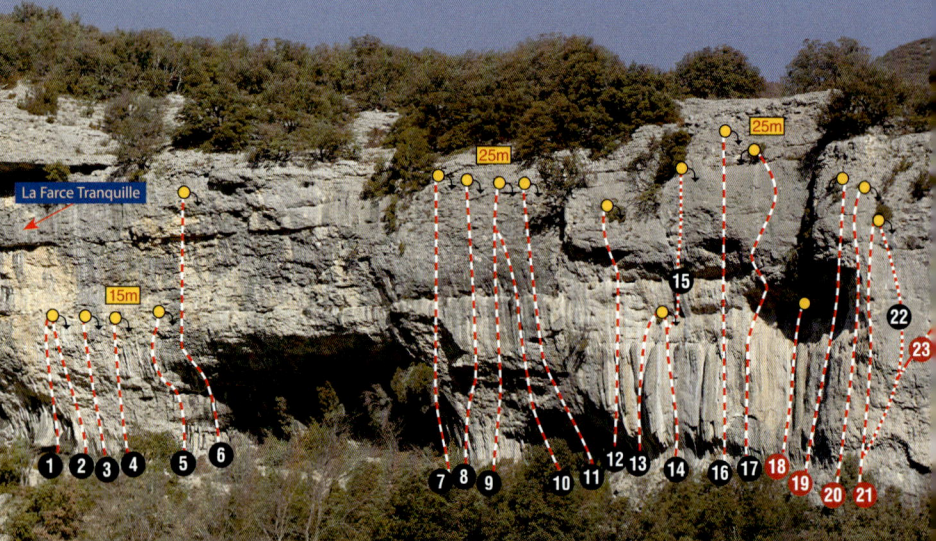

10 min · Lots of sun · Steep

La Farce Tranquille

25m · 25m · 15m · 15m

Milési. 6c

Lolita 6c

En Attendant Mozart . . . . 7a+

Chemin de Traverse 7a

Uni Vert, Minet Râle 7c

Laissez Passer les Rêves 7b

Gavroche et Mimi Pinson 7a
good route with a tough traverse on smooth rock.

Des Titis des Grisettes . . . . 6b+

Les Chevaux du Vent . . . . 7a+

Namasté. . . . . 8a+
an boulder problem to a rest then a nasty boulder problem to
top, or at least it is when you're pumped.

Baisers Volés 6c

T'as le Look Coco 6b

following 12 routes are to the right of a grassy gully.

La Pissotière. 8a
first of a pair of very bouldery routes.

33 **Perdu Sans Sa Loulou** 8a

34 **Navigue Sur la Flo** 7c
A grab cord on the third bolt says it all.

35 **Calm'ta Joie** 7b

36 **Entre Chien et Loup** . . . . 6c+
The wall just left of the prominent arete.

37 **Couenne Fraîche** 6c
The wall just left of the prominent cleft/corner. Poor.

38 **Psychopatatra** . . . . 6a+
The wall just right of the prominent cleft/corner.

39 **Une Histoire pas Terrible, Terrible**
. . . . 6b+
Start as for *Love Vibration*, then moves out left and up.

40 **Love Vibration** . . . . 6b+

41 **Le Retour du Printemps dans la Pairie**
. . . . 7a

42 **Porté Disparu** . . . . 6c+

43 **Cochon Rose** 6c

There are four routes passed on the walk-in in the 6c to 7b range.

Céüse

Sisteron

Volx

Orpierre

Bellecombe

Baume Rousse

Ubrieux

Saint Julien

Saint Léger

Malaucène

Combe Obscure

Les Dentelles

Venasque

Buoux

Géise
Sisteron
Volx
Orpierre
Bellecombe
Baume Rousse
Ubrieux
Saint Julien
Saint Léger
Malaucène
Combe Obscure
Les Dentelles
Venasque
Buoux

North Face

Lying on the opposite side of the river to the remainder of the crags, the North Face is mostly a summer venue. The routes are good, but there are very few warm-ups. Beyond the North Face are further crags, these are described in the local guidebook.

1 N'Oublie Pas Ton Blaireau	7b	
2 Le Retour de Maurice	7a	
3 Les Blaireaux au Photo	7a+	
4 Tenue Correcte Exigée	7a+	
5 East Side Story	7b	
6 Voilà l'Été	7b	
7 La Belle sous Dormantie	7b	
8 Soft Connerie	7b	
9 Joe's Rasnugueth Manettes	7b	

Céüse

Sisteron

Volx

Orpierre

Bellecombe

Baume Rousse

Ubrieux

Saint Julien

Saint Léger

Malaucène

Combe Obscure

Les Dentelles

Venasque

Buoux

Beuzz		7a
Albin		6c+
Si C'est PD, C'est Pas Dur		6c
Vite Fait, Bien Fait		7b+
Bouse de la!		7c+
Quand le Blues l'Emporte sur la Raison		
. . . .		8a

⑯ La Fruite en Avant		7c
⑰ Les Apnées de la Petite Grenouille		
. . . .		8a
⑱ J'Ecrins le Pire, Mi Amigo		7c+
⑲ El Dragon		8b
⑳ La Ballade d'Abdallah		8a+

La Ballade
d'Abdallah

Côtise
Sisteron
Volx
Orpierre
Bellecombe
Baume Rousse
Ubrieux
Saint Julien
Saint Léger
Malaucène
Combe Obscure
Les Dentelles
Venasque
Buoux

1 Les Petites Frappes de l'Alpe . . 8a

2 Petaos a Muerte 8a

3 Les Chercheurs d'Œufs . . . . 7c+

4 L'Assistanct 7c

5 Les Clowns 7c

6 Les Sumos Sont Parmi Nous 7c+

7 Bagdad Kofy Anann . . . 8b

8 Black Mamba 8a

9 Les Fêlés du Pack de Six . . 7c

10 Les Pédés du PACS à Six 7c

11 Chapeau Pointu 7c

12 Les Rifougneurs 7c
The extension is **7c**.

13 Roland Culet 7b

14 Macadam Cow-boy. 7a
The extension is **7b+**.

15 La Chevauchée Fantastique. 7a
Start left of the big tufa. The extension is **7a+**.

Side tabs (top to bottom): Céüse, Sisteron, Volx, Orpierre, Bellecombe, Baume Rousse, Ubrieux, Saint Julien, **Saint Léger**, Malaucène, Combe Obscure, Les Dentelles, Venasque, Buoux

Bille de Clown	✿ 🪜	☐	7b
Sacré Farceur	✿ 🧗	☐	6c+
Hold-up	✿	☐	6b+
Brady em Néonato	✿	☐	6c+
Strip-Tease	✿	☐	6c+
Mauvais Joueur	✿	☐	6a
La Voix des Sages	✿	☐	6a+

23 Mélodie	✿	☐	6a
24 Les Lionnes	✿	☐	6a+
25 Maquerelle du Bœuf	✿	☐	7c+
26 C'est ma Tournée	✿	☐	6b
27 Riche Art	✿	☐	6b+
28 Nom de Bluye	✿	☐	7a

The extension is **8a**.

Céüse

Sisteron

Orpierre

Bellecombe

Baume Rousse

Ubrieux

Saint Julien

Saint Léger

Malaucène

Combe Obscure

Les Dentelles

Venasque

Buoux

Papillon
Page 174

Mal aux Seins
Page 176

Malaucène

Du Bas
Page 178

Gros Zozo
Page 179

Céüse

Sisteron

Volx

Orpierre

Bellecombe

Baume Rousse

Ubrieux

Saint Julien

Saint Léger

Malaucène

Combe Obscure

Les Dentelles

Venasque

Buoux

	No star	✕	✕✕	✕
Up to 4+	1	-	1	
5 to 6a+	3	4	4	
6b to 7a	3	7	3	
7a+ and up	1	13	15	

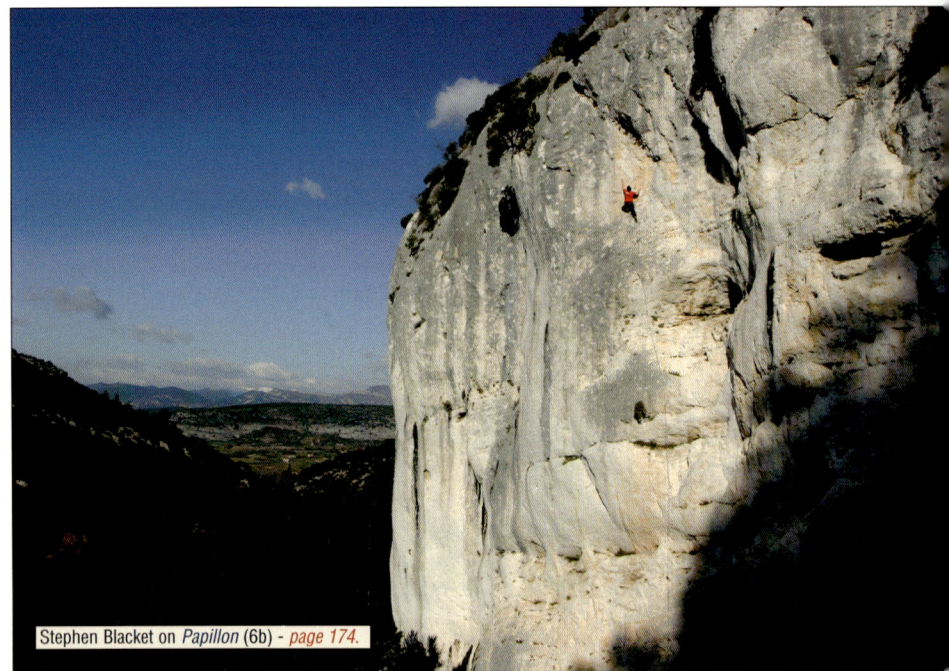

While Malaucène (strictly speaking 'Rochers du Groseau') isn't an extensive area, and is not exactly a 'happening place', the routes are quite brilliant, and it's not likely you will ever find it crowded.

Approach

From the town of Malaucène, take the road signed to 'Le Grozeau' and follow this until you reach a campsite and a bar with a small pond opposite it. Fifty metres before you reach the bar, a rough track leads off on the left, follow this and park near the old mine buildings. There are a number of tracks leading up towards the crags, the simplest way is to walk down to the road and follow it past the bar to the pond. From here pick up a trail leading through the woods, soon, the crags appear on the right. The first you come to is short, hard, vertical, and not described - continue to bigger and better things.

Conditions

Most parts of the crag get the mid-to-late afternoon sun, though many of the starts are well-sheltered by trees and some parts get none at all. In the winter the crag can get very cold. Malaucène often seems to get more wind than Saint Léger, so can be a good option for warmer days.

About 1km
N
D13
Entrechaux and Buis-les-Baronnies
D938
Malaucène
Rochers d Groseau
D974
P
D938
Mont Ventoux
GPS (N) 44°10'4.40" (E) 5° 8'56.18"
Carpentras

Céüse
Sisteron
Volx
Orpierre
Bellecombe
Baume Rousse
Ubrieux
Saint Julien
Saint Léger
Malaucène
Combe Obscure
Les Dentelles
Venasque
Buoux

Stephen Blacket on *Papillon* (6b) - *page 174.*

Céüse

Sisteron

Volx

Orpierre

Bellecombe

Baume Rousse

Ubrieux

Saint Julien

Saint Léger

Malaucène

Combe Obscure

Les Dentelles

Venasque

Buoux

Audrey Seguy on *Un Nouveau Monde Right* (7b+) - *page 174.*

Papillon

Some flawless routes are to be found in this area, following lines of pockets up immaculate clean rock, and often they aren't as hard as they look. The routes do have a 'new' feel about them, which on the plus side means nice shiny bolts and no polish, but take care with some the footholds that haven't been 're-enforced'.

❶ Quart de Cercle . . . . 🎏🔖 [ ] 8a
Nasty and going nowhere.

❷ Créscendo . . . . 🔖 [ ] 6c+
A good knee-bar might give you back enough for the finale.

❸ Hot Com 3 Pom . . . . [ ] 5+

❹ Sale Môme . . . . 🔖 [ ] 5+
A few pocket pulls lead to easy bridging all the way.

❺ Dam Ded . . . . 🔖 [ ] 6a
Slabby climbing up the pillar.

❻ Oiseaux de Passage . . . . [ ] 6c+
Take the left-hand line at the top.

❼ LHOOQ . . . . 🔖🔖 [ ] 7b+
Take the right-hand line at the top.

❽ Péril Jeune . . . . 🔖🔖 [ ] 7b
The extension is about **8b** and may be a project.

❾ Refarin Tire Toi . . . . 🔖 [ ] 7a
The extension is a good but sequency **7c+**.

❿ Le Mono . . . . 🔖 [ ] 8a
Extend at **8a+** above the first belay.

⓫ Un Nouveau Monde Left . . . . . . 🔖 [ ] 7c
The extension is **7c+**.

⓬ Un Nouveau Monde Right . . 🔖🎏 [ ] 7b
A brilliant little route - easier than it looks! The extension is 7c
Photo on page 173.

⓭ Moshé . . . . 🔖🔖 [ ] 7a
The left-hand finish feels nicely exposed.

⓮ Sarah . . . . 🔖🔖 [ ] 7a

⓯ L'Inachevé . . . . 🔖🎏🔖 [ ] 7b

⓰ La Scie des Lapins Bleus . . 🔖🎏 [ ] 7c

⓱ Chez Jolie . . . . 🔖🔖🔖 [ ] 7b
Eases significantly higher up - thank goodness.

⓲ Papillon . . . . 🔖 [ ] 6b
A great route which is a technical **6a+** to the mid-station.
Photo on page 172.

⓳ Potiron, Citrouille et Cie . . . 🔖🎏 [ ] 6c
A nice **6a** to the mid-station.

⓴ Salamadre . . . . 🔖🔖 [ ] 7a

㉑ Touche Pas á la Belle Mère . . . . 🔖 [ ] 6b

㉒ Pipougne . . . . 🔖🔖 [ ] 7a

Céüse

Sisteron

Volx

Orpierre

Bellecombe

Baume Rousse

Ubrieux

Saint Julien

Saint Leger

Malaucène

Combe Obscure

Les Dentelles

Venasque

Buoux

min Afternoon Vertical Steep

30m

25m

30m

20m

18m

19

18

18m

11

12

18m

14

11   12   13

15   16   17   18   19   20   21   22

Mal aux Seins

The shorter wall right of Papillon is less impressive but does have some good routes in the more amenable grades.

10 min | Evening |

15m

20m

1 Mistouflouette	☼			6b
2 Cayenne				6c+
3 Frisson d'Automne	☼			6a+
4 Manque de Tendresse	☼			5
5 Espèce Protégée	☼			4+
6 Entreprise de Travaux Public				4
7 Gros Comme une Maison	☼			5+
8 La Voie Lactée	☼			6c

9 Cailloux		☼		6b
Photo opposite.				
10 Vas-y-Mulet		☼		6a
11 Mal aux Seins	☼			6a+
A fun route, with big moves on big holds.				
12 Polarisant				6a+
A technical offering.				
13 Time Code				6b
A technical micro-climb.				
14 Preview				5
Follow the corner at the end of the crag.				

Adam Gill on *Cailloux* (6b) in winter conditions - *opposite.*

Céüse

Sisteron

Volx

Orpierre

Bellecombe

Baume Rousse

Ubrieux

Saint Julien

Saint Léger

Malaucène

Combe Obscure

Les Dentelles

Venasque

Buoux

1 Les Bruits du Silence . . . . . 6b+
A slightly wandering line.

2 9 Ans 9 Months et Toi . . . . 6b+
The holds improve the higher you get.

3 La Ligne Verte 7b
Save something for the powerful finish.

4 Boulémiquipement . . . . 7a+
The first of three grooves to finish.

5 Con Par Raison . . . . 7b+
A tough finish up the groove.

6 Taille Illusoire 7b

7 Pluie d'Enfer 7b

8 Respire . . . . 7c+
Some very powerful pulls on pockets.

9 Show Chaud 7a

10 Mon Elle du Désir . . . . 6b+
A surpisingly amenable route.

11 Petits Petons 7b
Not as hard as it looks, but still pretty tough.

12 Brise les Chaînes 7a

13 Fin des Stocks . . . . 7a+
The left-hand finish

14 Les Mini Pousses 7b
A pleasant shortie.

15 Politicopourri 7b
A sustained, and interesting line that keeps on going.

16 Une Journée de Merde 7a

17 Travaille Célébrale 6b
Head left after the second bolt.

25m

Du Bas and Gros Zozo

The first long wall you arrived at on the approach offers two distinct sections. A vertical grey wall with some intense and fingery climbing; and a steep wall which has several hard routes with bulging starts.

Ni Pute Ni Soumise 23   6a+
d right after the second bolt.

Deux Kilo Six 11   7b+

Et Plus Encore 11   7c+

Le Zoulou Blanc 11   8b

Le Gros Zozo 23   7b

Piétra Gala 23   8a

24 **Voyage au Centre de la Mère**
. . . . 11   8b

25 **La Complainte des Petits Enfants**
. . . . 11   7c

26 Putain de Toi 23   7b

27 Déroutage 11   7b

28 El Pitchoun 11   7a+

29 Jolly Jumpeur 11   7b

Céüse
Sisteron
Volx
Orpierre
Bellecombe
Baume Rousse
Ubrieux
Saint Julien
Saint Léger
Malaucène
Combe Obscure
Les Dentelles
Venasque
Buoux

Right Crag
Page 18

Left Crag
Page 184

Céüse

Sisteron

Volx

Orpierre

Bellecombe

Baume Rousse

Ubrieux

Saint Julien

Saint Léger

Malaucène

Combe Obscure

Les Dentelles

Venasque

Buoux

Combe Obscure

Céüse

Sisteron

Voix

Orpierre

Bellecombe

Baume Rousse

Ubrieux

Saint Julien

Saint Léger

Malaucène

Combe Obscure

Les Dentelles

Venasque

Buoux

	No star	✪	✪✪	✪
Up to 4+	-	1	-	
5 to 6a+	-	11	13	2
6b to 7a	-	7	8	3
7a+ and up	1	6	-	

Combe Obscure is a sweet little climbing spot consisting of easy-angled slabs of flawless grey rock. There are the odd hard routes in amongst the friendlier grades, but they will feel very technical at this angle.

Approach

Combe Obscure lies midway between Malaucène and Bédoin, off the D19. From Malaucène head south on the D938, turning left onto the D19 in the direction of Bédoin. After a few kilometres, you reach La Madeline. On a sharp bend in the road, a rough track, indicated by a yellow walking sign, leads off to the left. Drive a little way up the track and park at the end near an abandoned brick building. Don't leave anything valuable in the car! Walk past the building and continue in the same direction, following a coarse gravel track for about fifteen minutes until you reach the two crags.

Conditions

The cliffs are sheltered, and get the morning and midday sun. Seepage is unlikely to be a problem. The left crag gets the sun for longer than the right one.

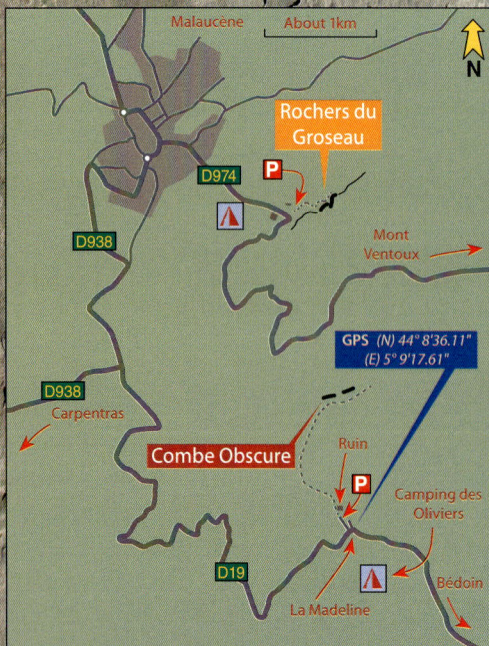

Malaucène   About 1km   N

Rochers du Groseau

P

D974

D938

Mont Ventoux

GPS (N) 44° 8'36.11" (E) 5° 9'17.61"

D938
Carpentras

Combe Obscure   Ruin

P

Camping des Oliviers

D19

La Madeline   Bédoin

Céüse · Sisteron · Volx · Orpierre · Bellecombe · Baume Rousse · Ubrieux · Saint Julien · Saint Léger · Malaucène · Combe Obscure · Les Dentelles · Venasque · Buoux

Céüse

Sisteron

Volx

Orpierre

Bellecombe

Baume Rousse

Ubrieux

Saint Julien

Saint Léger

Malaucène

Combe Obscure

Les Dentelles

Venasque

Buoux

Toby Dunn making the crux move on the untypically hard *Mariotte* (7c) - *page 187*.

36m · 35m · 30m · 30m · 15m

Left Crag

Perfect rock and an interesting combination of smeary slab climbing and steep jug pulling makes for some absorbing climbs. The longest routes require 70m ropes.

1 Percusion . . . . ☼1 ☐ **6a**
Weave around the blank rock on big pockets.

2 Jardin Secret . . . . ☼ 🔲 ☐ **6a+**
A short tricky section moving about the third bolt.

3 Pirate . . . . ☼ 🔲 ☐ **6b**
Follow the glue-in bolts. The steep section is a lot easier than what follows it, if it makes you feel any better.

4 De la Fruite dans les Ideés . . . . ☼1 ☐ **5+**
Follow the line that includes Petzl bolts.

5 2000 F le Kilo . . . . ☼2 ☐ **5+**
Some pleasant smearing, then jugs to the top.

6 La Domy . . . . ☼ 🔲 ☐ **6b**
A few thin moves early on.

7 Ralépas Grimpe . . . . ☼ 🔲 ☐ **6b**
Plenty of smearing to start.

8 Froggy One . . . . ☼1 ☐ **6a**

9 Vision . . . . ☼3 ☐ **5**
Fun flowing movements between big holds. *Photo opposite.*

10 Ziziben . . . . ☼2 ☐ **6a**

11 La Martine . . . . ☼ 🖐 ☐ **6c**
The grade is all packed into the finish.

12 Pas Glop Pas Glop . . . . ☼2 ☐ **6b**
Thin moves on crystals bar the way to an easy finish.

13 La Calade . . . . ☼2 ☐ **5+**
Clip the bolts on the left, layback and enjoy.

14 La Puce . . . . ☼1 ☐ **5+**
Good climbing for the lower slab, then better value as the climb steepens.

Céüse · Sisteron · Volx · Orpierre · Bellecombe · Baume Rousse · Ubrieux · Saint Julien · Saint Léger · Malaucène · Combe Obscure · Les Dentelles · Venasque · Buoux

Angoisse. . . . . ⚡ ☐ 5

..b through the alcove.

Solitaire . . . . ⚡ ☐ 5+

..re a few moves with *Angoisse* at the start.

L'Œil Bleu. . . . . ⚡ ☐ 6a

Les Ailes Brisées. . . . . ⚡ 🧗🧗 ☐ 7a+

..ything stops you ticking the wall, it's this one. The crux

..lves more strength from below your waist than above it.

19 Olimanu . . . . ⚡🧗▮▮ ☐ 6b

The crux comes quickly, and is probably the most interesting move on the crag - shorties will have to jump or make a very tenuous move to gain easier ground.

20 La Perle Noire. . . . . ⚡ ☐ 4

Easy-angle and very big holds.

21 Zut Plus de Piles . . . . ⚡ ☐ 5+

The difficult section is short lived.

Céüse
Sisteron
Volx
Orpierre
Bellecombe
Baume Rousse
Ubrieux
Saint Julien
Saint Léger
Malaucène
Combe Obscure
Les Dentelles
Venasque
Buoux

Stephen Blacket on *Vision* (5) - *opposite*

Cèüse
Sisteron
Voix
Orpierre
Bellecombe
Baume Rousse
Ubrieux
Saint Julien
Saint Léger
Malaucène
Combe Obscure
Les Dentelles
Venasque
Buoux

1 Le Lechant Mou 6a

2 La Dernière Minute . . . 6c

3 Hard Pepper . . . . 6b+

4 La Dalle dans le Ciel . . . . . 7b+

5 Ushuaïa 7b

6 Éléctric 7c

7 Picon Fatal . . . . 6a+

8 Soleil Levant . . . . 6a+

9 Fou du Pont 7a

10 Joe le Maxi 6b

11 La Biboufafait 6c

12 Truffe a la Tronçonneuse . . . 6b
A drilled pocket allows entry to some great jug-pulling up the headwall. One aid move required.

13 4487 après JC 7a

14 Saxo 7a

15 Vibration 6b
A few tough moves to enter the groove, but steady after that.

16 Que Fait la Police 7b

Right Crag

Similar to its left-hand neighbour but with more routes to go at and on even better rock.

Le Chandelier . . . . 6a+

...te that manages to feel bigger than it really is. Above ...ave, big moves on very big holds take you through some ...did positions.

La Gaffophone . . . . 6a+

Speed Sail 5

Élégance. . . . . 6b+

Mariotte 7c

...xacting fingery crux, and it's no picnic getting there either.
...o on page 183.

La Brise de la Pastille 6b

The Blue Breaker . . . . 6a+

24 Et Moi Alors 5

25 Les Soupirs 5
Photo on page 182.

26 Aymondoi 5

27 Dupont T 6a
A hard start leads to easier climbing.

28 Les Broques 6c
Balancy then a hard move off a mono leads to easy climbing.

29 Dupont D 6a

30 Naissance 6a

31 Bons Baisers de Kincon 6b

Chaine du Clapis
Page 206

Chaine de Gigondas
Page 198

Céüse

Sisteron

Volx

Orpierre

Bellecombe

Baume Rousse

Ubrieux

Saint Julien

Saint Léger

Malaucène

Combe Obscure

Les Dentelles

Venasque

Buoux

Les Dentelles de Montmirail

Chaine du Grand Travers
Page 192

Saint Christophe
Page 222

Cédse

Sisteron

Voix

Orpierre

Bellecombe

Baume Rousse

Ubrieux

Saint Julien

Saint Léger

Malaucène

Combe Obscure

Les Dentelles

Venasque

Buoux

	No star	☼	☼☼	
Up to 4+	11	9	1	
5 to 6a+	38	60	64	
6b to 7a	15	62	74	
7a+ and up	11	25	39	

The Dentelles is a spectacular area offering characterful climbing, far enough away from tarmac roads to make it feel unspoilt, but close enough to make it convenient.

Approaches

The approaches described are from Lafare but you can also approach from Gigondas.

Saint Christophe

From Lafare, follow the road to Gigondas. A small parking area on a very tight corner serves the impressive Cascade sector; walk up the road a little further and it leads almost to the base of the crag. There is limited parking on the right side of the road, alternatively continue for 100m to a larger parking area on the left. For the Tyrolienne wall, drop down a path from the second parking area to the top of the crag. Follow the clifftop to the right until you can descend the left side (looking in) of the crag.

Chaine de Gigondas

Continue along the road past Saint Christophe, which becomes increasingly rough until a large open parking area is reached - there is a large information sign here. The path to the north face of the Chaine de Gigondas leads up from the parking area

Rocher du Cayron

Continue past Chaine de Gigondas parking down the hill until it is possible to park on the left side of the road just before the road swings around to the right. Walk a short distance back up the road to find the path leading up on the right.

Rocher du Grand Travers

Approach as for Chaine de Gigondas, but before you reach the large parking area, a sharp turn leads off to the right - on your first attempt it is probably best to find the large parking area first, then turn around and take the track leading off on your left. Follow this track for a hundred metres or so until a parking area is reached. A trail leads up from here a short way to the crag.

Chaine du Clapis

Traveling south from Lafare, take the first right turn (easy to miss - if you reach the bridge you've gone too far) and follow a rough road with the impressive crags in full view. Continue until you reach a parking a[rea] on the right just opposite a sign that looks like a wine barrel. The footpath leads up fro[m] the parking area to the left side of the crag [-] follow a well-walked trail along the base of the crag to get to the various sectors.

Conditions

Offering both north and south-facing routes there is plenty to go at here whether you're here in the middle of winter, or summer. Th[e] north side of the Chaine de Gigondas will feel cool on all but hot summer days, and you can always opt for the full sun on the south face of the Chaine du Clapis or Sain[t] Christophe which are big sun-traps.

Accommodation

There are plenty of campsites in the region, the nearest is in **Beaumes de Venise**. The municipal campsite is open from the 1st March to the 12th November.
Also worth considering is the Gîte D'Étape in Lafare and the Gîte D'Étape in Gigondas. It is about an hour's drive from Buis, so a visit is a possibility if you are based over there.

Je Suis un Communiste (6c+) - *see page 20*[?]
Dièdre de Provence area of Chaine de Gigon[das]

Side tabs: Céüse, Sisteron, Volx, Orpierre, Bellecombe, Baume Rousse, Ubrieux, Saint Julien, Saint Léger, Malaucène, Combe Obscure, Les Dentelles, Venasque, Buoux

About 5km

Pierrelongue

Vaison-la-Romaine

D977

D4

L'Ouvèze

Mollans-sur-Ouvèze

D13

Entrechaux

Saint Léger

Sablet

Les Dentelles de Montmirail

D938

Malaucène

D977

D90

Malaucène

D7

D974

Gigondas

D90

Mont Ventoux
(1909m)

D8

Lafare

Vacqueyras

Combe Obscure

Montmirail

Beaumes
de Venise

Bédoin

D938

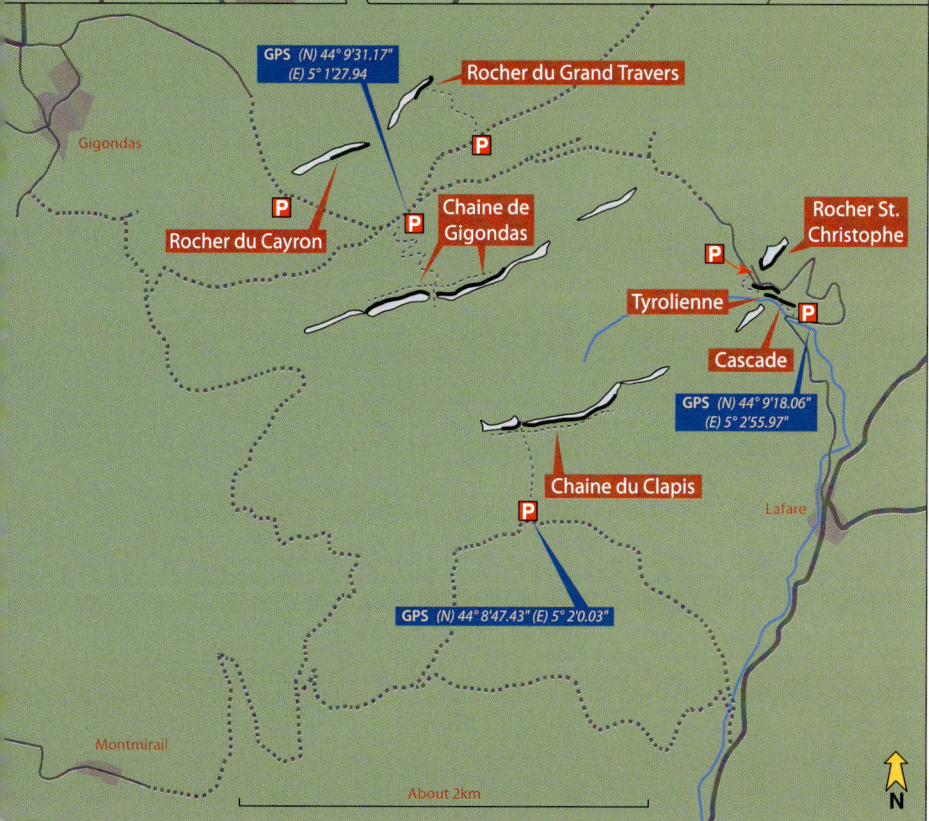

Céüse

Sisteron

Volx

Orpierre

Bellecombe

Baume Rousse

Ubrieux

Saint Julien

Saint Léger

Malaucène

Combe Obscure

Les Dentelles

Venasque

Buoux

GPS *(N)* 44° 9'31.17"
(E) 5° 1'27.94

Rocher du Grand Travers

Gigondas

P

P

**Chaine de
Gigondas**

P

**Rocher St.
Christophe**

Rocher du Cayron

P

Tyrolienne

P

Cascade

GPS *(N)* 44° 9'18.06"
(E) 5° 2'55.97"

Chaine du Clapis

Lafare

P

GPS *(N)* 44° 8'47.43" *(E)* 5° 2'0.03"

Montmirail

About 2km

N

Chaine du Grand Travers

Rocher du Cayron
Page 194

Les Dentelles

P
Parking for Chaine de Gigondas

Ceüse

Sisteron

Volx

Orpierre

Bellecombe

Baume Rousse

Ubrieux

Saint Julien

Saint Leger

Malaucène

Combe Obscure

Les Dentelles

Venasque

Buoux

Rocher du Grand Travers
Page 196

Céüse

Sisteron

Volx

Orpierre

Bellecombe

Baume Rousse

Ubrieux

Saint Julien

Saint Léger

Malaucène

Combe Obscure

Les Dentelles

Venasque

Buoux

Rocher du Cayron
A pleasant location featuring a collection of slabby routes on good compact rock.
Approach - See page 190.

❶ Agrhume . . . . ☐ 6a+

❷ Chicos . . . . ☐ 6a+

❸ Loloa . . . . 🔁 ☐ 6c+

❹ Virgule . . . . ☐ 5+

❺ Dessine-Moi Une Grenouille . . . 🔁 ☐ 6a+

❻ L'Astronef . . . . 🔁 🔨 🪝 ☐ 6b

❼ Bal du Roc . . . . 🔁 🔨 🪝 ☐ 6c

❽ Vol au Vent . . . . 🔁 🔨 🪝 ☐ 7a

❾ Funambulle . . . . 🔁 🔨 🪝 ☐ 6c

❿ Talons Aiguille et Bas Résille
. . . . 🔁 🔨 🪝 ☐ 7a+

⓫ Cachemire . . . . 🔁 🔨 🪝 ☐ 6
The start used to come in from the right (hence the oddly-positioned bolt) but chipped holds now lead directly.

⓬ Carence . . . . 🔁 🔨 🪝 ☐ 6
Photo opposite.

⓭ Les Quatres Saisons . . . 🔁 🔨 🪝 ☐ 6

⓮ Folle Envie . . . . 🔁 🔨 🪝 ☐ 6

⓯ Le Grand Mouvement . . 🔁 🔨 🪝 ☐ 7

⓰ Voyage-Voyage . . . . . . 🔁 🔨 🪝 ☐ 7

⓱ Captive . . . . 🔁 🔨 🪝 ☐ 6

⓲ L'Encre de Tes Yeux . . . 🔁 🔨 🪝 ☐ 6

Céüse Sisteron Volx Orpierre Bellecombe Baume Rousse Ubrieux Saint Julien Saint Léger Malaucène Combe Obscure Les Dentelles Venasque Buoux

25m

20m

18 19 20 21 22 23 24 25 26 27 28 29

Céüse
Sisteron
Volx
Orpierre
Bellecombe
Baume Rousse
Ubrieux
Saint Julien
Saint Léger
Malaucène
Combe Obscure
Les Dentelles
Venasque
Buoux

.es Jardins Suspendus		6a
Salsa		6a
.'Impérmanence		6a
Iiños		5+
.a Terre Après la Bombe		5+
Jnknown		?
.'Homme Volant		6a
Frankie Goes to Virginie		5+
Cuba Libre		6a
Chan Chan		5+
Compadres		5

Adam Gill on *Carence* (6b) - *opposite*.

Rocher du Grand Travers
Good rock and short, friendly routes following good lines plus a sunny aspect make this a popular spot for groups and families.
Approach - See page 190.

Large blocks

20m
15m
20m
15m

Warning - At time of writing, the threat of a rockfall posed by some large boulders at the top of the crag (belays of routes 16-18 are on these blocks) has closed the left-hand side of the crag.

Céüse · Sisteron · Volx · Orpierre · Bellecombe · Baume Rousse · Ubrieux · Saint Julien · Saint Léger · Malaucène · Combe Obscure · Les Dentelles · Venasque · Buoux

La Dalle de l'Arbre . . . . □ 5

Cracoucass . . . . 🎔 🏃 □ 6b+

La Lyon . . . . 🎔 🏃 □ 6b

Start en Feu . . . . 🎔 □ 6a+

La Gauche de la Droite . . . . . . 🎔 □ 6a

La Danone . . . . 🎔 □ 6a

La Fissure . . . . 🎔 □ 5+

Le Golot Critique . . . . □ 5

La Sophie . . . . 🎔 □ 5

L'Annie . . . . 🎔 □ 5

La D7 . . . . 🎔 □ 5

La G.G . . . . 🎔 □ 5+

L'Enfance de l'Art . . . . 🎔 □ 6a

35 L'Ivaldi . . . . 🎔 □ 6a

36 L'Octobule . . . . 🎔 □ 5+

The final five routes give pleasant easy climbing on the end wall.

37 La Niquedouille . . . . 🎔 □ 5
An easy initial slab leads to a prominent crackline.

38 La Garce . . . . 🎔 □ 4+
Scramble up past a detached block at 3m then follow the corner/crack up leftwards.

39 Le Vivier . . . . 🎔 □ 4+
Start left of the big tree, four bolts lead up past another tree, then continue to the top.

40 Super Mollasson . . . . □ 3
A very amenable line.

41 Les Mollasons . . . . □ 3
The final, ultra short, route on the right-hand side of the crag.

Ceüse

Sisteron

Volx

Orpierre

Bellecombe

Baume Rousse

Ubrieux

Saint Julien

Saint Léger

Malaucène

Combe Obscure

Les Dentelles

Venasque

Buoux

Dièdre de Provence
Page 200

Dièdre de
Provence

Chaine de Gigondas

guillette Lagarde
Page 202

Morizot-Parat
Page 204

Pierrelatine
Page 205

Dièdre des
Parisiens

Céüse

Sisteron

Volx

Orpierre

Bellecombe

Baume Rousse

Ubrieux

Saint Julien

Saint Leger

Malaucène

Combe Obscure

Les Dentelles

Venasque

Buoux

Left column sidebar tabs (top to bottom): Céüse, Sisteron, Volx, Orpierre, Bellcombe, Baume Rousse, Ubrieux, Saint Julien, Saint Léger, Malaucène, Combe Obscure, Les Dentelles, Vénasque, Buoux

1. Dièdre de Savoie . . . . 5+
2. Tibet Libre 7a
3. Dièdre de Provence 6a
   1) 6a, 2) 6a. *Photo opposite.*
4. Océane . . . . 7b+
   1) 4+, 2) 6b+, 3) 7b+
5. Le Jour et la Nuit 6a
   1) 5, 2) 6a
6. Le 5ème Guignol . . . . 6a+
   1) 6a, 2) 6a+
7. Super Cog . . . . 6b+
   1) 5, 2) 6b+
8. La Route de la Vie . . . . 5+
9. Faute de Prises . . . . 5+
10. La Savoyarde 5
    1) 5, 2) 4+
11. Bismilha . . . . 6a+

12. Hamdulilha 6b
13. Apollo 13 . . . . 6a
14. Vipère à Sonnette . . . . 5+
15. Jomo . . . . 5+
    1) 5+, 2) 4+
16. Montélimar . . . . 5+
    Approach from *Jomo.*
17. Solstice d'Été 6b
18. Dur la Reprise 6b
19. Lufalukejelcus 6a
    1) 6a+, 2) 6a+
20. Tierra del Fuego 6b
21. Williwaux 7a
22. Ourdes 96 . . . . 6c

[Icons: 25 min | Evening | Slabby | Vertical | Multi-pitch]

Dièdre de Provence

A mixture of routes following strong natural lines. *Diedre de Provence* is well worth doing and is probably the most popular route here.
Approach - See page 190 for main approach. Head left when you reach the top of the approach path.

Flèche à Jojo . . . . ⚡1 ☐ 6b
), 2) 5+

Nanie . . . . ⚡2 ☐ 6a+
a+, 2) 5

Homme à Lunettes . . . . 🔣🧗 ☐ 7c
as for *Nanie* or *Mauvais*.

Mauvais Jour . . . . ⚡1 🧗 ☐ 7a
), 2) 7a

De Champeville . . . . ⚡1 ☐ 5+
oach up *Nanie* which is 6a+.

Tour de Chauffe . . . . ⚡1 🧗 ☐ 7a+

La Griffe du Lion . . . . ⚡2 🧗 ☐ 7a

Petit Pilier . . . . 🪧 ☐ 6b

Je Suis un Communiste . . . ⚡2 🧗 ☐ 6c+
os on page 190 and 203.

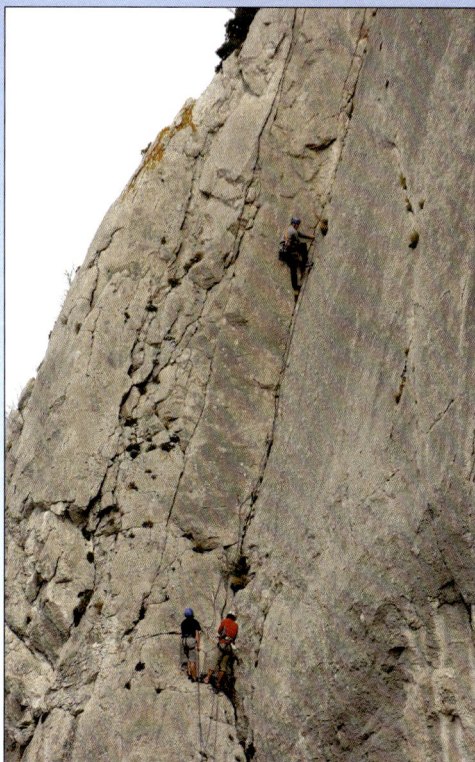

A team enjoying the classic *Dièdre de Provence* (6a) *opposite*.

L'Aiguillette Lagarde

Céüse
Sisteron
Voix
Orpierre
Bellecombe
Baume Rousse
Ubrieux
Saint Julien
Saint Léger
Malaucène
Combe Obscure
Les Dentelles
Venasque
Buoux

1. **Arete Lagarde** . . . . 2 ☐ 5
1) 5, 2) 5. Can be done in 1 long single pitch.

2. **Crack en Stock** . . . . 1 ☐ 5

3. **Tout Crapato** . . . . ☐ 4+
1) 4+, 2) 4+

4. **Week-end à Vichy** . . . . 1 ☐ 6b

5. **Spartacus** . . . . 1 ☐ 6a

6. **Oral au Moral** . . . . 1 ☐ 6b+

7. **Boule et Bill** . . . . 3 ☐ 5+
1) 5, 2) 5+

8. **Galinette** . . . . 1 ☐ 5

25 min | Evening | Slabby | Vertical

70m
45m
40m
35m
30m
30m
30m
28
28
27
27
27
26
25
24
23
23
22
21
20
19
18
18
17
16
16
16
16
15
14
13
12
11
10
10
9
8
7
7
7
6
5
5
4
3
3
3
2
1
1
1
20m
12m

Morizot-Parat
Dièdre de Provence

L'Aiguillette Lagarde
A wealth of short, slabby routes at the top of the approach path ensures popularity. The longer routes ta[ke] striking lines to the very top of the crag.
Approach - See page 190 for main approach.
This is the area just right at the top of the approach pat[h]

Géüse · Sisteron · Volx · Orpierre · Bellecombe · Baume Rousse · Ubrieux · Saint Julien · Saint Léger · Malaucène · Combe Obscure · Les Dentelles · Venasque · Buoux

Les Crados . . . . 1️⃣ ☐ 5+

Tintin Sous la Dentelle . . . . 2️⃣ ☐ 5+
+, 2) 5+

C'est Canon. . . . . 1️⃣ ☐ 5

Allons Z'Enfants. . . . . 1️⃣ ☐ 5+

Archimède . . . . 1️⃣ ☐ 5+

Lucky Luke . . . . ☐ 6a

Rantanplan . . . . ☐ 5+

Petite Émeline. . . . . 2️⃣ ☐ 5
, 2) 5, 2) 4+

Super Lolo . . . . ☐ 6a

La Belle Alexandra. . . . . ☐ 5
, 2) 5

Arete Est de L'Aiguillette Lagarde 2️⃣ ☐ 6a

Directe de L'Aiguillette. . . . . . . 2️⃣ ☐ 6a

Kébra le Loub . . . . 2️⃣ ☐ 6a+

Arete Ouest de L'Aiguillette. . . . 2️⃣ ☐ 6a

Garganta . . . . 3️⃣ ☐ 5+
+, 2) 5+

Le Socle . . . . 2️⃣ 🧗 ☐ 6c

Tischmacher . . . . 2️⃣ 🧗 ☐ 6c

Pilier Clair . . . . 1️⃣ 🧗 🗡️ ☐ 6c+

Citron Hallucinogène . . . . . 2️⃣ 🧗 ☐ 7a
a+, 2) 6b, 2) 7a

Vibration. . . . . 3️⃣ ☐ 6b
a+. As for *Citron*.... 2) 6b+, 3) 6b

Je Suis un Communiste (6c+) - *see page 201* -
Dièdre de Provence area of Chaine de Gigondas.

Céüse

Sisteron

Volx

Orpierre

Bellecombe

Baume Rousse

Ubrieux

Saint Julien

Saint Léger

Malaucène

Combe Obscure

Les Dentelles

Venasque

Buoux

80m

50m

16

15

29

30

35m

23

30m

40m

24

32

21

20m

26

15

45m

33

30m

9

31 32

29

20m

10

22

28

25 27

19

23

20

18

17 15

14

13

12

11

10

9

1 2 3 4 5 6 7 8 9

L'Aiguillette Lagarde

Morizot-Parat
A number of impressive wall climbs, many stretching to the summit ridge, make this feel a bit more adventurous than the average sport crag.
Approach - See page 190 for main approach. Walk right from the L'Aiguillette Lagarde sector.

1 Nulle Part D'Ailleurs		6c
2 Face Est		6b
3 Les Copains D'Abord		6b
4 L'Ivresse de la Victoire		6c
5 Le Mythe de la Beauté du Diable		6b
6 Hamburger		6b
1) 6b+, 2) 5		
7 Référentiel Bondissant		7a
8 Terre Étrangère		6c

Side tabs (vertical): Céüse, Sisteron, Volx, Orpierre, Bellecombe, Baume Rousse, Ubrieux, Saint Julien, Saint Léger, Malaucène, Combe Obscure, Les Dentelles, Venasque, Buoux

Approach to Pierrelatine Are

35m

38

20m

37

38

36

39

Céüse
Sisteron
Volx
Orpierre
Bellecombe
Baume Rousse
Ubrieux
Saint Julien
Saint Léger
Malaucène
Combe Obscure
Les Dentelles
Venasque
Buoux

Emprise Directe				7b
7b, 2) 7a+				
Baleine Sous Caillou				6c
6c, 2) 6c				
Ce Soir ou Jamais				6b
Radio Moquette				6b+
Jardinland				6c
Groupe Éléctrogène				7a+
Morizot-Parat				5+
4, 2) 5+, 3) 5+				
Larguez Tout				6b+
Ludwig				6a
Fleur de Lotus				6b+
Super Régina				6a
Dokter Gigi				7a
Mr. Wonderful				7c
Prince des Ténèbres				7a+
Voie du Surplomb				6c
6c, 2) 6a+				
Surplomb Variation				7a+
Glasnost				7b+
Managa				7c
Banana Split				7b
Temps Décadents				6c
Dièdre des Parisiens				5+
+, 2) 5+				
La Dalle du Banlieusard				6a+

31 Lobotomitique				7b
32 Petits Moutons				6c
1) 6c, 2) 6c				
33 À Titre Provisoire				6c
34 Le Dauphin D'Argent				6b+
1) 6b+, 2) 6b				
35 Rien Ne Va				6c
36 Croqueuse D'Hommes				7c
37 Arête Sur Image				7a+
38 Pierrelatine				7a+
1) 7a+, 2) 6a				
39 Soleil Couchant				6a

Ceüse

Sisteron

Volx

Orpierre

Bellecombe

Baume Rousse

Ubrieux

Saint Julien

Saint Léger

Malaucène

Combe Obscure

Les Dentelles

Venasque

Buoux

Dent Sarrazine -
not covered here.
Restricted climbing
due to nesting birds -

The Notch

Chagrin d'Humeur
Page 208

Vires Rouges
Page 210

Chaine du Clapis

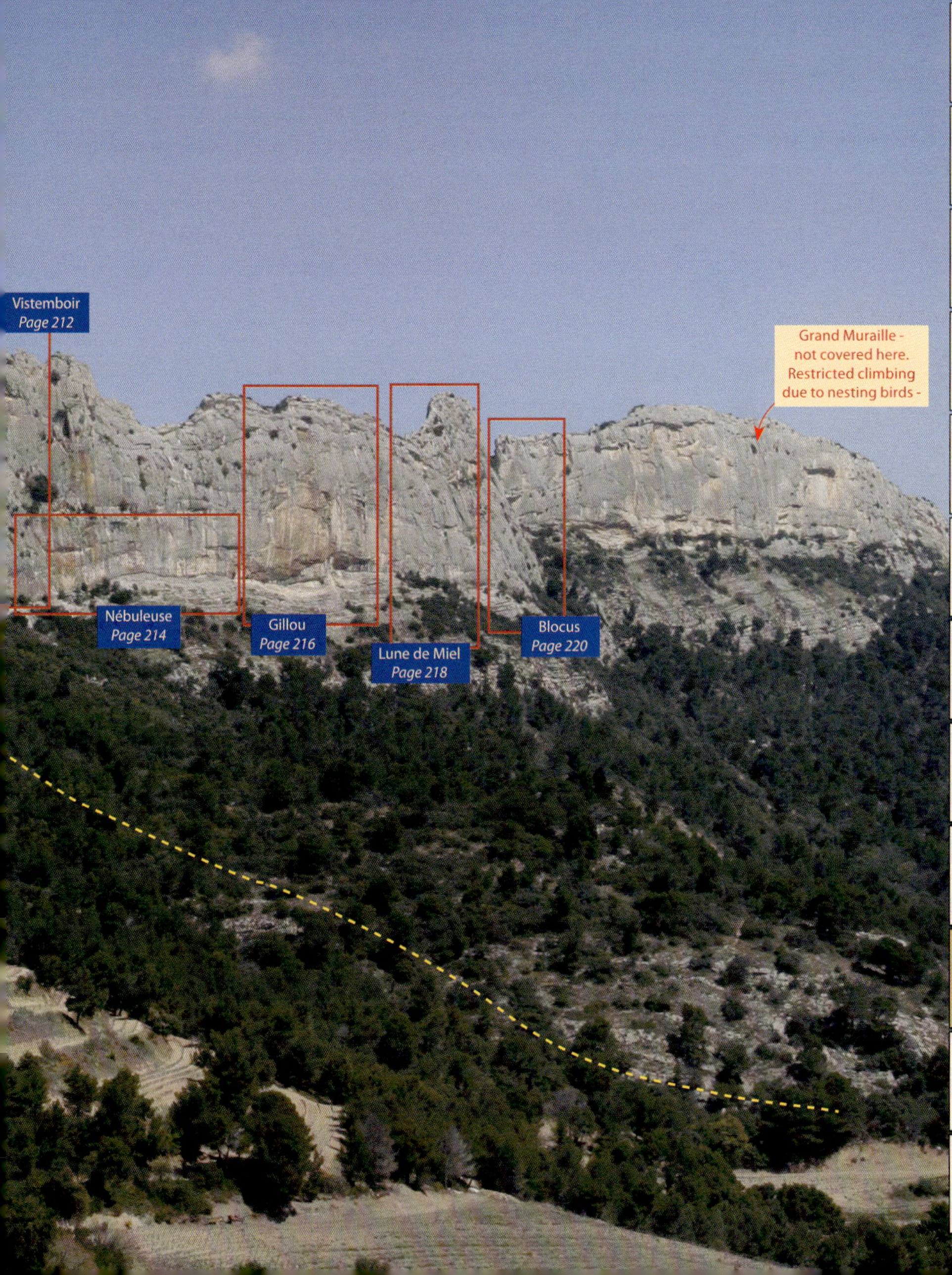

Vistemboir
Page 212

Grand Muraille -
not covered here.
Restricted climbing
due to nesting birds -

Nébuleuse
Page 214

Gillou
Page 216

Lune de Miel
Page 218

Blocus
Page 220

Céüse
Sisteron
Volx
Orpierre
Bellecombe
Baume Rousse
Ubrieux
Saint Julien
Saint Leger
Malaucène
Combe Obscure
Les Dentelles
Venasque
Buoux

1 Traversée . . . . ☐ 5
A long trad route for which few details are known.

2 Nike . . . . ☐ 5+

3 Ça Racle un Max . . . . ☒2 ☐ 6c
1) 5+, 2) 6c

4 Papé . . . . ☒2 ☐ 6b

5 Comme un Oiseau Sans Ailes . . ☒2 ☐ 6a+
1) 6a+, 2) 6a+

6 Électric Soupçon . . . . ☒2 ☐ 6a

7 Pan Bagnat . . . . ☒2 🧗 ☐ 7a+
1) 5+, 2) 7a+. The second pitch can be gained from the left.

8 Chagrin d'Humeur . . . . ☒3 ☐ 6a

9 Brazil . . . . ☒2 ☐ 6a

10 Silence. . . . . ☒2 ☐ 6a

11 Cheeseburger . . . . ☒2 ☐ 5+

12 Nid d'Écureuil . . . . ☒3 ☐ 6a
1) 6a, 2) 6a+

13 Ventre Gris . . . . ☒3 ☐ 6b
1) 6a. As for *Nid d'Écureuil.* 2) 6b, 3) 6b

14 Jeu d'Artifice. . . . . ☒2 ☐ 6a

15 N'Accablez Pas l'Os . . . . . . ☒1 🧗 ☐ 7a

Chagrin d'Humeur

The first sector you come across is a popular spot, with plenty of slabby routes up excellent rock. It might not be a good spot on a cool windy day as the wind funnels through the notch in the chain.

Approach - See page 190 for main approach. These walls are left of the notch.

| 15 min | Lots of sun | Vertical | Slabby |

Diane . . . . ⬡ ☐ 5+

ere are two continuation routes above Diane.

Tablier Rose . . . . ⬡ ☐ 6b

Charter Pour Ouaga . . . . ⬡ ☐ 6c
6a, 3) 6c

Des Gestes Pour le Faire . . ⬡ 🐾 ☐ 7a
5+, 2) 6b+, 3) 7a

Château de Sable. . . . . ⬡ ☐ 6b
6a, 2) 6b

Bayonnette . . . . ⬡ ☐ 6b
5+, 2) 6b

Sucre d'Orge . . . . ⬡ ☐ 6b
5, 2) 6b

Expo Système . . . . ⬡ ☐ 6b+
6a+, 2) 6b+

Traînée Marron . . . . ⬡ ☐ 6b+
5+, 2) 6b+

25 Orange Mécanique . . . . ⬡ ☐ 6a
1) 6a, 2) 5+

26 Jardin. . . . . ⬡ ☐ 5+
1) 5+, 2) 5+

27 Belote et Rebelote . . . . . . ⬡ 🐾 ☐ 6b ·
1) 6b, 2) 6a

28 Planplanette . . . . ⬡ 🐾 ☐ 6a
1) 6a, 2) 6a

29 Sémenova. . . . . ⬡ 🐾 ☐ 7a
A steep alternative finishing pitch.

30 Nikita . . . . ⬡ ☐ 6a+

31 Baramine et Belles Écailles . . . ⬡ ☐ 5+

32 Croissant Chaud . . . . ⬡ ☐ 6b
1) 6a. Can continue direct for a good 6b+ alternative. 2) 6b

33 Attention Fragile . . . . ⬡ ☐ 6a
1) 6a. Start up *Croissant Chaud.*
2) 6a. Can be done in one long run out.

Cèlise
Sisteron
Volx
Orpierre
Bellecombe
Baume Rousse
Ubrieux
Saint Julien
Saint Léger
Malaucène
Combe Obscure
Les Dentelles
Venasque
Buoux

Vires Rouges

Some brilliant technical wall climbs with some almost-as-good steep slabs to go at. This sector is often more sheltered from the wind than the previous one.

Approach - See page 190 for main approach. This wall is just right of the notch.

15 min | Lots of sun | Vertical | Slabby

The Notch

70m
35m
23
19
25
24
40m
18
23
35m
20m
25
35m
7
30m
20m
2
3
3
2
3
4
16 17
19
20
15
14
23 24 25
13
8 9 10 11 12
1 2
5
6 7
21 22
Vistembo

❶ Rictus	🔆		6c+
❷ L'Enfer des Roudoudous	🔆		6a+
1) 6a+, 2) 6a			
❸ Roudoudous Directos	🔆		6b+
1) 6b, 2) 6b+			
❹ Good Charlotte			?

❺ Fonction Nerf d'Acier	🔆		6c
❻ Georgette à Plat	🔆		7a
❼ Macroscope	🔆		6c+
1) 6c+, 2) 6b+			
❽ Tonton Tictac	🔆		6c

Side tabs: Céüse, Sisteron, Volx, Orpierre, Bellecombe, Baume Rousse, Ubrieux, Saint Julien, Saint Léger, Malaucène, Combe Obscure, Les Dentelles, Venasque, Buoux

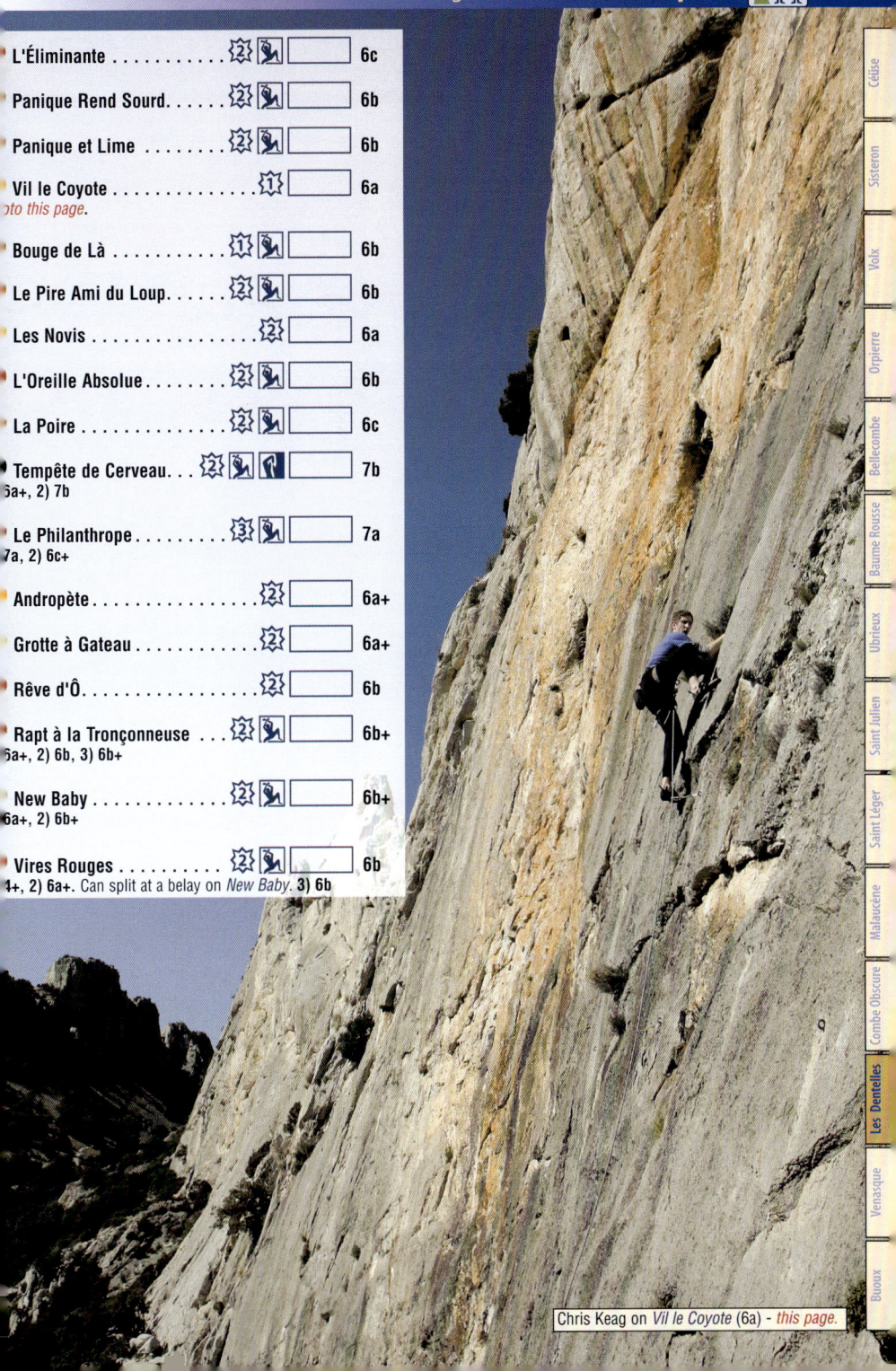

L'Éliminante 6c

Panique Rend Sourd. 6b

Panique et Lime 6b

Vil le Coyote 6a
oto this page.

Bouge de Là 6b

Le Pire Ami du Loup. 6b

Les Novis 6a

L'Oreille Absolue 6b

La Poire 6c

Tempête de Cerveau. . . 7b
6a+, 2) 7b

Le Philanthrope 7a
7a, 2) 6c+

Andropète . . . . 6a+

Grotte à Gateau . . . . 6a+

Rêve d'Ô 6b

Rapt à la Tronçonneuse . . . 6b+
6a, 2) 6b, 3) 6b+

New Baby . . . . 6b+
6a+, 2) 6b+

Vires Rouges 6b
4+, 2) 6a+. Can split at a belay on *New Baby.* **3) 6b**

Chris Keag on *Vil le Coyote* (6a) - *this page.*

Céüse · Sisteron · Volx · Orpierre · Bellecombe · Baume Rousse · Ubrieux · Saint Julien · Saint Léger · Malaucène · Combe Obscure · Les Dentelles · Venasque · Buoux

Céüse
Sisteron
Volx
Orpierre
Bellecombe
Baume Rousse
Ubrieux
Saint Julien
Saint Léger
Malaucène
Combe Obscure
Les Dentelles
Venasque
Buoux

Vistemboir

A justifiably popular sector with a number of good two and three pitch routes that feel quite airy. Bring a 60m rope and lots of quickdraws and you can try and link some of the pitches.

Approach - See page 190 for main approach. Follow the path right along the crag base.

70m

70m

80m

15

14

16

60m

12

13

2 3 5

55m

8

10

60m

1

7

6

5

10

14 16

2 3 4

15

1

30m

8

11

12 13

10

Vires Rouges

10

20m

14

30m

11

14

1

Vires Rouges

9 10

11

14

Nébuleuse

1 Philippus . . . . 6b+
1) 5, 2) 6a, 3) 6b+

The next seven routes all share the first pitch of Phillippus, 5.

2 Ésotéroc . . . . 6b+
1) 5, 2) 6b+, 3) 6a+. There may be a 4th pitch.

3 Bleu Pétrole . . . . 6c+
1) 5, 2) 6b+, 3) 6c+

4 Les Mémoires de Darwin . . 6c
1) 5, 2) 6c

5 Un Minou aux Yeux d'Océan 7a
1) 5, 2) 7a, 3) 6b

6 Rose Bonbon 7a
1) 5, 2) 5+, 3) 7a

7 Piano Postiche 7a
1) 5, 2) 5+, 3) 7a

8 Luna Speed . . . . 6b+
1) 5, 2) 5+, 3) 6b+

9 Viva la Vida 5

10 Vistemboir . . . . 5+
1) 5, 2) 4+, 3) 5+, 4) 5+

11 Égoïne . . . . 5+
1) 4+, 2) 5+

12 Solidarnosc 6a
Approach from *Égoïne*. 1) 5+, 2) 6a

13 Les Conquistadors 6a
Approach from *Égoïne*. 1) 5+, 2) 6a

14 Mégalomane Gaga 6b
1) 6b, 2) 4+, 3) 6a, 4) 6a+

15 Mégalomane 6b
1) and 2) as for *Mégalomane Gaga*. 3) 6a, 4) 6b

16 Bénédetti . . . . 6a+
1) 5+, 2) 6a+, 3) 6a

Céüse

Sisteron

Voix

Orpierre

Bellecombe

Baume Rousse

Ubrieux

Saint Julien

Saint Léger

Malaucène

Combe Obscure

Les Dentelles

Venasque

Buoux

Craig Entwistle on *Au Pays du Soleil Brûlant* (6c) - *page 215*
Mont Ventoux can be seen in the distance.

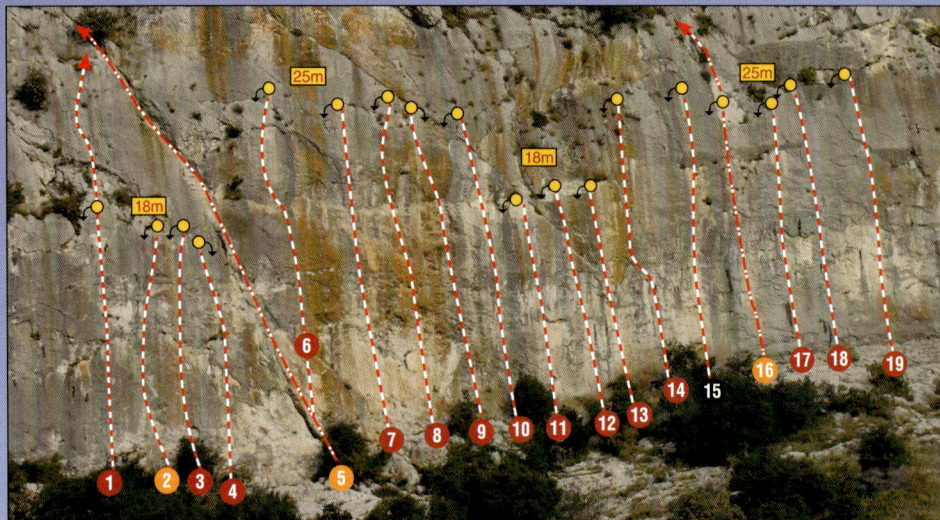

① **Mélomane Gaga (P1)** . . . . ⚡2️⃣ ☐ 6b
Three more pitches - see previous page.

② **No Comment** . . . . ☐ 6a+

③ **Mon Capo** . . . . ☐ 6b

④ **Unanime** . . . . ☐ 6c+

⑤ **Bénédetti (P1)** . . . . ⚡2️⃣ ☐ 5+
Three more pitches - see previous page.

⑥ **Hymnosens** . . . . ⚡1️⃣ ☐ 6b

⑦ **L'Enfant de Sable** . . . . ⚡1️⃣ ☐ 6b

⑧ **Karsherigène** . . . . ⚡1️⃣ ☐ 6b

⑨ **Tintin au Bidet** . . . . ⚡1️⃣ 🧗 ☐ 7a

⑩ **La Planète aux Scorpions** . . . . 🧗 ☐ 7a

⑪ **Camouflage** . . . . 🧗 ☐ 7a

⑫ **C'était un Roaw** . . . . 🧗 ☐ 7a

⑬ **Full Double Full** . . . . ☐ 6c

⑭ **On l'Appelle Fossile** . . . . 🧗 ☐ 7a

⑮ **Urgence du Pire** . . . . ⚡1️⃣ 🧗 ☐ 7a

⑯ **Pébroune** . . . . ⚡1️⃣ ☐ 6a
The route continues for two pitches on old gear.

Chagrin d'Humeur
Page 208

The Notch

Vires Rouges
Page 210

Nébuleuse
A wide wall with mostly single pitch routes that don't get a huge amount of attention. The quality generally improves as you move further to the right.
Approach - See page 190 for main approach.
Follow the path right along the crag base.

Plume		6b+
Rire en Dedans		6c
Le Zan		6c
Le Zain.		6b+
Ultimatum.		7a
La Vie au Chon		7a+
Nébuleuse (P1)		6a+
route continues for four pitches on old gear.		
La Loi du Caniveau		6b
Germinal		6c
Les Démons du Temps Immobile		7a

27 Le Local Loco		7a+
28 Profenator.		7a
29 Tous des Gosses		7a
30 Au Pays du Soleil Brûlant		6c
Photo on page 213.		
31 Gogol Blues		7a+
32 Sacrépuscule		6c+
33 Le Zèbre.		7a
34 Hula Hop		7b
35 Le Marquis		7b+
36 Le Lélo.		7b
37 Crise d'Autorité		7c

Nébuleuse

Gillou
Page 216

Lune de Miel
Page 218

Blocus
Page 220

Céüse

Sisteron

Volx

Orpierre

Bellecombe

Baume Rousse

Ubrieux

Saint Julien

Saint Léger

Malaucène

Combe Obscure

Les Dentelles

Venasque

Buoux

1 Petit Vérin 7b

2 Détour au Purgatore . . . 7b+

3 Masculin Singulier 7c

4 Bassora Fiesta 7c

5 La Transformation du Boulanger
. . . . 8a

6 Pas de Doute 7c

7 Osmose . . . .

8 Moxita 8a

9 Ticket Pour un Aller Simple
. . . . 7c+

Gillou

The most impressive sector at the Dentelles with plenty of big, steep, hard routes to choose from if you are up to them. Sheltered from the rain, the routes here tend to s well-chalked-up, making them look all the more inviting.
Approach - See page 190 for main approach.
Follow the path right along the crag base.

75m

30m

32m

20m

20m

30m

Nébuleuse

Regards de Profanes . . 🪙🧗🔧 [ ] 8a+

Over the Topinambours . 🪙🧗🔧 [ ] 8a+
+ to the first belay.

Rien à Cirer . . . . 🪙🧗🔧 [ ] 7c

Ocunu Beach. . . . . . . 🪙🧗🔧 [ ] 7a+

Outrage . . . . 🪙🧗🔧 [ ] 7c+?

Est-Ouest . . . . 🪙🧗🔧 [ ] 7a+

Saddam Kiki . . . . [ ] 7b

Gillou. . . . . 🪙🧗🔧 [ ] 7c
more pitches can be climbed at **5+**, **A1** if you want to get to
op of the wall.

⓲ C'était un Petit Bonheur 🪙🧗🔧 [ ] 7b+
The original start is up the previous route. The start shown is
Garagiste aux Mains Blanches, the grade is unchanged.

⓳ Tam-Tam . . . . 🪙🧗 [ ] 7b

⓴ Complicité d'un Paradoxe . . 🪙🧗 [ ] 8b

㉑ Le Lézard de Balthazar . 🪙🧗🔧 [ ] 7c

㉒ Bird's Beach . . . . 🪙🧗🔧 [ ] 7b+

㉓ J'ai Deux Amours. . . . . 🪙🧗🔧 [ ] 7b+

㉔ Gigondas New York . . . 🪙🧗🔧 [ ] 7b

㉕ Ça Cracotte . . . . 🪙🧗🔧 [ ] 7c

㉖ Poisson d'Avril . . . . . . 🪙🧗🔧 [ ] 7b

20 min | Lots of sun | Vertical | Steep | Dry in the rain

30m

12m

20m

Lune de Miel

16 17 18 19 20 21 22 23 24 25 26

Sidebar tabs: Céüse, Sisteron, Volx, Orpierre, Bellecombe, Baume Rousse, Ubrieux, Saint Julien, Saint Léger, Malaucène, Combe Obscure, Les Dentelles, Venasque, Buoux

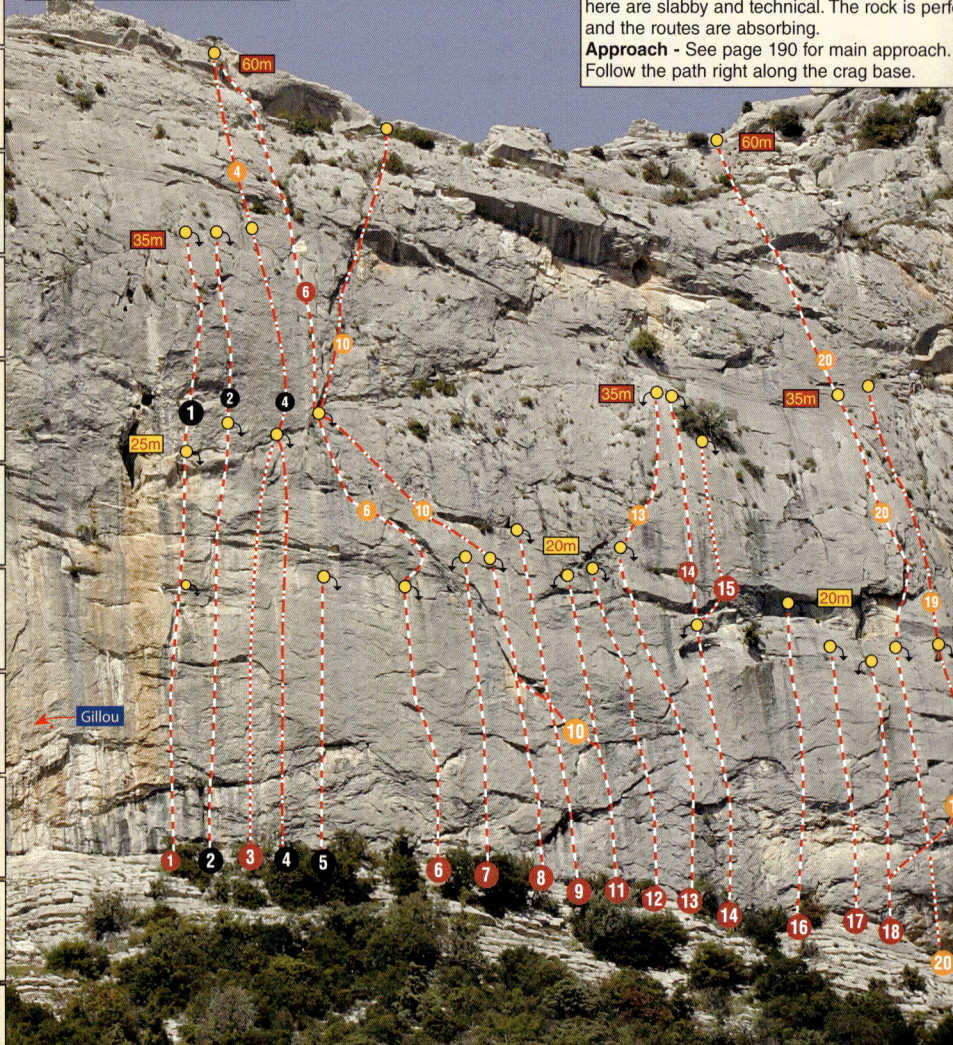

Lune de Miel

In sharp contrast to the wall to the left, the rout[...]
here are slabby and technical. The rock is perfe[...]
and the routes are absorbing.
Approach - See page 190 for main approach.
Follow the path right along the crag base.

❶ Loin de la Foule . . . . ☼ 🧗 ⬜ 7a+
1) 7a. Continue past the first belay. 2) 7a+

❷ Petits Doigts de Fée . . . ☼ 🧗 🪢 7b+
1) 7b, 2) 7b+

❸ Amis des Îles . . . . ☼ 🧗 ⬜ 7a

❹ Mini Prises, Maxi Vols ☼ 🧗 🪢 7b
1) 7b, 2) 7b, 3) 5+

❺ Invitation à la Danse . . ☼ 🧗 🪢 7b

❻ La Ballade du Mahabhartata ☼ 🧗 ⬜ 6b
1) 6b+, 2) 6a+, 3) 6b

❼ Les Chemins du Merveilleux ☼ 🧗 ⬜ 6c

❽ Courte Échelle . . . . ☼ 🧗 ⬜ 6b

❾ Crénoline . . . . ☼ 🧗 ⬜ 6b

❿ Lune de Miel . . . . ☼ 6a
1) 6a+, 2) 6a, 3) 6a. *Photo opposite.*

⓫ Tétanos . . . . ☼ 🧗 ⬜ 6c
Look out for bees.

Opéra Roc.	🏴	🧗		6c+
Logos	🏴	🧗		6b+
9+, 2) 6a				
Vertigo	🏴2	🧗		6b+
9+, 2) 6b				
Sueurs Froides	🏴	🧗		6b+
9+. As for *Vertigo*. 2) 6a				
Fée Folette	🏴	🧗		6c
Lagagne	🏴	🧗		6b+
Sacrilège	🏴	🧗		6b+
Supernova	🏴			6a+
a+, 2) 6a				
Mandragore	🏴			6a+
a, 2) 5+, 3) 5+				

Andy Gudgeon on pitch one of *Lune de Miel* (6a+) - *opposite*.

Céüse
Sisteron
Veaux
Orpierre
Bellecombe
Baume Rousse
Ubrieux
Saint Julien
Saint Léger
Malaucène
Combe Obscure
Les Dentelles
Venasque
Buoux

Blocus

A concentration of great slab routes, the best of which run for two pitches or more.

Approach - See page 190 for main approach. Follow the path right along the crag base.

1 Perverse Dévers	6c
2 Malpertuis	6c+
3 La Nova	6a+
1) 5+. Start up *Nucléus* to maintain the grade. 2) 5+, 3) 6a+	
4 Coup de Boule	6b+
1) 6c+. Start up *Malpertuis*. 2) 6b+	
5 Une Ideée en l'Air	6b

6 Nucléus	5-
7 La Berlue	5
8 Sans Issue	5-
9 Soupçons	5
10 Picots de Rose	6a
1) 5, 2) 5+, 3) 6a	

L'Ombre d'un Doute . . . . 5+

Agadir Rien à Dire 6a

L'art à Croft 6b

Pigne de Coucou . . . . 6b+

Rêve de Singe 6a
1, 2) 5+

Les Vautours 6a
-, 2) 5, 3) 6a

Gueule de Loup . . . . 5+

Italian Shoes . . . . 6a+
1+, 2) 5+

Turbostyle . . . . 6b+
1+, 2) 5

Pinpin et Yéyé 6b

Gargolot 6b
1, 2) 5+

Scorpigouille 6a
1, 2) 5+

Douce Romance . . . . 5+
-, 2) 5+

Histoire d'Aulx . . . . 6a+
1+, 2) 5+

Pilier Central Direct 6b
-, 2) 5+, 3) 6b

Dernier Tango au Clapis 6a
1, 2) 6a

Tango Direct . . . . 6a+

Mad Max 6b
1, 2) 6a

Blocus 6a
1, 2) 6a, 3) 5

Roc d'Azur 6a

Extrême Droit . . . . 5+
1, 2) 5+

next route is started by scrambling up an easy ramp to the
r right-hand side of the wall.

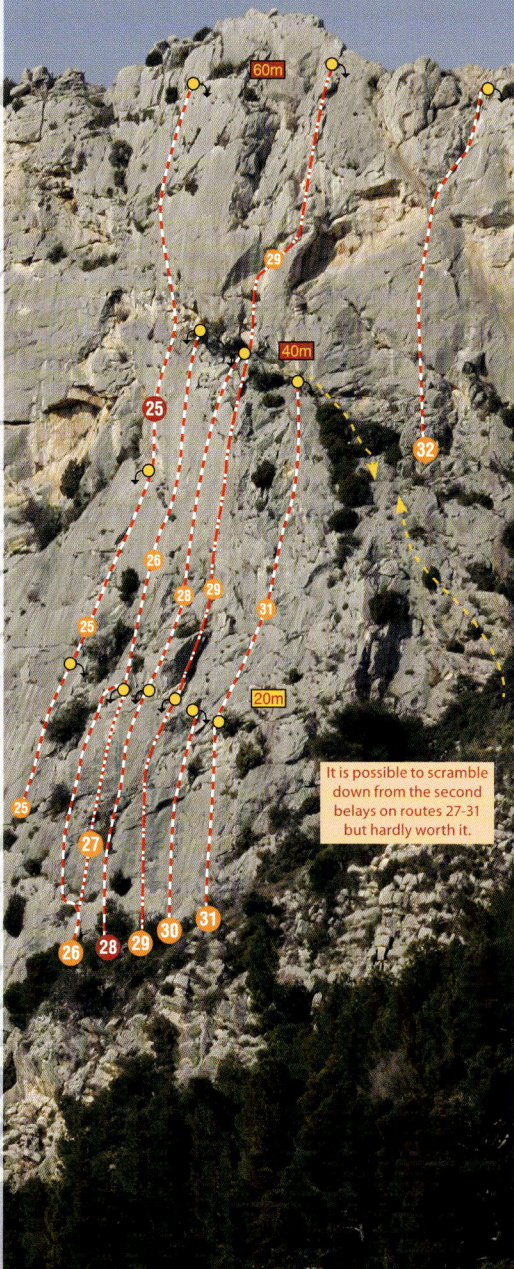

Hugo Délire . . . . 5+

Céüse
Sisteron
Volx
Orpierre
Bellecombe
Baume Rousse
Ubrieux
Saint Julien
Saint Léger
Malaucène
Combe Obscure
Les Dentelles
Venasque
Buoux

It is possible to scramble
down from the second
belays on routes 27-31
but hardly worth it.

Further to the right, there is a notch in the crag where
the wind often whistles through. Beyond here the
development is much less evident, though the rock is
good. The areas to the right are seasonally restricted
and not covered in this guide.

Saint Christophe

Céüse
Sisteron
Volx
Orpierre
Bellecombe
Baume Rousse
Ubrieux
Saint Julien
Saint Léger
Malaucène
Combe Obscure
Les Dentelles
Venasque
Buoux

Tyrolienne
Page 228

Cascade
Page 224

Le Grand Toit
Page 226

Saint Christophe
Page 230

Cèüse

Sisteron

Volx

Orpierre

Bellecombe

Baume Rousse

Ubrieux

Saint Julien

Saint Léger

Malaucène

Combe Obscure

Les Dentelles

Venasque

Buoux

5 min | Lots of sun | Vertical | Slabby | Multi-pitch

Tyrolienne - above

55m

45m

35m

30m

30m

4

7

16

30m

17

18

4

12m

7

15m

18

16

20

19

1

2

3

5

6

8

9

10

11

12

13

14

15

Le Grand Toit

Cascade

A sheltered, sunny spot with a collection of routes covering the gr[a] spectrum. The low grade slabby pitches at the base of the wall are popular with groups, so if there's a minibus at the parking area, you m find it wise to move onto somewhe else if you're looking for 4s and 5s.
Approach - See page 190.
From the limited parking on the be[n] follow the road which almost leads the base of the crag. A path leads under the wall from here.

Gougniaffier . . . . ☐ 6a+

Quelques Gouttes. . . . ☐ 6a

Les Pieds dans le Plat ☐ 6b

Pékin . . . . ☐ 7c
. Continue on from *Les Pieds...* 2) 6c

Mort aux Dents . . . . . ☐ 6a

Les Ratasi . . . . ☐ 6a+

Unknown. . . . . ☐ 7a+
+, 2) 7a+

Dièdre a Sec . . . . ☐ 5

Restosec. . . . . ☐ 5+

Alexandra . . . . ☐ 5

Sale Verdure . . . . ☐ 4

Pascal le Rappeur . . . ☐ 4

Rideau de Pluie. . . . . ☐ 5

Adheresec. . . . . ☐ 6a

Concrétion . . . . ☐ 5+

*ext three routes start up one of the easier
pitches.*

Unknown . ☐ 7b+
+, 2) 7b

Unknown. . ☐ 8a
e 7c+ to the first belay.

Unknown. . ☐ 7c

Project . . . . ☐ ?

La Main Droite du Diable
. . . . ☐ 8b

Unknown. . . . . ☐ 8b

Unknown. . . . . ☐ 8b

Unknown. . . . . ☐ ?

Unknown. . . . . ☐ ?

Tarvava . . . . ☐ 7b+

Unknown. . . . . ☐ 7b

27 Unknown. . . . . ☐ 7a+

28 Dièdre des Cascades . . . . . ☐ 6b+
1) 6b+, 2) 6a

29 Unknown. . . . . ☐ 7a
1) 7a, 2) 6c+

30 Unknown. . . . . ☐ 6b+
A finish to the *Dièdre des Cascades*.

Cascade

25m

25m

Approach the roof routes from here

① Unknown. 6a

② Unknown. 6c

③ Unknown. . . . . 6a+

④ Unknown. . . . . 7b+

⑤ Unknown. . . . . ?

⑥ Comme une mouche. . . . 8b
The centre of the huge roof.

⑦ Unknown. . . . . 7c+

⑧ Unknown. . . . . ?

⑨ Unknown. . . . . 7a+

⑩ Unknown. 7b

⑪ Unknown. 7b
Start up the previous route.

⑫ Unknown. 7b

⑬ Unknown. 7b
Start up the previous route.

⑭ Unknown. 7b

⑮ Unknown. 7

⑯ Unknown. 6

⑰ Unknown. 7

⑱ Unknown. 6

⑲ Drole De Brame. 6
There is a mid-height lower-off. Climb left of the upper roof.

⑳ Unknown. 7
The same lower-off is passed on the right. This one tackles the left-hand edge of the big roof.

The last four routes are on the foreshortened right-hand side the topo.

㉑ Thick + Soft. 6
Climb up to a hanging corner then follow the bolts out left.

㉒ Unknown. 6
Start up the previous route but go direct from the corner.

㉓ Pek Machine 6
The next line is fairly direct.

㉔ Unknown. 6
Start up *Pek Machine* and break out right.

Céüse
Sisteron
Volx
Orpierre
Bellecombe
Baume Rousse
Ubrieux
Saint Julien
Saint Léger
Malaucène
Combe Obscure
Les Dentelles
Venasque
Buoux

Le Grand Toit

The right-hand side of the Cascade area has a huge roof and some good blocky walls crossed by a series of horizontal breaks. The routes here tend to be short and powerful. It is a bit of a sun-trap but good in the winter.
Approach - See page 190.
From the limited parking on the bend, follow the road which almost leads to the base of the crag. A path leads off under the wall from here.

Céüse
Sisteron
Volx
Orpierre
Bellecombe
Baume Rousse
Ubrieux
Saint Julien
Saint Léger
Malaucène
Combe Obscure
Les Dentelles
Venasque
Buoux

5 min | Lots of sun | Slabby | Vertical

10m

15m

Tyrolienne

Just below the parking for Saint Christophe, Tyrolienne is a sort of miniature crag. The rock is good, but the routes are very short. A good, low-stress venue for novices.
Approach - See page 190.
From the upper parking, below St. Christoph, follow a short path to the clifftop, then descend down the left-hand side (looking in) of the crag to reach the base.

1 La Ragoût Tonton 3

2 L'Escagasse . . . . 4+

3 Les Filochons . . . . 6a+

4 La Mémé de là-Haut 5

5 À Fleur de Roc 6b

6 Giani . . . . 6a+

7 Désolé si J'Imisse 6a

8 Parpinasse à Gogo 6a

9 Vendage en Délire . . . . 5+

10 La Marc à Pinard 5

11 La Piquette 5

12 La Muscat d'Ici 5

13 La Fougasse 5
Photo opposite.

14 Mulot Intrépide 4

15 Les Blaireaux 5

16 Gaston 6

17 Salino 6

18 Les Escoubilles 6

10m

8m

13 14 15 16 17 18 19 20 21 22 23 24 25 26 27

Take care - big drop below!

Cascade

Céüse
Sisteron
Volx
Orpierre
Bellecombe
Baume Rousse
Ubrieux
Saint Julien
Saint Léger
Malaucène
Combe Obscure
Les Dentelles
Venasque
Buoux

Les Coucougnettes à Monsieur Bean			6b
Les Mollets de Daniel			5+
Morgan Aussi	☼		4+
Gratte-Cul	☼		5
Chibrette	☼		5
Figue Molle			4
Unnamed			4
Unnamed			4
Unnamed			4

Chris Keag on *La Fougasse* (5+) - *opposite.*

2 min Lots of sun Vertical Multi-pitch

Saint Christophe

An attractive roadside venue with a range of good
one and two-pitch routes on very good rock. The cr
is quite exposed, so best avoided on windy days.
Approach - See page 190.
A path leads direct from the upper parking to the cr

45m
35m
25m
18m
20m
35m

9 11 12 14 15 29 26 12 16 17 18 19 14 13

1 2 3 4 5 6 7 8 9 10 11

❶ Silence on Tourne 6b

❷ Canicule 6c

❸ É Té Ouf Toa 7a

❹ La Démission du Pachyderme . . 6c

❺ Oxygène 7a

❻ Le Phaléne . . . . 7a+

❼ Photographie Tendresse 7b

❽ Télé-Ragot . . . . 7a+
Finsh left or right.

❾ Orphée 6c
1) 6c+, 2) 6a+

❿ Éleusis 6c
You can extend it by continuing to join *Gilky*.

⓫ Gilky 6b
1) 6b+, 2) 6b+

⓬ Le Grand Méchant Look . . . 7a
1) 7a, 2) 6b

⓭ Citron Pressé 7a

⓮ Béatitude 6b
1) 6b+, 2) 6b+

Délicate et Zen 7a

God Bless You 6c

You Want Transport . . . . ?

Big Blair le Maléfique 7a

Le Dame de Flair 6b
o on page 21.

M.M. Charasse 6a

Tout est Bon a Prendre 7a

Génération Nictout 6c

L'Étrange Mutisme de l'Éolienne
. . . . 6c+

Kali Koba . . . . 7a+

En Route Pour Technotitlan
. . . . 7c

Le Forçat de Sainte Hélène 7b+

27 Amadorix et Clef au Plâtre
. . . . 7b

28 La Tautologie de Jacques 7b

29 Le Magicien d'Oz 7b

30 La Fraise des Doigts . . 7a+

31 Si Gargot Scie . . . . 7a+

32 La Rondeur des Jours 6c

33 Poison d'Avril 6a

34 Le Caprice des Vieux 6a

35 La Bidule . . . . 5+

36 Truc Mush 6a
Gain from the right or via *La Bidule*.

37 La Voie est Libre . . . . 6b+

38 Merci Nature . . . . ?

Les Dentelles de Montmirail

Malaucène

Malaucène

D974

Montbrun-les-Bains

Orange

Gigondas

Beaumes
de Venise

Mont Ventoux
(1909m)

Bédoin

Combe Obscure

D950

D938

Sault

Carpentras

Malemort du Comtat

D943

Venasque

Pernes-les-
Fontaines

Venasque

D4

A7

TGV

Avignon

D31

D938

Gordes

Apt

Châteaurenard

D900

Buoux

D943

Cavaillon

Bonnieux

N

Plan-d'Orgon

About 20km

Celse

Sisteron

Volx

Orpierre

Bellecombe

Baume Rousse

Ubrieux

Saint Julien

Saint Léger

Malaucène

Combe Obscure

Les Dentelles

Venasque

Buoux

Gaz Parry climbing *Chouca* (8a+) - *page 287* - at Buoux. Photo: David Simmonite.

The Buoux Area

Venasque - Buoux

though not right next to each other (around km apart) the climbing at Venasque and oux is very complimentary. The slopers Venasque are a perfect antidote to the cket-pulling fatigue that is an inevitable nsequence of spending too much time at oux.

etting there and getting around

ignon is on a direct TGV route from Paris, d Buoux is about an hour's drive from ere. There is a regular bus service from ignon to Apt, and around Easter there are ually plenty of climbers driving into Buoux ch day. If arriving by car, the A7 Autoroute Soleil allows access from the west, and e A51 allows access from the east. If riving by air, the closest major airports are mes, Marseille and Toulon.

here to stay

ou are dividing time between Buoux and nasque, you will probably spend more time Buoux, so it makes sense to base yourself Apt. The nearest campsite to Venasque n Malemort-du-Comtat (**Camping Font uve**) but there are also three campsites around Pernes-les-Fontaines, and one in Carpentras. For Buoux, the municipal campsite in Apt (**Les Cédres**) is walking distance from the shops and even has its own climbing wall. Some prefer the quieter setting of **Bonnieux** where the municipal campsite is also climber-friendly. The **Auberge des Seguins** is right under the crag of Buoux if you're looking for convenience and a little more comfort.

Local guidebooks

The **Buoux** guide (€20) is available from the campsites.

Web links

www.camping-les-cedres.fr
www.aubergedesseguins.com

Quinsan
Page 238

Céüse

Sisteron

Volx

Orpierre

Bellecombe

Baume Rousse

Ubrieux

Saint Julien

Saint Léger

Malaucène

Combe Obscure

Les Dentelles

Venasque

Buoux

Venasque

Place de l'Ascle
Page 242

Cèdise

Sisteron

Volx

Orpierre

Bellecombe

Baume Rousse

Ubrieux

Saint Julien

Saint Léger

Malaucène

Combe Obscure

Les Dentelles

Venasque

Buoux

	No star	⟨1⟩	⟨2⟩	⟨
Up to 4+	-	-	-	
5 to 6a+	13	9	1	
6b to 7a	7	35	17	
7a+ and up	5	13	9	

One of the least known areas in this guide, Venasque has a concentration of very high quality routes with very short approaches. The routes vary from those which are technical, vertical and festooned with slopers to jaw-droppingly steep walls with long sustained climbs. This is generally a shady spot but you can get some sun if you get there early enough in the day.

There are many more crags than described here, though a lot of the crags at Venasque are on private land and remain undeveloped. For three other developed areas, you may be able to acquire the local topo at the tourist information office in the town of Venasque, but this is closed off-season.

Approach

From either Venasque or the D4, follow the D247 south in the direction of Le Beaucet. A number of crags can be seen on the right. After about 1km, just beyond a bend, an unsigned minor road leads off to the left. To get to Quinsan take this turning and follow the road until a small parking area is found on the left. The path leads up opposite and splits at a bolted-on wooden sign allowing direct access to the left or right ends of the crag. To get to Place de l'Ascle continue driving to where a track leads off to the right just before the road meets the cliff. It is very easy to miss this turning, so slow right down when you see the road getting close to the rock.

More crags

Carpentras

D4

D247

Venasque

Place de l'Ascle

Quinsan

P

P

Le Beaucet

GPS *(N) 43°59'6.44" (E) 5° 8'43.00"*
GPS *(N) 43°59'9.63" (E) 5° 8'29.38"*

About 1km

Conditions

Quinsan gets some sun in the morning but is in the shade otherwise. In hot weather the shade will be welcome, but in the winter it will probably be too cold for comfort. Place de l'Ascle is a lot sunnier than Quinsan, though much of it falls into the shade in the afternoon. The starts of the routes are heavily sheltered by trees so whatever time of day you will probably have a shady belay spot.

Mont Ventoux from Venasque

Céüse

Sisteron

Volx

Orpierre

Bellecombe

Baume Rousse

Ubrieux

Saint Julien

Saint Léger

Malaucène

Combe Obscure

Les Dentelles

Venasque

Buoux

Craig Entwistle on *Petite Marie* (6c+) - *page 243*

1 Illustrator 6b

2 Magazine . . . . 6c+

3 Profil . . . . 7a+

4 Project . . . . ?

5 Ticket Repas . . . . 7b+

6 L'État de Grace . . . . 6b+

7 Macintosh 7a

8 Gangster d'Armour . . . . 7a+

9 Hyper Brown . . . . 6a+

10 Téchnofrite . . . . 7a+

11 Biodynamique 7a

12 1992 . . . . 7a

13 Virus 6c

14 Baby Relax . . . . 6b+
The rightwards-trending corner.

15 Nerveux S'Abstenir . . . . . . 6b+

16 Le Clan 7b
The rounded arete.

The next two routes are on the side wall.

17 Tube 7a

18 La Compil 6c

19 Jour Pour Jour 6c
The striking corner.

20 Action 7a

21 Séquence Passion 6b

22 Nicotine & Goudron 6c

23 Microcosme 6b
The inviting corner.

24 Le Pilier de Aléas 7a
Another corner, less inviting this time.

25 Les Arts Ménagers 6b

26 Unnamed 6a
A line of newer expansion bolts.

Side tabs (top to bottom): Céüse, Sisteron, Volx, Orpierre, Bellecombe, Baume Rousse, Ubrieux, Saint Julien, Saint Léger, Malaucène, Combe Obscure, Les Dentelles, Venasque, Buoux

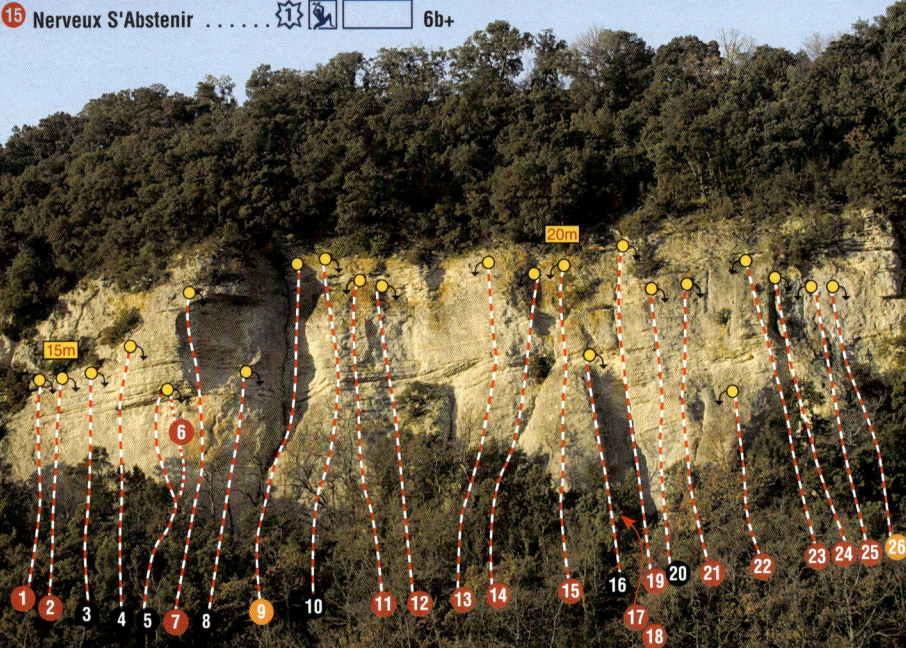

Exercise de Lecture . . . . 1 ☐ 6b

Gin Tonic . . . . ☐ 7b

Trop Uelie Pour Toi . . . . . . ☐ 7a
stunning crack.

Lucky 13 . . . . ☐ 6c

Dérapage Controlée . . . . . . ☐ 7a

Atha . . . . ☐ 6c+

Spormidable . . . . ☐ 6c

Ouvrez le Feu . . . . ☐ 6c
open corner and wall above.

Bad Dance . . . . 1 ☐ 7a+

20 Métres au Paradis . . 2 ☐ 7a

37 Kéksék Ksa? . . . . 2 ☐ 6b

38 Jazz Time . . . . 1 ☐ 6b+

39 Retour de Spectacle . . . . ☐ 6a+

40 La Mouche . . . . ☐ 6b

41 Urban Jungle . . . . ☐ 6b+

42 Little Big Man . . . . ☐ 6b+

43 Sympathy for the Devil . . . . ☐ 7b

44 Envie de Toi . . . . ☐ 6c
Start just right of the amazing cairn and follow the groove.

Quinsan

Apart from early in the morning, Quinsan doesn't get much in the way of sun - so a good venue for when you're chasing the shade.

Céüse · Sisteron · Volx · Orpierre · Bellecombe · Baume Rousse · Ubrieux · Saint Julien · Saint Léger · Malaucène · Combe Obscure · Les Dentelles · Venasque · Buoux

1 Mauvais Coup . . . . 7a+

2 Allo Mamanm Boseettes . . . . ?

3 Acromégalie 7a

4 Plat de Résistance 7b
The distinctive brown groove to start, then the grey bulge.

5 On n'est pas des Zéros . . . . . . 6c+

6 Amicalement Vôtre 6b

7 Rockland . . . . 7a+

8 Silencers . . . . 7a+

9 La Déchirure 7b

10 Jeu de Paume 7a

11 Platine 7b

12 Platonique 6c

13 Nulle Part Ailleurs 6c

14 Papy Bosseur 6c

15 Déclaration de fin de Chatier . . . . . ?

16 Mamie Brossa 7a

17 Faut pas en Faire un Plat 6c

18 L'Astronaute 6b

19 Pleine Lune. 6b

Envei de Toi

Craig Entwistle on *33 Huit* (6b+) - *page 243*

Céüse

Sisteron

Volx

Orpierre

Bellecombe

Baume Rousse

Ubrieux

Saint Julien

Saint Léger

Malaucène

Combe Obscure

Les Dentelles

Venasque

Buoux

Routes 31 -
35 are start
from a led
accessed b
knotted ro.

Place de l'Ascle - Left

brilliant collection of routes covering a range of climbing m steep, sustained jug-pulling up impressive orange lls, through to slabby technical offerings that are always the shade. The wall is right next to the road but it is ually very quiet.

Les Vilains Petits Canards . 　　　　　**7a**
eep start then move out left from the crack at the third clip.

Power Flower . . . . 　　　　**7a**
ve out of the crack to the right at the third clip.

33 Huit . . . . 　　　　**6b+**
to on page 241.

Allo? Colchita? . . . . 　　　　**6c**
over the ditch to start then follow the right-hand line of bolts.

Hasta Siempre. . . . . 　　**6b+**
t as for *Allo? Colchita?* then traverse out right after the third and climb the groove.

Sirocco . . . . 　　**7a+**
t down in the ditch and follow either line of bolts to finish.

Elle Chante dans le Vent . . . 　　　　**7b+**
lder onto the ledge and follow the leaning wall. Probably best et a belay from the ledge and avoid the rope drag.

Les Petits Qui Frétillent . . . 　　　　**7b**
illiant uncompromising line, mind out for the bird's nest.

Aller Plus Haut . . . . 　　　　**7b+**
ther brilliant line with fewer rests, a couple of smaller holds, mostly jugs all the way.

Misanthropies Thérapeutiques 　　　　**7b**
uably the best line of the crag straight up the middle of the wall.

Champ du Possible . . . 　　　　　　**7b+**
od link-up. Start as for *Vole* then move left after the third bolt ollow bolts into the finish of *Misanthropies Thérapeutiques*.

Vole . . . . 　　　　　　**7b**

Petite Marie . . . . 　　**6c+**
king line just left of the arete with several good rests along the . Photo on page 237.

Blacks Blancs Beurs . . . . . . 　　　　**6c+**
right side of the arete. A different style of route from those s left.

Unknown. . . . . 　　**?**
k-up starting up *Rêves Brulés* and finishing as for *Blacks cs Beurs*.

16 Rêves Brulés. . . . . 　　**6a+**
Take a line just left of the prominent crack.

17 Lasissons les Dire . . . . 　　**6a**

18 Beacuoup de Bruit Pour Rien. . . 　　**6a+**

19 Jusqu'au Bout . . . . 　　**6a+**

The following five routes are above the worn steps in the gully. The routes are short and always shady. A popular walk passes through here so mind out for walkers.

20 Le Moldus au Balcon . . . . 　　**6a**
Follow the arete, moving left to the belay.

21 Camino de Piedra . . . . 　　**6a**
Start 1m right of the previous route, which it soon joins.

22 Con la Luz. . . . . 　　　　**6a**
Short steep and juggy. Worth a start for the novelty.

23 Mieux Vaut en Rire . . . . 　　**6a**
Several metres right of the previous route.

24 À la Fraîche . . . . 　　**6a**

25 GaMeuBuZo . . . . 　　**5+**

26 Mauvais Virus . . . . 　　**6b+**

27 Je Reviens Demain . . . . 　　**6a+**

28 Jumbo Appetite . . . . 　　**6c**

29 Cap Chevalier . . . . 　　**6a+**

30 Unknown. . . . . 　　**5**

The following six routes start from a ledge, which is accessed via a knotted rope. They are quite recent additions and may take a little while to clean up. They are short but interesting, not unlike English gritstone but with plenty of bolts.

31 Unknown. . . . . 　　**5**

32 Unknown. . . . . 　　**5**

33 Unknown. . . . . 　　**5+**

34 Unknown. . . . . 　　**6a**

35 Unknown. . . . . 　　**6a**

Céüse Sisteron Volx Orpierre Bellecombe Baume Rousse Ubrieux Saint Julien Saint Léger Malaucène Combe Obscure Les Dentelles Venasque Buoux

Céüse
Sisteron
Volx
Orpierre
Bellecombe
Baume Rousse
Ubrieux
Saint Julien
Saint Léger
Malaucène
Combe Obscure
Les Dentelles
Venasque
Buoux

Place de l'Ascle - Right

The right side of the crag is characterised by a series of closely-packed routes up sloping holds on vertical rock followed by the final 'must see' wall that is the epitome of a sport crag and a 'must climb' venue for those with the requisite arms and motivation.

1 Sur la Route . . . . 6b?

2 Duel Végétale . . . . 6a+

3 La Dame du Lac 6c

4 La Partie Continue 6a
A real gem at this grade.

5 Play-List . . . . 6b+

6 Chez Francis 6c
Some tough moves to get the the first bolt.

7 Tireur d'Élite 6c

8 Le Quart d'Heure Américain . . . 6b

9 Allô?! La Terre 6c-
On the side wall.

10 Fête de Pères 7a

11 Trésor Caché 7b

12 Blédina Carotte 7b

13 La Restanque 6c
The steep extension is **7a+**.

Célise

Sisteron

Volx

Orpierre

Bellecombe

Baume Rousse

Ubrieux

Saint Julien

Saint Léger

Malaucène

Combe Obscure

Les Dentelles

Venasque

Buoux

Boule de Calin. 7a

Eh Tardado Mucho 7a

Mise au Vert . . . . 6b+

Terminator 6b

Colère de Lait . . . . 5+
or start, it improves a bit, then it finishes.

Feu . . . . 6a+

Sortie Ouest . . . . 6a+
up the vegetated runnel.

Bézingougne . . . . 7a+

22 L'Intégrale de Peuterey . . . 7b
Continue up the wild extension at **7b+**.

23 Aprés Moi le Déluge. . . . . . 7c+
Continue past the first belay.

24 Unknown. . . . . 7c+

25 Ça Ira Mieux Demain 7c

26 Lou Gardeù . . . . 7c+

27 Unknown. 8a
Use the hanging rope to get onto the holds.

28 Merci d'Être Passé. . . . 8a+

29 Roule Bamboule 8b
Two metal steps lead into the action.

La Derive
Page 250

Autoroute
Page 253

La No - DSF
Page 254 to 259

GVB - PGF
Page 260 to 263

Les Diamants
Page 266

Excalibur
Page 270

Les Diamants
Page 266

Pilier des Fourmis
Page 274

Céüse

Sisteron

Volx

Orpierre

Bellecombe

Baume Rousse

Ubrieux

Saint Julien

Saint Léger

Malaucène

Combe Obscure

Les Dentelles

Venasque

Buoux

Buoux

Styx Wall
Page 282

TCF
Page 278

Cédise

Sisteron

Volx

Orpierre

Bellecombe

Baume Rousse

Ubrieux

Saint Julien

Saint Léger

Malaucène

Combe Obscure

Les Dentelles

Venasque

Buoux

	No star	✵	✵✵	✵
Up to 4+	3	1	-	
5 to 6a+	8	22	28	
6b to 7a	1	21	101	
7a+ and up	2	27	81	

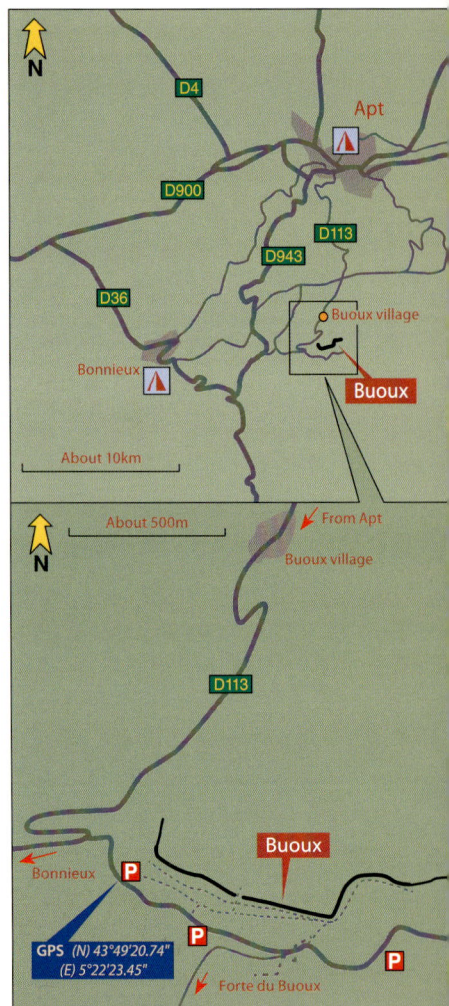

Buoux (pronounced "*bee-you-ks*") is the pocket-pulling capital - a mixture of limestone and sandstone, the rock has a dazzling array of pockets, some tiny, some huge - in Buoux even the pockets have pockets in them! In other words it helps to like pockets if you climb here. It isn't all pockets though since the red and brown rock gives even more variety, especially on the middle section of the cliff.

For a while, the word 'Buoux' was synonymous the golden age of sport climbing, and an icon of sport climbing itself. Sadly though, it became a victim of its own success when sections of the cliff were banned due to cheapskate climbers dossing and polluting the woods around the crag. These access difficulties have now been resolved but it goes without saying that climbers still need to show respect and behave sensibly.

Approach

In the town of Apt, follow the D900 east through the town, by the river, until you reach a tree-lined car park just before a large Intermarché supermarket. Turn left here (signed 'Buoux') and follow the signs through the one-way system, past the Gendarmerie, and out on the D113 to the village of Buoux. Pass through the village and continue for a short distance to a left turn on a bend. The first parking area is found up this road on the left, just after a corner. A little further on is another parking area on the right. The first two parking areas are well-placed for climbing at the sectors on the left side of the crag (La Derive to Les Diamants). The next parking area is reserved for visitors to the Fort, but continue up the road and a third parking area is found near a collection of bins, this is good for the sectors on the right side of the crag (Les Diamants to Bout du Monde).

Conditions

Though some sectors get afternoon shade, Buoux is mostly a sunny venue. The fact that is in a valley does provide shade at the end of the day, but for the most flexibility aim to visit in the spring or autumn. A sunny winter's day can be perfect, but you may be unlucky and find it freezing cold, or even snowing.

N

D4

Apt

D900

D113

D943

D36

Buoux village

Bonnieux

Buoux

About 10km

About 500m

N

From Apt

Buoux village

D113

Buoux

Bonnieux

P

P

GPS (N) 43°49'20.74"
(E) 5°22'23.45"

Forte du Buoux

P

Céüse

Sisteron

Volx

Orpierre

Bellecombe

Baume Rousse

Ubrieux

Saint Julien

Saint Léger

Malaucène

Combe Obscure

Les Dentelles

Venasque

Buoux

Marcella Belletti on *Rose des Sables* (7a) - *page 282.*

From mid morning
20 min
Slabby
Vertical

30m

20m

25m

15m

Cèlise
Sisteron
Volx
Orpierre
Bellecombe
Baume Rousse
Ubrieux
Saint Julien
Saint Léger
Malaucène
Combe Obscure
Les Dentelles
Venasque
Buoux

Brazil 2 **6b**
w the flake left then the technical slab to the top. The big
et on the slab is a highly effective water collector, so beware
as been raining recently.

La Présanteur ou la Grâce . 2 **6c+**
ort bouldery route aiming for the prominent scoops.

Rambo . . . . 3 **7b+**
iking line up the arete.

La Conjuration des Imbéciles
. . . . 2 **7b**
her fingery exercise.

Xénofolie 2 **6b**
o the left side of the corner before venturing out onto the
May feel a little run-out if the climbing's at your limit.

La Gibottière . . . . 3 **5+**
ssic line up the corner

Ambre d'Anus . . . . 2 **6a+**
o the groove to an initial belay (**5** to this point) then move
and follow the crack with interest.

Canard WC **5**
y short route, can be extended at **6a+** by continuing as for
re d'Anus.

9 La Calfouette. 3 **6a**
A superb route following the prominent crack/flake.

10 Bon Anniversary Enté . . 2 **7a+**
A technical test-piece up the wall/steep slab just right of *La Calfouette* (start hidden on the topo).

11 La Dérive des Incontinents . . . . 2 **6a+**

12 Ring'art 1 **6b**
Start in the corner, and finish up the slab.

13 Germanophobie 2 **6c**
Technical slab climbing.

14 Unknown. **5**
Pointless. The worst route at Buoux?

15 Unknown. . . . . 2 **7a+**
Some tough slab moves.

16 Afrique physique 2 **6b**

17 Podium. 1 **6c**

18 Embouillasse 1 **6a**
Start in the chimney formed by the large block (start hidden on the topo).

19 Doutte a Goutte . . . . . . 2 **7b+**
A very thin piece of slab climbing.

La Dérive

uiet sector with some great routes following strong
s up clean and unpolished rock. If you're over-used to
p pocket pulling, the grades of the slabby routes will
ably feel quite harsh. There are a few routes in the
6b+ range further left of *Brazil* which are featured in
ocal guide.

Autoroute
Page 253

Songe
Page 252

La Dérive

Songe
A classic Buoux slab wit
some steep finishes.

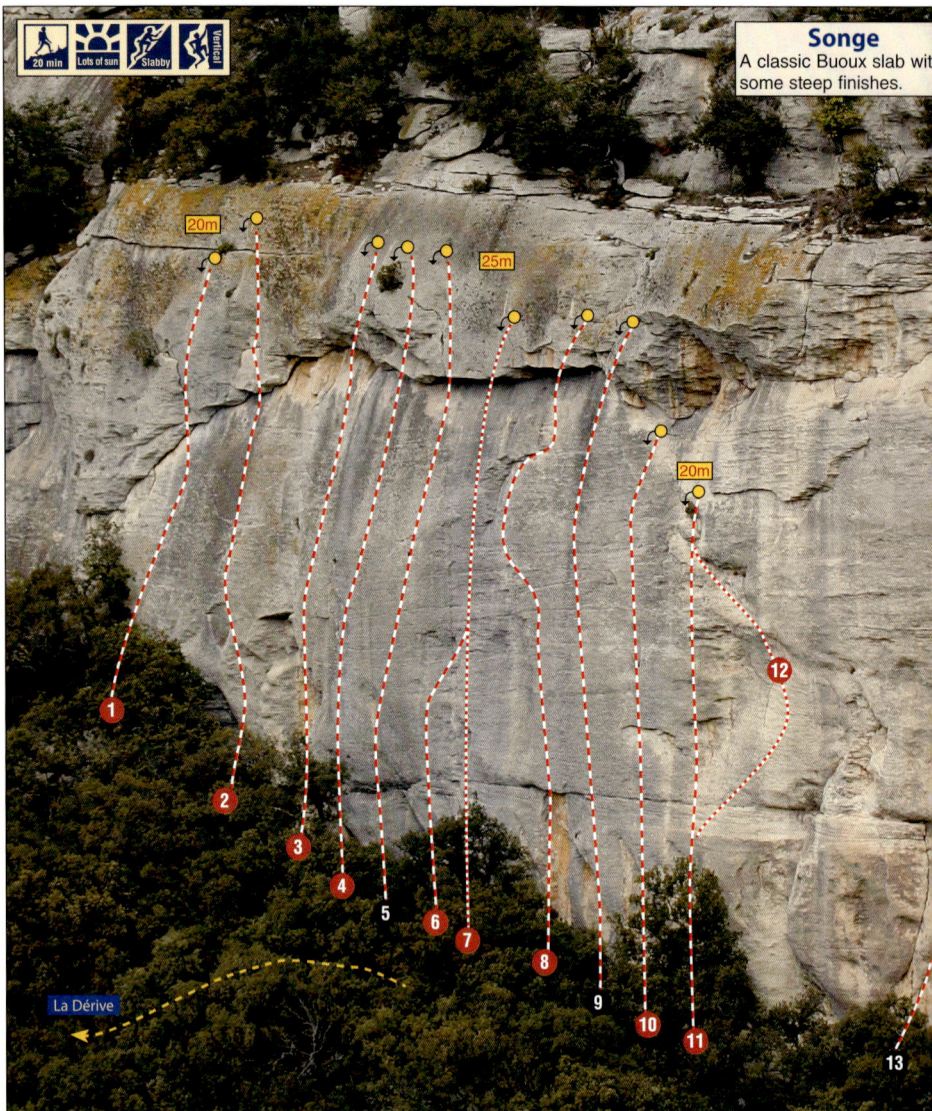

20 min | Lots of sun | Slabby | Vertical

20m
25m
20m

La Dérive

① Là-Bas si j'y Suis 6b

② Complicité d'Évasion . . . . . 6b+

③ Vol au Vent . . . . 6b+

④ Salsa du Démont . . . . 6c+

❺ Drôle de Drame 7b

⑥ Marteau sans Maître 2 . . . . 7a

⑦ Alertez les Bébés 6c

⑧ Songe Sucré 7

❾ Polka des Ringards . . . 7

⑩ Be Bop Tango 7

⑪ Top Club 7
A few hard pulls on pockets. It is possible to avoid the harde
moves my stepping one move to the left onto holds shared v
Be Bop Tango making the route **6c**.

⑫ Dernier Problème des Alpes . . . 6
A cunning line. When it starts to feel improbable, jugs are jus
out of sight.

Autoroute

famous sector with an array of hard wall climbs
an impressive imposing sheet of perfect rock.

Cadise

Sisteron

Volx

Orpierre

Bellecombe

Baume Rousse

Ubrieux

Saint Julien

Saint Léger

Malaucène

Combe Obscure

Les Dentelles

Venasque

Buoux,

artie Carée . . . . ⚡🧗🧗 ☐ 7b+
d line on superb rock, with a bouldery finish.

roject . . . . ☐ ?

octeur Jacques Hob 🧗🧗🧗🧗 ☐ 8a

iol de Corbeau . . . . . . ⚡🧗🧗 ☐ 7b+
the good rests on the way up the wall, an exacting slab
awaits: jumping for the belay is not uncommon.

utoroute du Soleil 🧗🧗🧗🧗 ☐ 7c
ux classic following the dark rock all the way.

elle de Cadix . . . . 🧗🧗🧗 ☐ 7b

⑲ **Valse aux Adieux** . . . . . 🧗🧗🧗 ☐ 7a+

⑳ **La Mimi aux Champs** . . . . . 🧗🧗 ☐ 6b+

㉑ **Les Gens d'Ici** . . . . 🧗🧗 ☐ 6c

㉒ **Le Cœur en Bandoulière** 🧗🧗🧗 ☐ 6c

㉓ **L'Armour à la Plage** . . . . ☐ 6a+

㉔ **Noël au Balcon** . . . . . . 🧗🧗🧗 ☐ 7a

㉕ **Nomades** . . . . 🧗 ☐ 5+

Céüse

Sisteron

Volx

Orpierre

Bellecombe

Baume Rousse

Ubrieux

Saint Julien

Saint Léger

Malaucène

Combe Obscure

Les Dentelles

Venasque

Buoux

La No

A pair of short walls at the left end of the main crag. The lower wall is an infamous Buoux slab with all that entails, but the crack taken by *La No* is worth hunting out, if you fancy something a bit different. The upper wall pitches can be approached by walking around to the left.

12m

10m

1 13 9 14 15 16 12 7 6 17

15m 15m 10 20 min Lots of sun Slabby

8

1 2 3 4 5 6 7 9 11 12

Béda *Page 256*

PGF
Page 262

La No

GVB *Page 260*

DSF *Page 258*

Cédise

Sisteron

Volx

Orpierre

Bellecombe

Baume Rousse

Ubrieux

Saint Julien

Saint Léger

Malaucène

Combe Obscure

Les Dentelles

Venasque

Buoux

a Risqueuse	2		5+
, 2) 5+			
anaris des Îles	2		5+
haton	2		5+
Émoro	2		6a
Oiseau Bleu	2 🧗		6b
ex Pistol	2 🧗		6b+
, 2) 6a			
léniskoté	2 🧗		6b
2) 6a+			
es Tontons Macoutes	1 🧗		6c
K Carol	3		5+
ss-popular upper pitch is **6b**.			
anabis	1		6a
yanolite	1		6c
a No	3		6a
A Buoux off-width to start. *Photo this page*. 2) 5+			
pium	2		6b+
Intruse			7b
uages Blancs	1		6b
Petits Pas de Bloc	1		6b
ol Qualifié	2		5+

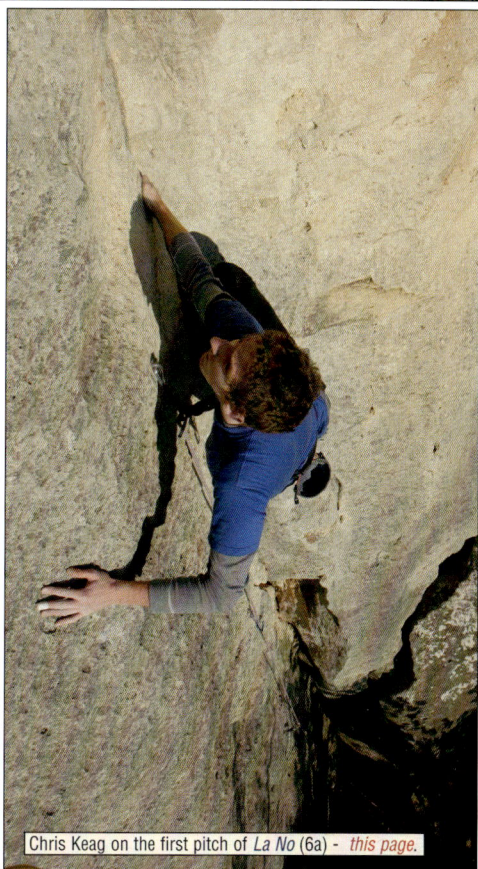

Chris Keag on the first pitch of *La No* (6a) - *this page*.

15 min | Lots of sun | Vertical

Céüse
Sisteron
Volx
Orpierre
Bellecombe
Baume Rousse
Ubrieux
Saint Julien
Saint Léger
Malaucène
Combe Obscure
Les Dentelles
Venasque
Buoux

La No

La No

25m to ledge

8

8

1 9 10

11 12

3 2 5

35m

8

20m

6

8

Secteur DSF

Le Goitre

1 2 3 4 5 7 8

Béda

A beautiful piece of orange and grey rock with some very strong crack and corner lines. The second pitches are not often connected up since they require a bit of a scramble through the woods to join them. The upper section can also be approached by scrambling in from La No.

1 **L'Abreuvoir aux Oiseaux P1** 6a
1) **6a.** Lower-off or scramble a long way through the woods to the upper wall. 2) **6a**

2 **La Béda** . . . . 6a+
1) **6a.** Lower-off or continue to the upper wall.
2) **6a**, 3) **6a+**. Only this pitch requires trad gear.

3 **La Kajozoazo** 6a
1) **6a.** Lower-off or continue to the upper wall. 2) **6a.**
There are more bolts above. *Photo on this page.*

4 **C'est à Cause des Garçons** . . . . 6c+

5 **L'Archi Hyper Ultra Extra** . . . 7a
1) **7a.** Lower-off or continue to the upper wall. 2) **5+**

6 **L'Archi Variation** . . . . 6c+

7 **Comme des Bêtes** 7b

8 **Franco-Belge** 6a
1) **6a**, 2) **6a**. Lower-off or continue to the upper wall.
3) **5+**, 4) **5**

The rest of the routes are on the upper section.

9 **Honneur aux Zappeurs** 6a

10 **L'Émoro (p2)** 6a
The first pitch is on Sector La No (previous page).

11 **Pleure Donc Pas Petit** . . . . 6a+

12 **Carnaval des Orchidées** 6a

Céüse
Sisteron
Volx
Orpierre
Bellecombe
Baume Rousse
Ubrieux
Saint Julien
Saint Léger
Malaucène
Combe Obscure
Les Dentelles
Venasque
Buoux

Pulling past the roof on pitch one of *La Kajozoazo* (6a) - *this page*.

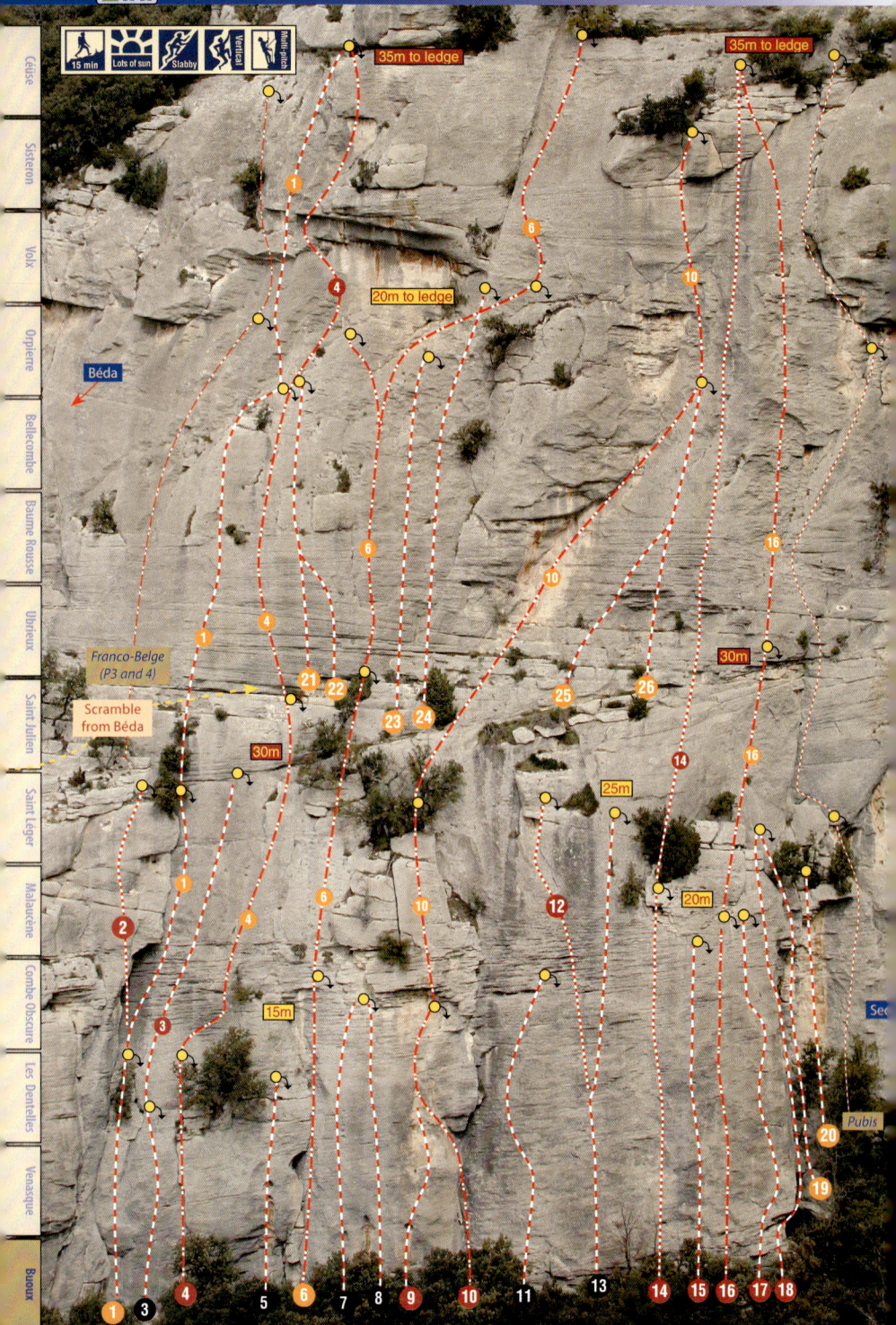

15 min | Lots of sun | Slabby | Vertical | Multi-pitch

35m to ledge

35m to ledge

20m to ledge

Béda

Franco-Belge
(P3 and 4)

Scramble
from Bèda

30m

30m

15m

25m

20m

Sec

Pubis

Céüse · Sisteron · Voix · Orpierre · Bellecombe · Baume Rousse · Ubrieux · Saint Julien · Saint Léger · Malaucène · Combe Obscure · Les Dentelles · Venasque · Buoux

Secteur DSF

llection of brilliant routes up perfect rock that often
ve technical and sustained climbing. There are also
e excellent multi-pitch routes which weave all the way
his superb wall.

Le Goître . . . . 5+
-, 2) 5, 3) 5+, 4) 5

Le Goître Direct 6b

La Berlut des Berlots . . . . 7b+
+, 2) 6b+

OSF . . . . 6b+
+, 2) 5+, 3) 6a, 4) 6b+

Chrysalide 8a

La Marabounta 6a
, 2) 5, 3) 5+. Optional finish on the left on this pitch. 4) 5+

Tout Va Bien . . . . 7b+

Pas de Pet 7b

Vague de Chaleur sur L'Antarctique
. . . . 6c

Touloum . . . . 6b+
+, 2) 6a, 3) 5, 4) 6a+

Rein ne va plus . . . . . . 7b+

Escouba 7a

C'est l'Histoire d'un Mec 7a+

Souche à Mex 6c
, 2) 6b. A very long second pitch.

Prise d'Otages 7a

Pepsicomane 6b
, 2) 5+, 3) 6a

Congé Chimique 6c

Golot Fou . . . . 6b+
the wall to the right of the arete for much of the route,
e returning to the left wall to finish. *Photo on this page.*

Cœur de Pierre . . . . 5+

Dièdre Rouge 6a

The following routes can be accessed from the ledges on the left, or by one of the routes below.

21 **Duel au Soleil** . . . . 6a+

22 **Stratagème** 6a

23 **La Balade des Amoureux** . . . . . 5+

24 **Cœur en Ballade** 6a

25 **Le Retour de 007** 5

26 **Zapping** . . . . 5+

Gill on *Golot Fou* (6b+) - *this page.*

Cëuse
Sisteron
Volx
Orpierre
Bellecombe
Baume Rousse
Ubrieux
Saint Julien
Saint Léger
Malaucène
Combe Obscure
Les Dentelles
Venasque
Buoux

15 min | Lots of sun | Slabby | Vertical | Multi-pitch

55m to ground

40m to first ledge

28m to second ledge

Secteur PGF

Second ledge

15m to first ledge

First ledge

12m

Secteur DSF

Pepsicomane

Secteur GVB (Grande Veine Bleue)

routes on three levels, there is plenty to go at here.
headwall pitches can be linked into from the pitches
w to produce some superb long climbs.

⁂ubis . . . . 🔳3🔳 ⬜ 6a+
+, 2) 5+, 3) 6a+ (left finish) or **6a** (right finish).

⁂ubis - Variante Érotique . . . . . 🔳2🔳 ⬜ 6a+
re direct line.

⁂agdad Café . . . . 🔳2🔳 ⬜ 6c
, 2) 6b+, 3) 6c

⁂'Uterus . . . . 🔳2🔳 🔳 ⬜ 6c

⁂all Street . . . . 🔳2🔳 🔳 🔳 ⬜ 7a

⁂ine & Bar . . . . 🔳2🔳 🔳 ⬜ 6c+

⁂irst ledge can be reached by from the right.

⁂bjectif Lune . . . . 🔳2🔳 🔳 ⬜ 6b+
. An easier first pitch can be done on its own. **2) 6b+**

⁂liss Terre . . . . 🔳1🔳 🔳 🔳 ⬜ 7a

⁂aisseau de Pierre . . . . 🔳2🔳 🔳 ⬜ 6b+
+, 2) 6b+

🔟 **Dévers Gonde** . . . . 🔳2🔳 🔳 ⬜ 6a+

⓫ **Grande Veine Bleue** . . . . 🔳1🔳 ⬜ 6a+
1) 6a, 2) 6a+

⓬ **Bloc Note** . . . . 🔳2🔳 ⬜ 5+
Photo below.

⓭ **Poème Givré** . . . . 🔳2🔳 🔳 ⬜ 6b
1) 5+. The easier first pitch can be done on its own. 2) 6b

⓮ **La Baleine et les Glaçons** . . . . ⬜ 5

⓯ **Le Miel dans les Oreilles** . . . . . . ⬜ 4+

⓰ **Premières Fessées** . . . . ⬜ 4+

⓱ **Le Choix de Sophie** . . . . . . 🔳2🔳 🔳 ⬜ 6c

The second ledge can be reached by scrambling up the gully.

⓲ **La Géomètre** . . . . 🔳2🔳 ⬜ 6a

⓳ **Luhora** . . . . 🔳2🔳 🔳 🔳 ⬜ 7b

⓴ **Maître au Jeu** . . . . 🔳2🔳 ⬜ 6b

㉑ **Lotus Bleu** . . . . 🔳2🔳 🔳 🔳 ⬜ 7b+

Céüse
Sisteron
Volx
Orpierre
Bellecombe
Baume Rousse
Ubrieux
Saint Julien
Saint Léger
Malaucène
Combe Obscure
Les Dentelles
Venasque
Buoux

Phil Vickers climbing *Bloc Note* (5+) - *this page*.

15 min | Lots of sun | Slabby | Vertical

Secteur Diamant

Secteur PGF (Pilier de la Gueule Ferm
Above some good short slabs is the upper wall contain
long, soaring lines up fine, grey rock.

30m

25m

20m

20m

15m

11

12

9

8 **10** **11** **13** **14** **15** **16** **17** **18** **19** **20**

1

2 **3** **4** **5** **6** **7**

Secteur GVB

Mur Zappa

Céüse
Sisteron
Volx
Orpierre
Bellecombe
Baume Rousse
Ubrieux
Saint Julien
Saint Léger
Malaucène
Combe Obscure
Les Dentelles
Vénasque
Buoux

Tout à Fait Theirry . . . . 4+

Eh Oui Jean-Michel! . . . . 4+

Que d'Émotions! . . . . 4+

Petit Prince 5

La Confiture pour Cochon . . 5+

o on this page.

Lapin des Sables . . . . 5+

Quatre Quarts 5

main wall in this area is reached by scrambling up the easy
' to gain the wide higher ledge.

Bascule Infernale . . . . . . 7a+

Infernale Bascule 6c

Le Routard Galactique . 7a+

Pilier de la Gueule Fermée

. . . . 7a

a, 2) 5+

Boulevard du rock 7b

Join à Venture . . . . 7b+

Age of Dream 7b

L'Éspoir Vit en Exil 6b

Saccageur de Rêve . . . . . . 6b+

Zygène Pourpre 6c

Patte de Coin . . . . 5+

Édition Spéciale 6a

Prise Matique 6a

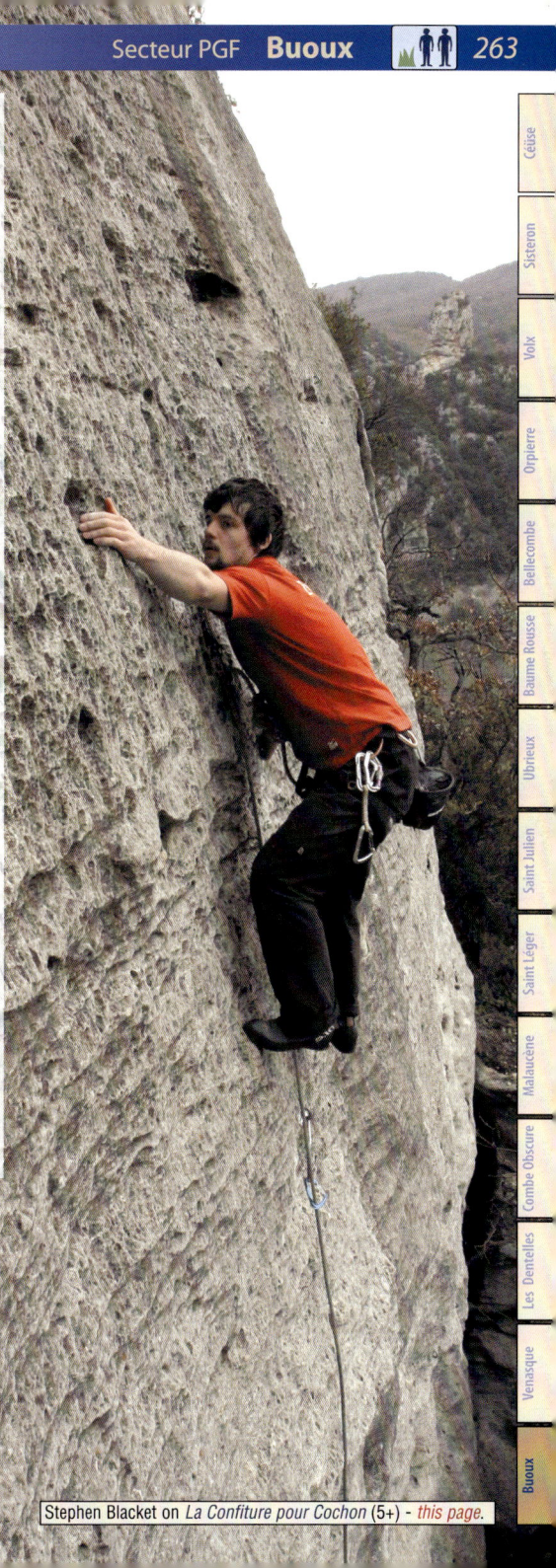

Céüse · Sisteron · Volx · Orpierre · Bellecombe · Baume Rousse · Ubrieux · Saint Julien · Saint Léger · Malaucène · Combe Obscure · Les Dentelles · Venasque · **Buoux**

1	Minouchette Chérie			6a
2	Poupon la Peste			6a
3	Pilier de la gueule Fermée			6b
4	Kadjet Tropic			6a+
5	Ainsi Parlait Zarathoustra			6b
6	Zarathoustra Direct			6b
7	Couleur 3			6b+
8	Zappa Maniac (Left)			6b+
9	Zappa Maniac			6b+
10	L'Ombre d'un Doute			6b
11	Bal des Lazes			6a
12	Schabada Swing			6b+
13	La Quête de l'Oiseau du Temps			6b

14	Paulo, si t'Assures C'est pas Dur!			6b
15	Dardibule			6a
16	Bas les Masques			6b
17	La Bonté du Forgeron			6b
18	Skud			6a
19	La Marine			6a
20	Aptitudes			6b
21	Tentation d'Éxister			7a
22	Procession des Sous-Hommes			7b
23	Nutso-mato			6b
24	Enty-prises			6c

See photo opposite.

15 min   Lots of sun   Slabby

Les Diamants

18m

15m

18m

Mur Zappa

Mur Zappa

Zappa Wall is the home of many of Buoux's most feared slabs, stay away from it when it is warm unless you wan to suffer. The 6b's aren't much harder than the 6a's, thou that says more about the 6a's than it does about the 6b'

Gélise

Sisteron

Volx

Orpierre

Bellecombe

Baume Rousse

Ubrieux

Saint Julien

Saint Léger

Malaucène

Combe Obscure

Les Dentelles

Venasque

Buoux

Céüse

Sisteron

Volx

Orpierre

Bellecombe

Baume Rousse

Ubrieux

Saint Julien

Saint Léger

Malaucène

Combe Obscure

Les Dentelles

Venasque

Buoux

Adam Gill on the technically absorbing *Enty-prises* (6c) - *opposite*.

15 min | Lots of sun | Slabby | Vertical

35m from ledge

20m from ledge

30m

25

26

20m from ledge

25

25

24

23

Secteur PGF

26 27 28 29 30 31 32

34

35

33

36 37 38

39

17

17

Mur Zappa

Enty-prises

20m

13

10

1

15m

2 3

4 5 6 7 8 9 11 12 14

17

Les Diamants

A concentration of brilliant routes await at this easily
missed sector. The *Partie Gratuite* wall has a number of
recommended routes, often combining steep and powerful
starts with technically absorbing 'grey' finishes. Les
Diamants has some incredible soaring pitches that would
be completely polished were they closer to the beaten
track, so they are well worth the effort! Approach either by
walking along the ledge from the left, or doing one of the
routes below and continuing upwards.

Lédise | Sisteron | Voix | Orpierre | Bellecombe | Baume Rousse | Ubrieux | Saint Julien | Saint Léger | Malaucène | Combe Obscure | Les Dentelles | Venasque | Buoux

Belsunce. 6c

Belsunce Direct 7a

Cap'tain Crochet 7b

Super Brown 6b
oo many bolts on this Yosemite style off-width.

Antinéa. 6b

Javanaise 6c

Northern Light 7b

Salinas (P1) 6b

Amour Bleu. 6c

Transat 6c

The Cruiser . . . . 6c+

Partie Gratuite. . . . . 6a+

Borinqueno . . . . 7a+

Samba . . . . 6c+

Music of Moves . . . . 7a+

En Montant Chez Kate. . . . . . . 7a+

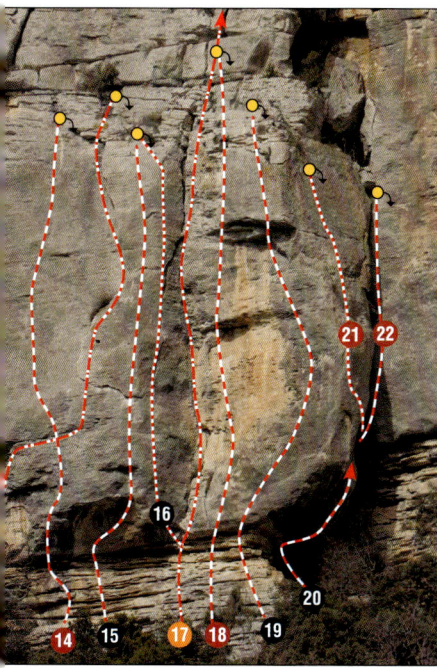

17 La Volière. 7b
1) 5+, 2) 5+, 3) 7b. Two easier pitches to a hard finish.

18 Pigalle la Blanche . . . . 6b+

19 Fire Works . . . . . . 7b+

20 Joe Weider's Rock Principle 7c+

21 La Balance 6c
Start on the left wall back in the cave, and follow the bolts left to a junction with *Joe Weider*, then take the left-hand finish.

22 Vieux Debris . . . . 6c+
Same start as *La Balance*, but continue straight up to finish as for *Joe Weider*.

The rest of the routes begin from the mid-height ledge reached by one of the lower pitches, or from Secteur PGF on page 265.

23 Terre Sauvage . . . . 7a+

24 Jungle 6b

25 Africa . . . . 7a+
1) 6b+, 2) 7a+

26 La Marine . . . . 7a+
2) 7a+, 3) 6b

27 Akoulina . . . . 7a+

28 Sensuelle et Sans Suite 7a+

29 La Nostalgie Camarade 7a+

30 Koweit and See 7c

31 Pêcheur d'Étoiles. 6c

32 La Petite Graine . . . . 6b+

33 Salinas (P2) . . . . 7a+

34 Fréquence Môme. 7a

35 Les Diamants sont Éternels 7a
One of the finest 7a's in the world, it has a little bit of everything.

36 Lieux Secrets et Vilains Messieurs
. . . . 7c+

37 La Bourse ou la Vie 7b+

38 Tempête du Désert . . . . 7a+

39 C'est une Andalouse. . . 7b

Céüse
Sisteron
Volx
Orpierre
Bellecombe
Baume Rousse
Ubrieux
Saint Julien
Saint Léger
Malaucène
Combe Obscure
Les Dentelles
Venasque
Buoux

Fakir

A fine wall of orange rock with constantly interesting climbing on large pocketed features. Although the first pitches get most of the traffic, it's worth carrying on up.

Vertical · Steep · Multi-pitch

15 min · Lots of sun

55m

Les Diamants

40m

60m

60m

45m

28m

25m

20m

28m

Excalibur

Knotted rope gains ledge

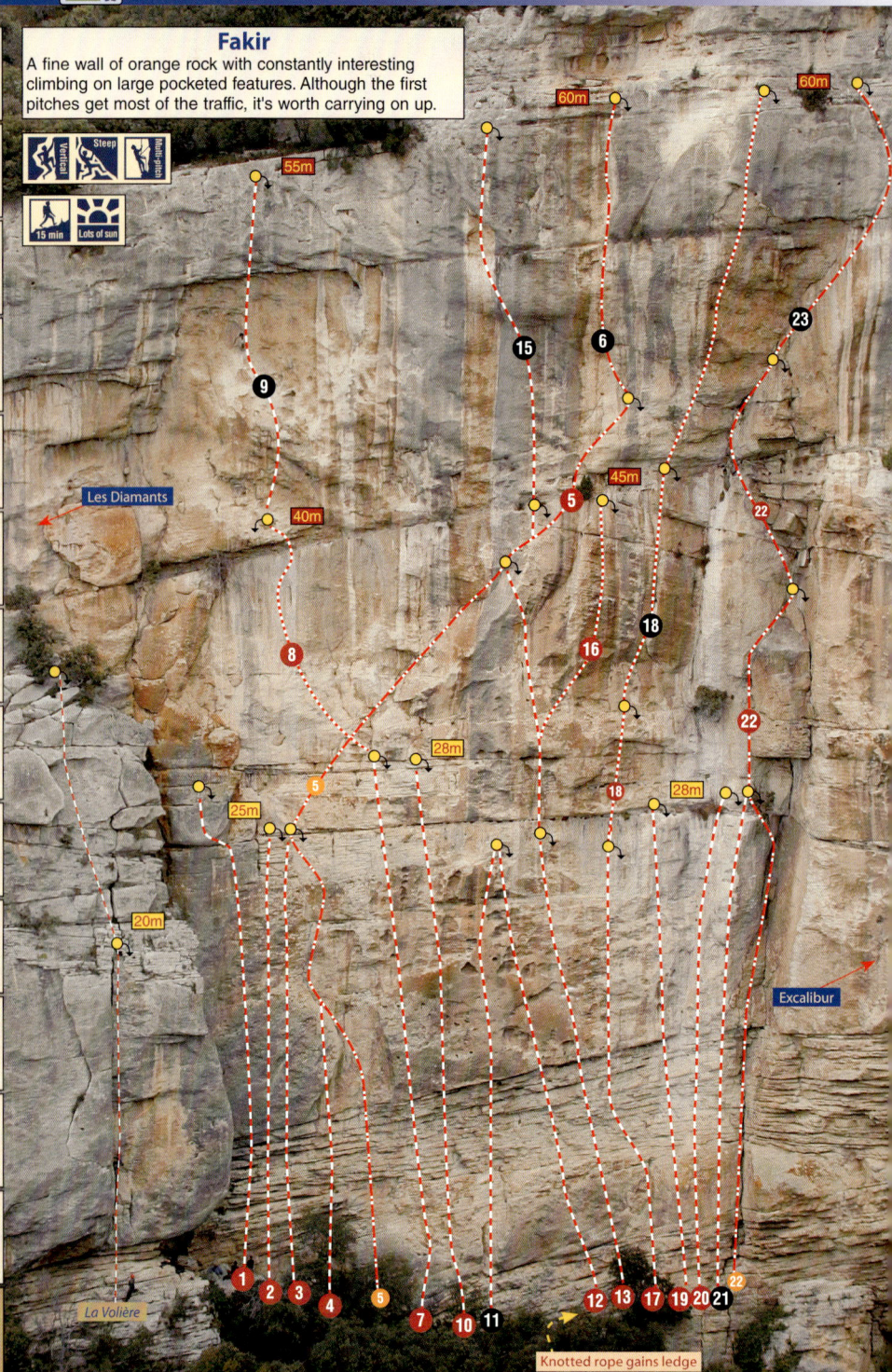

La Volière

Céüse
Sisteron
Volx
Orpierre
Bellecombe
Baume Rousse
Ubrieux
Saint Julien
Saint Léger
Malaucène
Combe Obscure
Les Dentelles
Venasque
Buoux

Le Père Noël est une Ordure
. . . . 🔲 6c

Rivage . . . . 🔲 6c

Encore et Toujours . . . . 🔲 6b+

Bleu Tomate . . . . 🔲 6b

La Fakir . . . . 🔲 6c
a+, 2) 5+, 3) 6c

La Fakir (P4) . . . . . 🔲 7c+

Invasion Nordique . . . . 🔲 6b+

Big Bang. . . . . 🔲 6c
ow on from *Invasion Nordique*.

Big Crunch . . . . 🔲 7a+

Que Fait la Résistance? . . . 🔲 6c

Ici Londres . . . . 🔲 7a+

Signé Farax. . . . . 🔲 6c
n 6b in the local guide, but the start is desperate.

Cri de Guerre . . . . 🔲 6b+
erb. There are a couple of options for continuing further.

14 Slogan de Combat . . . . 🔲 6c+
Follow on from *Cri de Guerre*.

15 Tout, Tout de Suite . 🔲 7c+
Follow on from either *Slogan de Combat* or *Fakir*.

16 Prix de Détail . . . . 🔲 7a
Another follow on from *Cri de Guerre*.

17 Désespoir . . . . 🔲 6c+
A great pitch that weaves around a lot more than the line indicates. Start at the finger crack.

18 De Camino a la Vereda
. . . . 🔲 7b
1) 6c+. Climb *Désespoir* but continue to a higher lower-off.
2) 7b, 3) Unclimbed.

19 Dérision . . . . 🔲 7a

20 La Solution Finale . . . . 🔲 6b+

21 Djihad . . . . 🔲 7a+

22 Le Tozal . . . . 🔲 6b
1) 6a, 2) 6b, 3) 6b

23 Le Tozal (P4). . . . . 🔲 7b

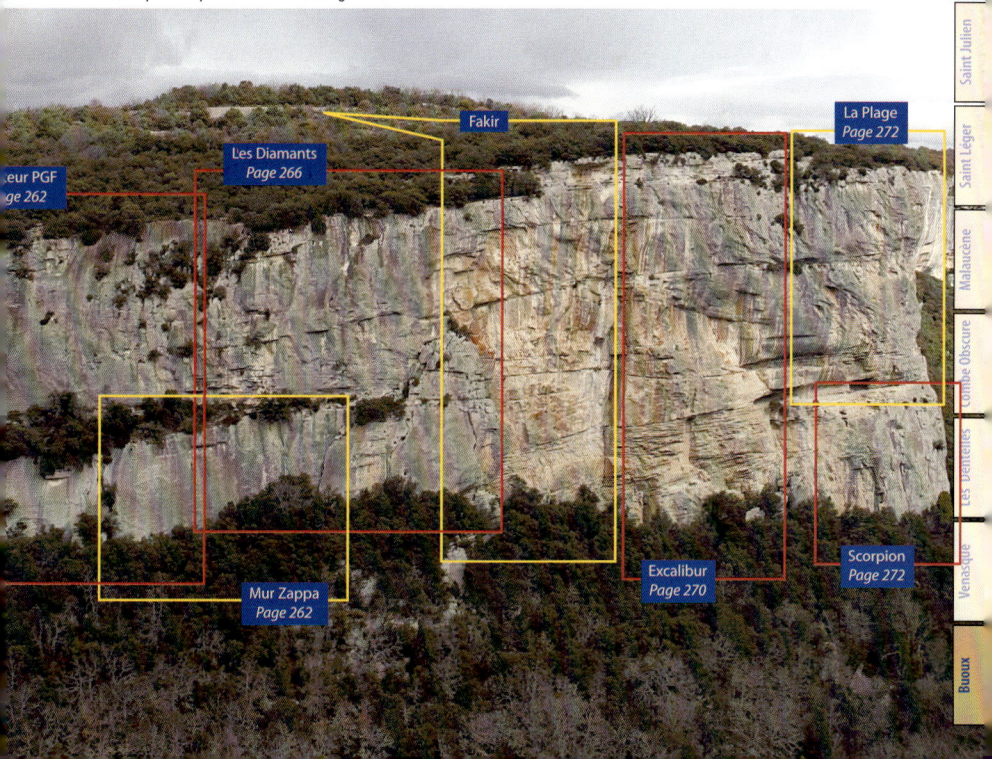

Fakir

La Plage
Page 272

Les Diamants
Page 266

eur PGF
ge 262

Mur Zappa
Page 262

Excalibur
Page 270

Scorpion
Page 272

Céüse · Sisteron · Volx · Orpierre · Bellecombe · Baume Rousse · Ubrieux · Saint Julien · Saint Léger · Malaucène · Combe Obscure · Les Dentelles · Venasque · Buoux

15 min | Lots of sun | Vertical | Steep | Multi-pitch

Excalibur

Some great link-up that lead to the top the crag, well almo The first pitches around here are popular, taking ste lines with hardly a pocket in sight.

70m · 65m · 50m · 45m · 35m · 25m to ledge · 25m · 10m

Geüse · Sisteron · Volx · Orpierre · Bellecombe · Baume Rousse · Ubrieux · Saint Julien · Saint Léger · Malaucène · Combe Obscure · Les Dentelles · Venasque · Buoux

Le Tozal

Fakir

La Plag

Le Vieil Homme est Amer . . ⚡🔧 [ ] 7a
a. Continue past the first lower-off. 2) **6c**

Le Pilier Déglingue . . . . ⚡ [ ] 7a
+, 2) 7a, 3) 7a

J'aime, J'aime, J'aime . . . . . . ⚡ [ ] 6c
be started from the ground.

Leave it to the Lawyer . . . . . . ⚡ [ ] 6c+

Fingers of Fate . . . . ⚡🔧 [ ] 7a

Into the Waves . . . . . . ⚡🔧🔧 [ ] 7b

Feeling Fine . . . . ⚡🔧 [ ] 7b

next routes are started on the ledge at the top of the steps.

Mr Bricolage . . . . ⚡🔧▮ [ ] 7a+
c+, 2) **7a+**. The symbols are for the second pitch.

La Siesta . . . . ⚡ [ ] 6c+

Homo-sapiens Néandertalis . . . ⚡ [ ] 6c+

La Concièrge est dans l'Escalier
. . . . ⚡🔧 [ ] 7a

Excalibur . . . . ⚡🔧 [ ] 7b+
0+, 2) **6a**. A short pitch. 3) **6c**

Séquence Frisson . . . . . . ⚡🔧 [ ] 7a+

e are three exposed pitches high on the wall.

20 year old project . . . . [ ] ?

Fesse et Geste . . . . . . ⚡🔧🔧 [ ] 7c+

Les Flammes du Désir . . . . ⚡🔧 [ ] 7b
perb orange groove leads to a technical finale.

next long route gains more harder pitches higher up.

Les Clandestins . . . . ⚡🔧 [ ] 6c

La Diagonale du Fou . . ⚡💪🔧 [ ] 8a
connection from *Les Clandestins* is **6a+**.

Synergie . . . . ⚡💪🔧🔧 [ ] 8b+

Les Joies Simples . . . . ⚡🔧 [ ] 6c+

Projection Privée . . . . ⚡🔧 [ ] 7a+

t at ground level, four routes lead up the horizontal breaks.

La Jonction . . . . ⚡💪 [ ] 6b+
eat pitch, steep but they're all big holds.

Audrey Seguy pitch 2 of *Le Rut* (6b) - *this page*.

㉓ Baston Général . . . . ⚡ [ ] 6a
A good one to get started on, with just one tricky bit.

㉔ Ramboutan Farcis . . . . . . ⚡🔧 [ ] 6b+
A few tough pulls.

㉕ Roadhouse Blues . . . . ⚡ [ ] 6a

The upper wall on this side has a series of hard pitches gained from the access route of Le Rut.

㉖ Sid Vicious . . . . ⚡🔧 [ ] 6b+
A short section of pocket-pulling.

㉗ Le Rut . . . . ⚡ [ ] 7a
A good set of pitches. Start by climbing *Ramboutan farcis* or climb the first two pitches (see next page) to La Plage and walk left along the ledge. *Photo this page.*
3) 6b+. A few sharp pocket pulls. Can be linked to pitch 4.
4) 6b. Move left and follow the superb groove.
5) 7a. Exposed but never desperate.
6) 6b. Can be a bit dirty.

㉘ Mauvais Sang . . . . ⚡💪 [ ] 8b
A beautiful, exposed pitch.

㉙ Spécialisé Funky . . ⚡💪🔧🔧 [ ] 7c+

㉚ Le Grand Petrarkos ⚡💪🔧🔧 [ ] 7c+

㉛ Petit Cali . . . . ⚡💪🔧🔧 [ ] 8a

㉜ La Casse d'Eau . . . ⚡💪🔧🔧 [ ] 7c

㉝ SOeScalade . . . . ⚡🔧 [ ] 7a+
1) 7a+. Break left from the third pitch of *Le Rut.*
2) 6c+. Not a pleasant start, but the slab above is fun.

Céüse
Sisteron
Volx
Orpierre
Bellecombe
Baume Rousse
Ubrieux
Saint Julien
Saint Léger
Malaucène
Combe Obscure
Les Dentelles
Venasque
Buoux

La Plage

La Plage is a sort of 'Bout du Monde lite' and a popular hangout with a concentration of good bouldery routes mainly in the upper 7s. Approach via the old stairs from below, approaching from the right is not recommended.

| 15 min | Lots of sun | Steep | Multi-pitch |

50m from ledge

30m from ledge

20m from ledge

Le Rut

Le Rut

Excalibur

Scorpion

This popular sector has a go spread of route including some great easier tic

| 15 min | Afternoon |

La Gougousse

Approach scramble up old stairs

25m

25m

Pilie
Fou

Side tabs (left margin): Céüse · Sisteron · Volx · Orpierre · Bellecombe · Baume Rousse · Ubrieux · Saint Julien · Saint Léger · Malaucène · Combe Obscure · Les Dentelles · Venasque · Buoux

Route numbers: 1 2 3 4 5 6 7 8 9 10 11 12 13 14 15 16 17 18 19 20 21 22 23 24 25 26 27 28 29 30 31 5 5 5 5 5

7 Deverdur. 7a

8 La Nuit des Morts de Rire . . 8a

9 Des Verts Pépères 6c
Great moves throughout the route, then a frustrating finish where a long reach may make things a bit easier.

10 Kamikaze . . . . 6c+
Always be wary of routes named 'kamikaze'!

11 Imitation Granit . . . . 5+
Start at the prominent granite-like flake.

12 Bourreau d'enfants. 6b

13 Le Rut 6a
1) 6a, 2) 5+. Can be continued to the top of the crag - see previous page.

14 L'Anamour 7a

15 J'ai du Vague à l'Âme . . . . . . 6b+

16 La Gougousse (P1). 6a
See next page for following pitches.

La Plage

17 Project . . . . ?
An infamous project, that remains unclimbed...

18 Acapulco. 7c

19 Excès de Zèle 7c

20 Sous les Pavés . . . . . . 7c+

21 Passage . . . . 7c+

22 La Ouate. 8a

23 Cadeau Empoisonné. . . 7b+

24 Gedeon. . . . . 7a+

25 Chocolat Moto 7a

26 Il Moro de Venezia. . . . 7a
1) 7a, 2) 6c, 3) 7a

27 Kookabura . . . . . . 7a+

28 Cool Raoul 7a

29 Relax Max . . . . 6b+

30 Paradis Artificiel . . . 7b+

31 Tranquille Bill 6b

gh Sibbring on the first pitch of *Scorpion* (5+) - *this page*.

orpion

Crank Frank. 7b

Comme Papa. . . . . 4+

La Montée aux Enfers. . . . . . . 6b+

Carton Jaune. . . . . 6a+

Scorpion. . . . . 6c+
+. *See photo on this page*. 2) 5+, 3) 7a, 4) 6b, 5) 6c+

La Flèche 6c

Célèse
Sisteron
Volx
Orpierre
Bellecombe
Baume Rousse
Ubrieux
Saint Julien
Saint Léger
Malaucène
Combe Obscure
Les Dentelles
Venasque
Buoux

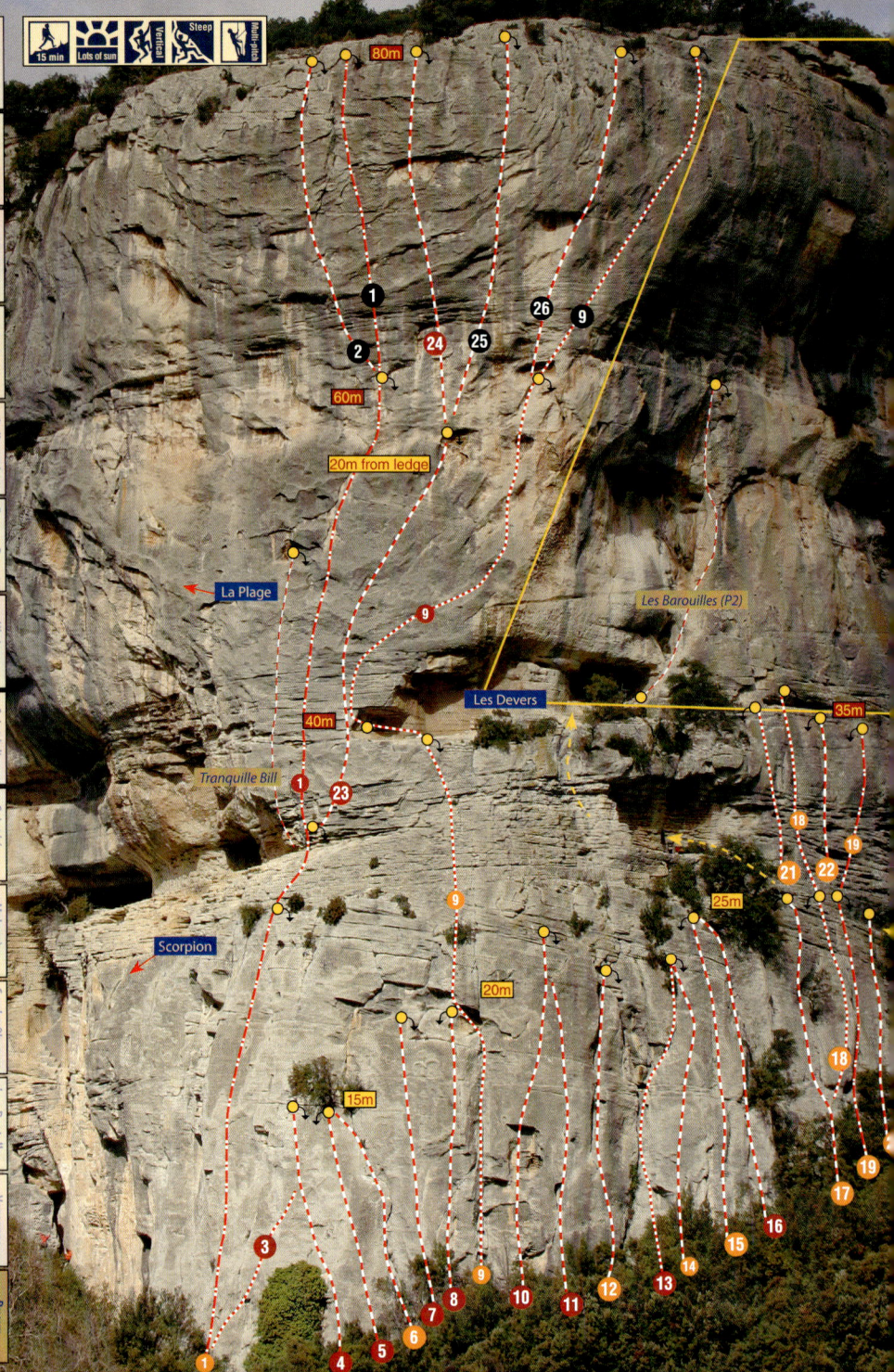

15 min | Lots of sun | Vertical | Steep | Multi-pitch

80m

60m

20m from ledge

La Plage

Les Barouilles (P2)

Les Devers

40m

35m

Tranquille Bill

25m

Scorpion

20m

15m

1
2
24
25
26
9
9
23
9
18
19
21
22
18
3
4
5
6
7
8
9
10
11
12
13
14
15
16
17
18
19
1

Pilier des Fourmis

e grandest sector on Buoux with a wealth of brilliant routes a few of which continue all the way to the top. *Le Pilier Fourmis* is perhaps the best multi-pitch route at Buoux and well worth getting on even if you have to use direct aid the crux move on the final pitch. The lower slabby walls are popular.

La Gougousse . . . . 7a+
a. Lower-off or make an easy scramble to the next belay
b, 3) 7a+

Amour à Sens Unique . . 7b
alternative final pitch to *La Gougousse*.

Le Roi de la Jungle 6b

Mise Amour 6b

Sourire Hawaii . . . . 6b+

Téléthon . . . . 5+

Backstage . . . . 6b+

Tora-Torapas . . . . 6b+

Le Pilier des Fourmis . . . . . 7a+
a. A good pitch in its own right up the corner.
, 3) 6b, 4) 7a+. A wild finalé, can be aided at **6b+**.

Vaugreray's Sister . . . . 6c+

Comme un Loup Blessé . . . 6c+

Joe Klaxon . . . . 6a+

Bonne Nouvelle des Étoiles 6c

Les Barouilles (P1) . . . . 6a+
ontinues higher up but is seldom climbed as a multi-pitch
e. Pitch 2 is described on the next page.

15 **Vice et Verseau** . . . . 6a+

16 **Tendance Actuelle** 6b

17 **Tremplin** . . . . 5+

18 **Décadanse** . . . . 5+
1) 5+, 2) 5+

19 **Surfin'Rock** 5
1) 5, 2) 5

20 **Quelle Corrida!** 6a

Two continuation pitches are available.

21 **Soleil de Nuit** . . . . 5+

22 **Le Petit Sauvage** . . . . 5+

There are four more pitches higher up on the wall.

23 **Carpe Diem** . . . . 6b+

24 **Belle de Seigneur** 7a

25 **Les Étoiles se Cachent Pour Mourir**
. . . . 7b

26 **Le Schlafzack et le Bierkenstock**
. . . . 8a

Devers
Page 276

TCF
Page 278

Rêve
Page 280

Styx Wall
Page 282

No Man's Land
Page 284

Bout du Monde
Page 286

Pilier des Fourmis

Célise | Sisteron | Volx | Orpierre | Bellecombe | Baume Rousse | Ubrieux | Saint Julien | Saint Léger | Malaucène | Combe Obscure | Les Dentelles | Venasque | Buoux

Céüse
Sisteron
Volx
Orpierre
Bellecombe
Baume Rousse
Ubrieux
Saint Julien
Saint Léger
Malaucène
Combe Obscure
Les Dentelles
Vénasque
Buoux

15 min | Morning | Vertical | Steep

60m

19
20 21
22 23
24
25m to ledge
25 26 27 28
30m
17
18
16
13
15m
14 15
9 10 11 12
7 8
1 2 3 4 5 6

Surfin' Rock
Décandance
Pilier des Fourmis

Les Devers

A varied and imposing wall with
a number of popular mid-grade
routes low down, but capping the
at the top of the crag are some
the most significant hard routes
the history of sport climbing.

Le Vieux qui Lisait des Romans d'Armour

. . . . 6a

to on this page.

Prises Éléctriques . . . . 6a+

Homo-Grimpus-Lubéronus 6b

S'il te Plaît, Dessine-moi Un Mutant

. . . . 6b+

Mega Top 7a

Colonel Six B 6b

more routes start from the cave above.

Imitation Saussois . . . . 6c+

La Tradition du Geste . . 7a+

the next routes follow the precarious approach walk (take t care) to the higher ledge. The ledge can also be reached by route Décandence (see previous page).

Taupe Niveau . . . . 7a+

Humanoïdes . . . . 6c+

Le Prophète est sur le Parking

. . . . 7b+

Action Directe 7c

Elvis Dévisse 6b

Elvis Ognome 7a

Barouilles (P2) 6c
first pitch is described on the previous page.

Elvis Cartonne 7a

Cri Cri le Holy 6c

La Victoire de l'Homme sur les WC

. . . . 6b+

rest of the routes are mega-hard lines high on the wall hed by one of the lower pitches.

Et Dieu Créa l'Infame 8a+

Total Transfer 8b

Agincourt 8c

Anaïa Aubry on *Le Vieux qui Lisait des Romans d'Armour* (6a) - *this page.*

㉒ La Chiquette du Graal 8b+

㉓ Le Spectre du Sur-Mutant

. . . . 8b+

㉔ Miss Catastrophe . . 8c

㉕ La Mission 8b

㉖ Dévers Pervers . . . . . . 7b+

㉗ Jextraordinaire . . . . . . 7c+

㉘ Les Caprices d'Anatole 7c+

Secteur TCF (Turbo Cibi Facho)

A justifiably popular wall with some truly great routes. The popular ones are getting quite polished now, but they are still superb. Come in the morning for sun, wait until the afternoon for shade.

15 min | To mid afternoon | Vertical | Steep

Ceüse
Sisteron
Volx
Orpierre
Bellecombe
Baume Rousse
Ubrieux
Saint Julien
Saint Léger
Malaucène
Combe Obscure
Les Dentelles
Venasque
Buoux

40m

16

40m

35m

40m

24

22

23

14

R

Devers

19

20 21

20m

15

17

22m

18

14

Re

4

6

13

14

12

11

10

9

8

7

5

3

2

1

La Tradition...

Le Juif Architecte. 6c

Jolinouille 7a

Requiem. . . . . 7c+

Requiem sur vos Tombes 8a+
rder, right-hand finish to *Requiem*.

J'Irai Crâcher sur vos Tombes
. . . . 7c+
eft-hand branch.

La Cage aux Orchidées 7b
easier right-hand branch.

Un Zeste d'Inceste . . . . 7b+
hes much lower than the other routes.

Dresden . . . . 7a+
oux classic.

TCF 7a
her Buoux classic - getting a bit shiny too. *Photo below.*

Papa Pas Pou 6c

Le Zoo des Robots 6c

Alambic, Sortie Sud 6b
asiest face route here, and hence popular.

13 Zéphir . . . . 6a+
A long pitch into the corner.

14 La Conque 6a
1) 6a, 2) 6a

15 Le Corps Électrique . . . 7b+

16 Le Complexe d'Icare . . 7c

17 Docteur Folamour . . . . 7b+
A logical extension of *Requiem*.

18 Les Évadés de la Cage 7c+
A short hard extension.

19 La Fée du Logis. . . 7c+
A hard and steep extension.

20 Monsieur Propre . . . . 7b+
A powerful extension.

21 Camambert Fergusson 7a
A wild extension on big holds.

22 La Chèvre et le Chou . . 7c
A harder right-hand variant to *Camambert*.

23 Mécanique des Fluides 7b+
A steep link up into *Le Chevre*.

24 Les Clowns . . . . 6b+
Move out right from the second pitch of *La Conque*.

Roberts on *TCF* (7a) - *this page*. Photo: Richard Betts

Céüse

Sisteron

Volx

Orpierre

Bellecombe

Baume Rousse

Ubrieux

Saint Julien

Saint Léger

Malaucene

Combe Obscure

Les Dentelles

Venasque

Buoux

10 min | To mid afternoon | Vertical | Steep

18m to ledge

35m

18m to ledge

30m

25m

Secteur TCF

Styx

1
2
3
4
5
6
7
8
9
10

Routes 3 to 6 are normally belayed from the bottom of a large easy slab which is much lower than shown, but you will need to scramble up to the start of the bolts to lower-off with a 60m rope.

Ceüse
Sisteron
Volx
Orpierre
Bellecombe
Baume Rousse
Ubrieux
Saint Julien
Saint Léger
Malaucène
Combe Obscure
Les Dentelles
Venasque
Buoux

Rêve

A mixture of routes following strong lines. Get here early for the sun, or stroll up in the afternoon for cooler conditions. *Rêve de Papillon* is essential for all aspiring 8a badge wearers but beware, entire trips have been spent on this route alone!

steep starting moves on *Rêve de Papillon* (8a) - *this page*.

Bonnet d'Ane . . . . 🔆 🏳 🧗 ☐ 7b

Kaderlita . . . . 🔆 🏳 🧗 ☐ 7b+

Le Glantier . . . . 🔆 ☐ 6a

Les Fruits de la Passion . . . . . 🔆 ☐ 6c

Le Condor . . . . 🔆 ☐ 6a

Meurte dans un Jardin Anglais

. . . . 🔆 🏳 🧗 ☐ 7b

The following routes are gained by scrambling up to the start of Vent de Sable. Bring your camera if someone's on Rose des Sables (next page).

7 La Vache Multicolore . . 🔆 🏳 🧗 ☐ 7b

8 Rêve de Pates . . . . 🔆 🏳 🔩 ☐ 7c+

9 Rêve de Papillon . . 🔆 🔩 🏳 🧗 ☐ 8a

An iconic route, almost a rite of passage. An inability to use your feet may actually come in useful at the start, but you'll need them to clip the belay. *Photo on this page.*

10 Vent de Sable . . . . 🔆 🏳 🔩 ☐ 7c

Céüse · Sisteron · Volx · Orpierre · Bellecombe · Baume Rousse · Ubrieux · Saint Julien · Saint Léger · Malaucène · Combe Obscure · Les Dentelles · Venasque · **Buoux**

Styx Wall

A justifiably popular wall, with line after line of brilliant climbing, just beware of the slabby sandbags at the right-hand end of the wall.

1. Tupinambis . . . . ① ☐ **6a**
2. La Mouche à Bière . . . . ② 🧗 ☐ **6c+**
3. Le Nombril de Vénus . . . . . ③ 🧗 ☐ **6c**
   The direct line is more like **6c+**.
4. Bienvenue sur Aflolol . . . . . ② 🧗 ☐ **6b+**
5. L'Aspic . . . . ① ☐ **6a**
6. Regards et Sourires . . . . . . ② 🧗 ☐ **7b+**
7. Rose des Sables . . . . ③ 🧗 ☐ **7a**
   One of the best routes here. *See photo on page 249.*
8. Courage, Fuyons . . . . ③ 🧗 ☐ **7a+**
   The ability to jam will help at the top.
9. Os Court . . . . ③ 🧗 ☐ **7b+**
   Chipped, but still very good.

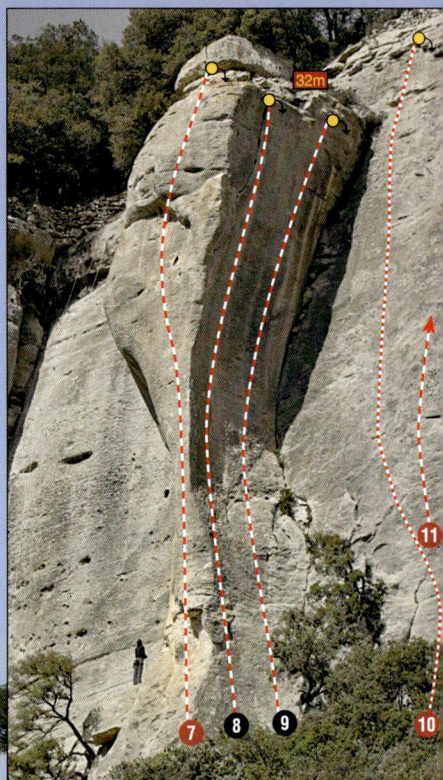

Mamie Nova 2 7a

Mélodie Gaël . . . . 2 6b+

Désidia. 2 6c

Andeavor 2 6b

Récréactivité. 3 6b

Buffet Froid. 2 6c

Ultime Violence . . . . 2 6c+

Antidote . . . . 2 7a+

Rhinoféroce 2 7a

Vieux Campeur . . . . 2 6c+

Ravi au Lit . . . . 7c+

21 Le Hasard Fait Bien les Choses
. . . . 1 7b

22 Plus de Trois Fois, C'est Jouer Avec…
. . . . 2 7a

23 Scaravangeur 2 7a

24 Cupule Radiale . . . . . . 2 7a+

25 La Dame aux Camélias. . . . 2 6c

26 Handisport . . . . 2 6c+

27 Kilo de Frites Physique. . . . 1 6c+

28 La Salska du Styx 7b

29 Proxima Nox . . . . 1 6c+

30 Le Voyage de L'Incrédule . . 1 6b

15 min · Lots of sun · Vertical

30m   30m   30m

No Man's Land

19 20 21 22 23 24 25 26 27 28 29 30

Célise · Sisteron · Volx · Orpierre · Bellecombe · Baume Rousse · Ubrieux · Saint Julien · Saint Léger · Malaucène · Combe Obscure · Les Dentelles · Venasque · Buoux

No Man's Land

This fine wall has one of the iconic routes at Buoux - *No Man's Land* is popular though, so expect to have to share it with others. On the plus side, there's a good chance that the clips will be in, so you can have a go and not worry about pumping out at the end of the traverse and having to get your clips back. If it all seems a bit hard here, you might want to leave your pack behind if you intend walking around the corner to the next section....!

30m

35m

35m

35m

28m

28m

15m

Bout du

Styx Wall

Celse

Sisteron

Voix

Opierre

Bellecombe

Baume Rousse

Ubrieux

Saint Julien

Saint Léger

Malaucène

Combe Obscure

Les Dentelles

Venasque

Buoux

Project . . . . ?

Pacemaker 7c
o on this page.

No Man's Land 7b
ga classic, and no pushover. Photo on page 1.

Méthode Rose . . . . 7a+
wild extension through the roof.

Harlem Desir 7c
rder, more direct version of No Man's Land.

Anja's Platte . . . . 7b+
ect start to No Man's Land.

Stranger than Paradise
. . . . 7b+

Franky Paradise . . . 7b+
ternative start to Stranger then Paradise.

Franky Z'aplat 8a

Terrain Naturel Tentant (TNT)
. . . . 7c

Corbeau Technique National (CTN)
. . . . 8b

Project . . . . ?

Project . . . . ?

Céüse
Sisteron
Volx
Orpierre
Bellecombe
Baume Rousse
Ubrieux
Saint Julien
Saint Léger
Malaucène
Combe Obscure
Les Dentelles
Venasque
Buoux

Classic Buoux - *Pacemaker* (7c) - *this page.*

Bout du Monde

Probably the world's best-known hard-climbing sector, Bout du Monde has long been a forcing ground. Although no longer the *only* place to test the best, if you're dedicated enough, it's only a matter of time before you're going to pay these routes a visit.

15 min   Lots of sun

40m

40m

40m

32m

30m

25m

5

20m

15m

15

2

4

7

9

12

1

3

6

8

10

11

13

14

15

16

17

No Man's Land

Grése · Sisteron · Volx · Orpierre · Bellecombe · Baume Rousse · Ubrieux · Saint Julien · Saint Léger · Malaucène · Combe Obscure · Les Dentelles · Venasque · Buoux

1 Fissure Serge . . . . 7c+

2 La Directe del'Idole . . . 7c

3 Gratton Labeur . . . . . . 8a+

4 Promenade au Bord du Gouffre
. . . . 7c+

5 Les Croisements de l'Été 7a

6 Tabou . . . . 8a+

7 Tabou Zizi 8b
Continue without resting for the extra grade.

8 La Rose et le Vampire 8b
One of the most famous sport climbs in the world, chipped, but chipped well.

9 La Rage de Vivre . . . . . 8b+
The extension to *La Rose* without resting. If you take the belay the second pitch is *La Secte* and gets 8a+.

10 Il Était Une Voie . . 8c

11 Bout' de Chou . . . . 8b+

12 Chouca . . . . 8a+
Another mega classic. The crux could once be done by a figure-of-four from an 'hourglass' pocket. The middle bit broke off leaving a less useful pocket and now all but the tallest and strongest will have to jump. *Photo on this page and page 232.*

13 Le Minimum 8c
Les Paul, 8c - finish as for *Bout' de Chou*.

14 Hierogriffe . . . . 7b+

15 Total Khéops 7c
Join *Hierogriffe* for a while then continue to the top in one pitch.

16 Trop n'est Jamais Assez 7b+
1) 7a+, 2) 7b+

17 Tiens Bon La Rampe . . 7b

Céüse

Sisteron

Volx

Orpierre

Bellecombe

Baume Rousse

Ubrieux

Saint Julien

Saint Léger

Malaucène

Combe Obscure

Les Dentelles

Venasque

Buoux

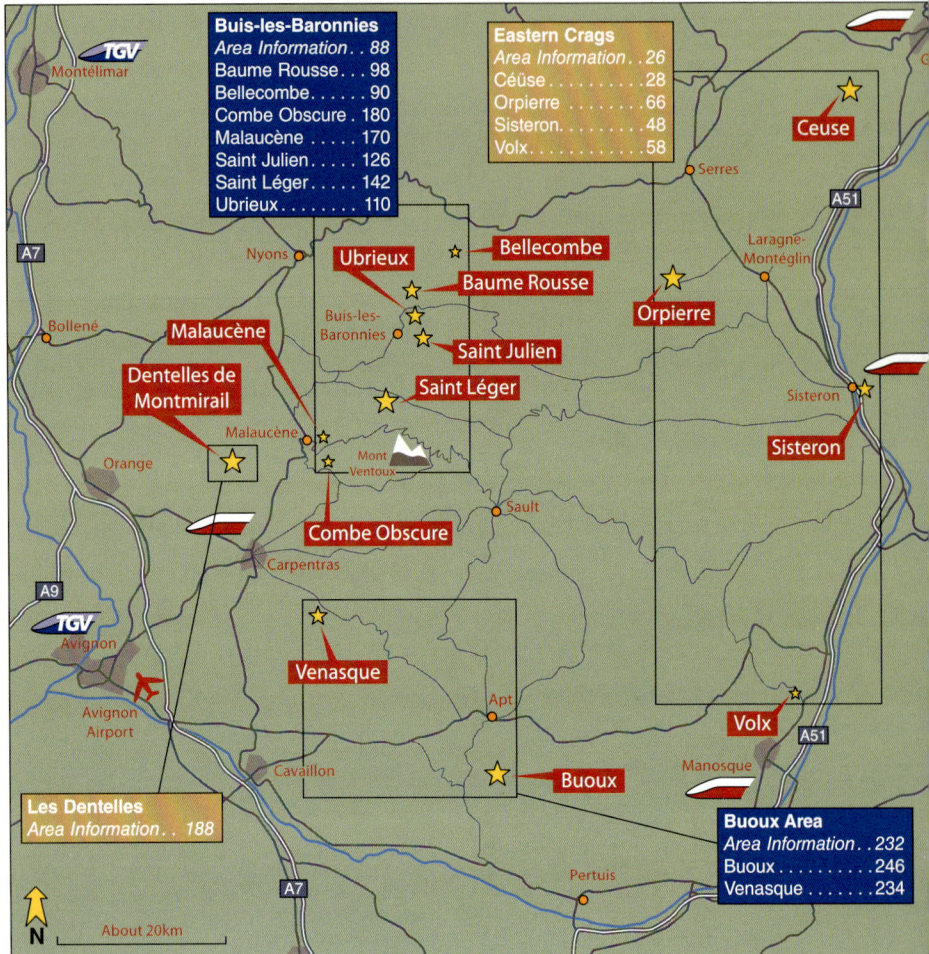

Side tabs (left margin, top to bottom): Céüse, Sisteron, Volx, Orpierre, Bellecombe, Baume Rousse, Ubrieux, Saint Julien, Saint Léger, Malaucène, Combe Obscure, Les Dentelles, Venasque, Buoux

Buis-les-Baronnies
Area Information . . 88
Baume Rousse . . . 98
Bellecombe 90
Combe Obscure . . 180
Malaucène 170
Saint Julien 126
Saint Léger 142
Ubrieux 110

Eastern Crags
Area Information . . 26
Céüse 28
Orpierre 66
Sisteron 48
Volx 58

Les Dentelles
Area Information . . 188

Buoux Area
Area Information . . 232
Buoux 246
Venasque 234

Map labels: Montélimar, TGV, Nyons, Bollène, A7, Orange, Malaucène, Avignon, TGV, Avignon Airport, Cavaillon, A9, Carpentras, Mont Ventoux, Sault, Apt, Pertuis, A7, Serres, Laragne-Montéglin, A51, Sisteron, Manosque, Volx, A51

Crag markers: Ceuse, Ubrieux, Bellecombe, Baume Rousse, Orpierre, Saint Julien, Saint Léger, Malaucène, Dentelles de Montmirail, Buis-les-Baronnies, Sisteron, Combe Obscure, Venasque, Buoux, Volx

N — About 20km

Mountain Rescue

Dial 112 - Ensure you have details of your location and what the incide involves. This number works on any mobile on a French network.